40 Winks

40 Winks

A Narcoleptic's Journey Through Sleep, Dreams & Spirituality

Brenda A. Moore

Disclaimer

This is the story of my personal journey through life living with narcolepsy and discovering not only the hardships, but also the beautiful experiences intense and excessive dreaming can create. The memoir recreates events and conversations from my memories, diaries and dream journals. Some names and identifying details have been changed to protect the privacy of individuals. Although I provide information to help educate individuals of the many aspects of sleep disorders, this book is not intended as a substitute for the medical advice of physicians. The reader should consult a physician in matters relating to his/her health and particularly with respect to any symptoms that may require diagnosis or medical attention.

40 Winks: A Narcoleptic's Journey Through Sleep, Dreams & Spirituality

Copyright © 2017 by Brenda A. Moore. All rights reserved.

All Rights Reserved. No part of this book may be copied or reproduced by any means, electronic or mechanical, including photocopying, recording, or any information storage and retrieval system, without prior permission in writing by the publisher except for the use of brief quotations in a book review.

ISBN: 978-0-692-79288-9

Cover and interior page design by Jeff Brandenburg
Illustrations by Brenda A. Moore
Edited by Leigh Saffold

Published by 40 Winks Press
40winksjourney@gmail.com
facebook.com/40winksthebook

First printing: 2017

Printed in the United States of America

Dedication

To my husband, my life's dream was made possible
by your unconditional love and support in
good times and in bad 'til death do us part.

Contents

Dedication — v

Acknowledgments — ix

Introduction — xi

CHAPTER 1: Scare the Daylights out of Me — 1

CHAPTER 2: Sleep Like a Baby — 19

CHAPTER 3: Put it to Rest — 31

CHAPTER 4: Sweet Dreams — 43

CHAPTER 5: Living in a Dream World — 59

CHAPTER 6: The American Dream — 73

CHAPTER 7: Cry Myself to Sleep — 89

CHAPTER 8: Up All Night, Sleep All Day — 109

CHAPTER 9: Eat, Sleep & Breathe… — 145

CHAPTER 10: Let Sleeping Dogs Lie — 165

CHAPTER 11: Dream On — 189

Afterword: Sleep on It — 217

Acknowledgments

I am extremely blessed to have had such a loving and supportive family, as well as wonderful friendships throughout my lifetime. My parents' love for each other and strong family values taught me valuable lessons and provided a solid foundation for me to grow with confidence and security.

I am grateful to my friends throughout the years who looked out for me, stood by me, and even simply helped me stay awake when I needed to. You never made me feel judged or inadequate, only loved.

I want to especially thank my best friend and husband for creating this beautiful story of ours with me. No matter where life took us, you were always by my side. Thank you for being patient as I struggled to keep up with life's demands. Thank you for listening to the countless, crazy dream adventures I felt I had to share, and believing my amazing sleep paralysis experiences that I know were hard to understand. Thank you for believing in me.

In my quest to find knowledge and support during my struggles with narcolepsy, I discovered the organization Narcolepsy Network. I sincerely want to thank the board members, staff, volunteers and all the contributing doctors and researchers for their ongoing efforts to provide support, advocacy, education, and awareness for the people with narcolepsy. I have witnessed the impact you have made in medical advances as well as in the lives of those suffering by providing a sense of family.

Sharing so many intimate and emotional experiences in my life so that I could help others understand the power of dreams was a very scary and difficult decision to make. I am so lucky to have had Leigh Saffold, my amazing editor. Her hard work and genuine concern for the book's success have provided a wonderful experience transitioning my words into a beautiful creation I can be proud of.

Introduction

As I walk around the corner, I glance up the stairs and down the hallway. I'm pleased to see my beautiful, overgrown Belgian Malinois, Sara. She is lying quietly with her head down between her paws. Sara's been gone for over a year now, so any chance I get to see her is a blessing. The hallway is dark, and I can't make out who the young girl lying on the floor in PJ's with her arms around Sara is. Sara looks sad, however. Her ears are dropped back, and she doesn't lift her head when she sees me. Her eyes are glowing from the distant light behind me, but they are not her usual gold color. They are red. "Sara," I say cautiously yet loudly enough so she can hear me, "if that's you, come here please." The young girl gets up and does several quick backbend flips out of the hall and into a nearby bedroom. Sara still does not move. I reach to flip a light switch for the hallway. No light turns on. I try another switch next to it, but again, no light. Wonderful, I realize, there's evil here. Although I know I'm dreaming, I still have to try. "Sara, if that's you, come here." I wake up.

Scientists have proven that important chemical processes take place during the REM stage of sleep that support our health in both mind and body. Benefits include creativity and problem solving, memory consolidation, and growth development. Researchers have also found that without REM, we will die. Beyond that, we are left with mysteries that many researchers are too afraid to examine for fear the answers will take them beyond their medical expertise. Dreaming is the component of REM that has been studied for centuries, and yet only theories exist. Some people regard dreams as spiritual encounters, while others view them simply as random images produced by the brain to form stories. As a person with narcolepsy, I regularly experience vivid dreams as well as the blending of REM and wake states of consciousness. At one time, I thought this was a curse, but have since discovered how much potential there is within this state of mind.

This is the story of my journey. As a child and young adult, I struggled with an undiagnosed chronic sleep disorder characterized by overwhelming daytime sleepiness, vivid dreams and nightmares, paralysis upon waking or falling asleep, and hallucinations. Not only was I challenged by my sleepiness during the day, but also the anxiety of having evil encounters in nightmares. At the age of twenty, just as I was beginning to deal with the hardships of adulthood—starting a family, managing a home and finances, and losing my mother to cancer—I was diagnosed with narcolepsy. Learning to manage the disorder became just one more thing on my list of responsibilities. As life's hardships increased, dreams grew to include premonitions and became a source for self-analysis and emotional healing. Sleep paralysis with hallucinations became more frequent, but the experience was no longer simply terrifying; it started to spur my curiosity.

Through lucid dreaming and sleep paralysis, I began to experience after-death communication (ADC) with passed loved ones. Unanswered questions about dreams and their connection to the afterlife set me on a path to educate myself and search for truths behind what was yet unknown.

I began a quest to not only become the master of my own sleep, but also teach others about sleep disorders and the possibilities dreams had to offer. I furthered my education in sleep with a degree in polysomnography and began working as a sleep technologist.

With my knowledge of sleep and personal experiences with dreams and sleep paralysis, I began to form my own theories about the role REM plays in our connection to the spiritual world. My story provides the evidence needed to bridge the gap between medical advances in sleep and neurology and spiritual teachings of the afterlife. Dr. Kevin Nelson's neurological research on near-death experience (NDE), spiritual teachings from world famous medium James Van Praagh, and collective experiences of after-death communication (ADC) provided the missing links I'd been searching for to develop a well-rounded theory for the spiritual nature of dreams and sparked a drive for me to share my experiences with others.

You don't have to have a sleep disorder or be religious to take interest in this story. You just have to be human. We all have hardships. We all sleep, dream, have a soul, and die. What makes us unique is how we deal with our hardships, develop our spirituality, and heal our soul. Whether we seek counseling from professionals, comfort in friends, or turn inward to examine our own psyche, I hope that my journey to healing my soul and finding my path will help others discover theirs.

CHAPTER 1

Scare the Daylights out of Me

Matt is so cute. My friends are all sitting around staring at us, waiting for something. I'm not sure what's supposed to happen. He's sitting next to me, but I'm lying on the ground. Matt slowly leans down toward my face. I'm so nervous. I think he's going to kiss me, I'm about to feel his lips touch mine. I put my hand against his face and push away hard. I wake up.

"Brianna!" I opened my eyes to see my mom standing over me with her hands on her hips. "That's not very nice! All I wanted to do was to give you a little kiss!" I'd come into her room to take a nap while she was putting her make-up on. I must have hurt her feelings pushing her away like that—I thought I was pushing Matt away! I couldn't tell her that I was having a dream about Matt trying to kiss me, that would have been too embarrassing.

I followed her downstairs to the kitchen. "Mom! I can't take it anymore! There really *is* something wrong with me!" I pleaded as I watched her cook dinner. I knew she thought I was blowing things out of proportion, but she also knew that I was the sleepiest person she'd ever known. Between our weekly battles of getting me up for Sunday mass, my nightly struggles with staying awake to do homework, and all of the random times and places she'd seen me fall asleep, she had to take me seriously. She also knew about my crazy dreams. She told me she got goosebumps all over her arms after I told her my nightmare about the box turning into a gun and pointing at my head. I thought she understood I needed help, but just didn't know how. I tried to explain how difficult school was, but none of the teachers had said anything to her and I wasn't failing or anything. "OK," she said. "I'll make a doctor's appointment." *Finally, I would have my answer!*

My mom and I waited more than an hour before being called in, but at least I'd finally get a doctor's diagnosis and the help I needed. The doctor asked me a few questions about my activity level and sleeping habits, then took a sample of my blood. I had been totally honest with my answers, but couldn't help noticing that he didn't seem very concerned. I heard my mother laugh a little as they talked privately on the other side of the room; I was afraid she wasn't painting an accurate picture of the severity of my condition. Yes, I was an A/B student, and yes, I played all kinds of sports, but that didn't mean it was easy! Feeling very anxious, I sat bolt upright when the doctor approached me. "Well, dear, you are borderline anemic. Other than that, you are a perfectly normal, young lady." *Noooo...! This wasn't happening! He's a doctor! He had to know.* My mother turned to him, and they began talking quietly. A large lump formed deep in my throat. I fought back the tears as best as I could. The ride home was a quiet one, so I drifted off to sleep.

From the time I was two years old, I lived in a three-bedroom, Raised Ranch–style home my parents had built in a small, suburban town. I didn't particularly like my room. Well, my room was OK, but I had a really hard time sleeping at night. I could fall asleep and stay asleep, but my dreams were killing me! I was plagued by nightmares almost every night, the kind that made my hair stand straight up on my arms. I would tuck my Blankie, my bear Harry, and my bunny Snuggles in around me to feel safe and warm, but as soon as I closed my eyes to sleep, it was as if they weren't there. Sleep was a scary place. Once I closed my eyes, no one was there to protect me.

I welcomed any amount of light to help ease my fears. My eyes wouldn't tear away from the closet door across from my bed where the glow from the streetlight outside my bedroom window filtered in through the curtains. I feared that I might see a light appear in the crack like it does in the movie *Poltergeist* just before the girl gets sucked in. I knew I was too old to be scared like this, but my big sister Renee had filled me with scary stories like telling me that our house was built on an ancient Indian burial ground. "Get out of my room!" she'd scream every time I tried to sneak into her bed at night. Didn't anyone understand what it was like being too scared to sleep? It wasn't about being alone, it was about seeing what waited for me when I closed my eyes. Staying up half the night trying to find peaceful sleep could've had something to do with me being sleepy all the time.

> *I walk in the entryway and head towards the steps that lead to our downstairs recreation room. It gets darker the further down I go because there are no windows in the basement. At the bottom of the steps, I turn into the rec room and reach for the light switch. I flip the switch, but the light bulb stays dark. It's here. I don't know what "it" is, but fear fills my head and makes me dizzy. The evil presence snatches the sound from my voice. My body feels heavy as I try to turn and go back up the steps. An invisible force is pulling my body toward the basement where the evil awaits. I wake up.*

Seventh grade was back to school as usual. Although junior high was much harder than elementary school, I loved that I could choose my own classes, had a locker and a locker partner, and walked freely from class to class. I did have anxiety dreams about school, however, like forgetting my locker combination and not knowing my schedule. In most of my classes, I would fall asleep every day while taking notes. Gym and art were easy to stay awake in, and study hall was a perfect time to nap. I always looked forward to the end of the school day when volleyball or basketball practice would begin. My friends knew and accepted me as "the sleepy one." They loved to hear about my adventures in dreamland. "What did you dream last night, Brianna?" my locker partner would ask each morning. One morning she asked whether or not we dream in color. "I don't know," I said. "I guess I've never really paid attention before."

On the days when we had a spelling test, I'd found that if I ran through the list of words a few times during lunch, I could usually ace the exam. But one afternoon, studying during lunch wasn't quite enough. "Take out a blank sheet of paper and put your name in the upper right hand corner," the teacher instructed, "then number from 1 to 10." *OK, did that.* "The first word is…" she went on to name a word, use it in a sentence, then gave us time to write it down. My concentration level was at an all-time low! I heard the word and began to write. Again, I heard the word and began to write. Finally the test was over. She walked through the aisles picking up each of our papers as she went. I looked down at my paper. Horrified, I saw that there were only scribbles next to each number. Not one letter of one word was written except my name! I knew how to spell all of the words. I slowly looked up to see my teacher looking down at my paper with a puzzled look on her face. I could not think of anything to say, so I managed a half smile of embarrassment. She collected my paper and moved on to the next desk.

Thinking about sitting still and paying attention in class made me nervous, even panic when I thought about really long standardized tests. Something had to be done. One day after school, some friends and I took a walk to a nearby QuikTrip. I had seen the caffeine pills NoDoz before, but had been too scared to actually purchase them. I didn't think you had to be a certain age or anything, but still thought it was wrong to take drugs. I believed the "This is your brain. This is your brain on drugs." campaign that showed a raw egg, and then that egg being fried. But a kid had to do what a kid had to do! We were all at the counter purchasing soft drinks, gum, and candy bars when I reached for the pack of NoDoz that were hanging on a rack close to the register. One of my friends gave me a funny look, then smiled and took one for herself.

Standing alone in a giant prairie, I take in all of my surroundings. I feel a slight breeze on my face and see the grass sway with the wind. The tall grasses are green! Yes, definitely green. There are a few varieties of wild flowers. There's red, yellow, purple… definitely color. I walk around the field and try my best to look carefully at everything before I wake up. *Nothing unusual is happening in this dream, I'm just exploring my senses. So peaceful. There's a tree close by. The green leaves feel soft and rubbery on my fingertips.* I wake up.

"OK, class, you can take out your books and choose a spot on the floor if you wish for personal reading time," my teacher announced. *Yes! Perfect!* I thought, grabbing my book and heading to the back of the classroom. Sprawled out on the floor, I opened my book. "Brianna?" I opened my eyes to see the entire class back in their chairs staring at me. Some had smiles on their faces, while others looked sorry for me. "Would you care to join the rest of the class?" she asked with an exhausted look. I slowly got up, picked up my book, headed back to my desk, and thought, *This is my life, I guess.*

The older I got, the more my parents allowed me to watch scary movies. We had all watched *Jaws* together. I lived in Missouri so we mainly went to lakes, yet I still freaked out occasionally when swimming. But *Amityville Horror*, *Fear No Evil*, *Exorcist*, and *Rosemary's Baby* were a whole different ballgame. I'm pretty sure someone should have censored those. In the scariest of horror films, a demon typically tried to possess an innocent girl and a priest tried to cast the evil spirit out, or someone would do a ritual and summon a demon to acquire supernatural powers.

Despite the gruesome endings of these movies, I had recreated a similar scenario. I tried summoning a demon by making up my own ritual and chant to invoke special powers. Not that I really believed it would work, but I was curious. I sat in my room and made up a dumb chant. It didn't make sense or even mean anything, "Uhmmm … kubalaiha … nottistah … Uhmmm … kubalaiha … nottistah … tutubahya …," I sang in a low monotone, while at the same time opening up my mind to let some powerful, evil spirit come and fill me with supernatural powers. A feeling of being watched came over me and a cold chill ran up my spine, giving me goosebumps. I quickly left my room.

I'm in my room standing at the end of my bed. Music from the clock radio starts blaring so loud that I jump and look up. My insides feel queasy as I realize I'm not alone. On the opposite side of my room, there's a shadow of a man with a hatchet standing next to my dresser. I turn and try to run

into the hallway, but I can barely move. I see my dad sitting in the big, round, purple chair watching TV in the living room at the end of the hall. If I could just get to him.... I open my mouth, but only soft squeaks come out. I'm pulled to my knees by a force so strong it feels like a giant vacuum sucking me backwards. As I crawl away from my room towards my dad, the Hatchet Man gets closer. I inch my way slowly down the hallway as the pressure of the suction takes my breath away. There is no chance of flying this time like I had in other dreams. Just keep pushing forward. On my hands and knees, I reach my arm out to touch my dad's leg. "Hey, there you are!" He reaches down and pulls me up into his lap. I wake up.

Looking around, I noticed how incredibly accurate the room had been in my dream. I wondered what would happen if I reenacted the beginning of my dream now that I was wide awake. I positioned myself at the end of the bed and closed my eyes. Nervous energy flowed through my veins. I took a deep breath, opened my eyes and looked toward the clock radio sitting on my dresser. Nothing happened. I didn't know what I'd expected. I guess I'd wanted to prove to myself that I was safe. Even though I could tell the difference between dreams and wake, my dreams felt so intense and real. In fact, I considered everything about them "real," they just weren't in my waking reality. I once had a dream where a monster was able to get too close and bit me! It bit me *hard*, right on the back! I woke up with the worst back pain. How could something from my dreams have actually hurt me? What if the Hatchet Man had caught me?

I was starting high school, which meant being able to enroll in the classes of my choice. Of course, I took study hall to make sure I could fit a nap into my day; gym class to give me some exercise; and art, which, although I loved it, I must not have been fully awake when I decided to sign up because I stank at drawing. I also had the opportunity to take my first psychology class. The anticipation of having a class where I could find an answer to my sleep problems practically killed me.

On the first day of psychology, the teacher walked down the aisles and passed out our textbooks. *Forget old doctors who were simply waiting to retire*, I thought, *I'll figure out what's wrong with me since no one else seems to care.* Thumbing through the chapters, I looked for anything that had to do with sleep. I found the word "Narcolepsy" in bold-faced letters. Excitedly, I read the description. My heart sank. *This isn't me*, I thought to myself. *How can this not be the answer I'm looking for? Yes, I'm tired all the time, so I do have excessive daytime sleepiness. But I don't have "Cataplexy," a sudden collapse of the muscles or muscle weakness associated with extreme emotion such as laughing. And I don't have problems with sleeping at night. I sleep all night long (except, of course, when I'm too scared).*

I felt so defeated. I stared at the page for a while, hoping I was missing something. That had to be the answer! The section was on sleep disorders; it was a small section, but it talked about a condition that made you sleepy all the time. *But how could this be my diagnosis if I don't have cataplexy?* I felt like crying. I thought for sure my psychology class would have the answer for me. I had nowhere else to turn. I continued to stare hopelessly at the pages until I started to feel sleepy. I perked up as the teacher announced he wanted to do some sort of experiment with the class. He asked us to close our eyes and think of something, but I couldn't remember what.

> *The smoke is thick and the smell of sulfur is in the air. I hear gunshots and screaming in the distance. Still bodies lie scattered across the grassy plains. They are uniformed men, some in blue and some in red. I notice the cannons and men with rifles and understand that I'm somehow standing in the middle of a Civil War battlefield.* I wake up.

"Alright, open your eyes," the teacher said as he walked around the front of the class. His eyes searched the class to see who he wanted to call on. *Not me, not me, please don't call on me*, I prayed. He wanted to know what we were thinking about! I'm not sure how he would have handled the truth if I told him, even if he was a psychology teacher. How on earth did I fall asleep, and so fast? I didn't think I was *that* tired. A better question was, how did I dream so fast?

My friend Lynn lived far out in the country and had a big house on lots of land. One night, she invited a group of girls over for a slumber party. We jumped on her trampoline until it was too dark to see, watched for falling stars in the pitch-black sky, and listened for coyotes. As the night got late, we went inside to try to make each other levitate. It was just a dumb thing young teenage girls did for entertainment. Kelly lay down on the floor while the rest of us sat around her with our hands under her body. We took turns chanting: "Light as a feather, stiff as a board." If we all concentrated hard enough, she was supposed to start rising up into the air. When it didn't work, we gave up and moved on to the next brilliant idea, the Ouija board.

Why parents allowed kids to have this "game," I'd never understand. It was basically a bunch of kids performing a séance. The four of us sat in a circle on the floor of Lynn's room with only a small lamp on to set the mood. Each of us placed our fingertips lightly on the plastic game piece that sat on a game board printed with the letters of the alphabet. Michelle spoke up. "If there is anyone else in the room with us, give us a sign." We waited patiently for spirits to communicate with us by moving the piece across the board to spell out words. Slowly the piece started moving. We looked at each other, wondering which one of us was directing it. We all knew *someone* had to be moving it. With a serious face, Michelle repeated, "Give us a sign if there is a spirit here with us in this room." I wasn't scared because I knew it was silly, yet I couldn't help but be excited at the same time. The lamp light flickered twice. All eyes shot up, staring at each other. Then the screams began. The thrill was awesome! Two of the girls had planned to turn the lamp on and off with the floor switch, they admitted later. However, they never expected the light to actually "flicker." By the terrified look on their faces, I wondered if someone or something *was* actually in the room with us that night.

> *I wake up and notice that Lynn's sheets with the little purple flowers are pulled up over my head. My legs are stretched out straight and crossed at the ankles. My arms are above my head and crossed at the wrists. I can't move, it's as if my hands and feet are bound together. I can hear a faint*

drumming sound and chanting. The sounds slowly become louder in my ears. I feel the tip of a steel blade being dragged along the fronts of my legs. The blade now moves slowly along my arms. My whole body is paralyzed, all I can do is lie there. This seems like a dream, but I know I am awake because I'm staring at Lynn's sheets with the little purple flowers. The chanting starts to fade. My body comes to life again. I wake up.

I opened my eyes to see the little flowers on the sheets that had been pulled up over my head. I slowly pulled them down to reveal the morning sun that lit up the room. I lay there quietly, processing what had just happened: I felt like I had just been the victim of a witch's voodoo spell. I clearly remembered feeling the blade on my legs and arms and the sound of drums in my ears. My hands and feet had felt like they were bound together tightly, making it impossible for me to move. I went over this again and again in my head. I knew I was awake, I was staring at Lynn's sheets when it happened! As I thought about the voice I'd heard chanting, I wondered if we somehow invited some kind of spirit into Lynn's room. The light did flicker, after all. I hoped this witch, if that's what it was, stayed in Lynn's house and not with me! I had enough trouble with nightmares in my own room. My friends already thought I was weird with all of the dreams I shared with them, so I decided to keep this experience to myself.

I heard a senior at my school, John Morrison, wanted to go out with me. Being a sophomore, this seemed really cool. He was the complete opposite of me—he talked to everyone and although he blew off just about all his classes, the teachers still loved him. I liked to think of myself as a "good girl," always trying to do the right thing and please my parents and teachers. He was definitely in the "bad boy" category. He always wore the same combination of ripped up jeans, flannel shirt with a white T-shirt underneath. He had longer hair in the back and was considered a "gear head" because he always worked on cars. He didn't care much to impress with style, but was smooth with words. I wasn't sure why exactly, but it seemed like most girls liked bad boys.

He told me he'd rather go work for his older friend Richard and make money than sit all day in boring classes that didn't matter to him. I, on the other hand, was the typical rule follower, very shy, and had to try so hard just to finish my homework. I read, reread, and still had no idea what it was I was learning. Since my grades were good, teachers weren't mean like they had been when I was younger. They just let me sleep in class. I had lots of friends, and I guess you could say I was one of the popular kids. Well, at least I was friends with the popular kids. If opposites attract, John and I were definitely a great match!

I started hiding from him in the bathroom after school when he was waiting to talk to me before my volleyball games. I knew he never kept a steady girlfriend, but dated lots of girls; I didn't want to be just another girl to check off his list. I could tell he was starting to lose interest, which was actually upsetting to me, so I agreed to go on a date with him. What a crazy first date! Kelly and I were only fifteen, and her parents made her bring a friend if she was to go on a date with Chris (also a senior), so we made it a double date. Luckily, when John and Chris came to pick us up, my parents didn't notice that they had been drinking.

"You two have to get in the back," John said once we were outside. Kelly was upset because she really liked Chris, but since they were acting mean, I tried to show that I didn't care. We just drove around while the guys drank. What kind of double date had she brought me on? Chris turned around and stuck the bottle out to Kelly, "Want a drink?" She gave me a quick look before she took the bottle from him and drank. She handed the bottle back to Chris and he turned to me, "You want some, too?" I heard the words *Say no!* clearly and right in my ear, yet they didn't come from anyone in the car. I wasn't about to *not* listen to some mysterious voice in my ear, so I said no. Chris didn't seem to care either way and turned back around. Kelly apparently didn't hear the message not to drink. In fact, no one but me seemed to hear the voice. And I certainly wasn't going to ask anyone about it either or they might have thought I was crazy!

Kelly's date went from bad to worse. She resorted to heavy drinking, probably to make up for the bad date that consisted of nothing but driving around and listening to the guys tell dumb stories about themselves. We had to pull over into a parking lot so she could be sick. John and I sat in the car and talked. With John having the reputation he did, I knew talking wasn't what he expected. I was really glad I hadn't drunk with them, and felt good to be able to think clearly and be in complete control of myself. Talking was what he got.

At the end of the night, while my friend's date was holding her hair back as she threw up, John and I kissed.

I had the guys drop us off at my house—no way could Kelly go home in her condition. While she was in the bathroom puking, I called her parents to see if she could spend the night. Unfortunately, they didn't believe Kelly was "just" in the bathroom. My parents were asleep upstairs and clueless about what was going on when her parents busted in through the basement doors and searched for Kelly. I had never been so scared for a friend before! The yelling woke my parents and had them running down the steps to the basement. "They are drunk!" Kelly's mom yelled. "Brianna? Are you drunk?" my dad asked with a disappointed look on his face. "Not at all, Dad." My grin couldn't have been bigger.

I was grateful to my guardian angel for speaking up at a time when I'm not sure if I would have made the right decision. At least, that's what I called it, my guardian angel. What else could it have been? Who knows what decisions I would have made if I had chosen to drink like Kelly did. What if John had lost interest in me because I had drunk too much that night or lost control? That night could've steered my life in a very different direction.

John and I began spending more time together. I didn't have my license yet, so one day after school he volunteered to drop me off at a tanning salon. After talking with a friend of his that worked at the front desk, she walked me back to a room to get settled for my 30 minute tanning session. John said he'd be back to pick me up in about thirty to forty-five minutes. Although the beds were very uncomfortable and hot, I always liked how at peace they made me feel. What a great place to feel warm and sneak a little nap in without getting in trouble. I jumped a little when my eyes opened and I realized that I was closed in a dark, cold tanning bed. My naked body felt sore from the hard, glass bed. What happened? Why was it cold? Quickly, I got dressed and headed to the lobby. I didn't recognize the girl behind the front desk.

Outside the sky was dark. What time was it? Or worse yet, what day was it? My heart pounded. Panicked and nervous, I asked the girl at the front desk if I could use the phone. "Brianna, where are you?" John asked. "I went to pick you up but the girl said no one was back there! It's six o'clock at night!" He sounded really worried. Embarrassed, I explained that I must have fallen asleep and the buzzer from the bed turning off didn't wake me up like it usually did. After he dropped me off at home, he told me to call him later. Little did he know that this crazy "sleepy Brianna incident" wasn't the first and certainly wouldn't be the last.

When he teased me about the tanning bed incident, I told him stories about falling asleep in the dentist's chair, nodding off while getting my hair cut (my bangs were always crooked), and the time my dad caught me asleep on the toilet. "Brianna Sleeping Pictures," I said. "My mom has a whole stack of them," I usually fell asleep in the car, too, but sometimes, I would wake up when we got home. I'd pretended I was asleep so that my dad would carry me inside. "Katherine, I'm not carrying her in," my dad would say as I tried not to crack a smile, "I know she's awake." "Oh, Wayne, she's asleep. She's always asleep." My dad would then give in and carry me to bed. Before getting off the phone, John asked me to call him back later that night since he couldn't call me because my parents didn't want the phone to ring past 9:30 p.m.

> *Lying in bed, I reach over and pick up the phone. Dialing John's number, I notice that the buttons aren't working right. It's like the phone won't let me dial what I want to dial. Oh, this must be a dream, I think. I give myself a "one, two, three, wake up!" command. I wake up and reach over to pick up the phone to call John. As I start dialing, I notice that the dial pad doesn't look quite right. I keep getting wrong number recordings. Darn it! Still a dream! Again ... Again ... Again ... Lying in bed, I pull the phone towards me and tuck it under the small night light behind the headboard of my bed. I'm not going to be fooled this time. I turn the switch to light the numbers on the pad. Carefully, I dial John's number. It works! I talk with John briefly, telling him about the crazy dream I had. We hang up. I wake up.*

"Hello?" John answered groggily. "Hey, it's me." *Finally*, I thought, *it's for real this time*. "What are you doing? It's two o'clock in the morning!" In disbelief and anger I yelled, "Oh my gosh! I've been trying to call you all night!" We were still newly dating so I didn't dare go into details about the dream, but he must have thought I was a freak by now. We abruptly ended the conversation with "OK, see you tomorrow," and I went back to sleep.

I was a free bird! With my driver's license in hand and the car my parents had bought me, I had no limits. Who was I kidding? I didn't go far because I had never paid attention to street names or directions. I mainly drove to and from school, friends' houses, and John's house. I had to be careful not to drive for too long when I was sleepy. Yawning was my sign that sleep was coming on quickly, and I had to get off the road right away.

Driving home one afternoon, I noticed myself yawning. I turned the radio up really loud and sang along; then I rolled the windows down to get the air flowing and make it cold. So often, I prayed to God to help me get home without killing myself or someone else. This was one of those times. The sting in my eyes and heaviness of my lids were overwhelming as I pulled up to the traffic light. *I'm just going to close my eyes for one minute while the light is red,* I thought. I knew it was a bad idea, but I had no choice—sleep was coming whether I liked it or not. *Wake up!* The words filled my ears. My eyes flew open just in time to see the passing car and slam on my brakes. I had rolled into the middle of the intersection! My heart raced and adrenaline pumped through my veins, but my thoughts were not on the near miss. I wanted to know who woke me up. I didn't recognize the voice, it was just a quick and clear whisper. Somebody, my guardian angel perhaps, was definitely watching over me.

> *My body is heavy, pulling me to my knees. I'm at the end of the hallway again, right outside my bedroom. I can see my dad sitting in the round, purple swivel chair at the end of the hallway, he's facing into the living room watching TV. I'm being sucked backwards toward my bedroom. The force is so strong that it's hard to move forward. I feel the evil presence, I know it's creeping up behind me. I know screaming isn't an option, the vacuum force steals the sound from my voice; I can't move like I want either. I have an idea: if I can do something that gets my dad's attention, then he'll turn around. The evil behind me is coming closer. I look a little in front of me and concentrate. It works! A large vase appears on a small table to my right. My hand reaches for the table and pushes, knocking the vase off. A second evil presence appears directly in front of me. All hope is lost.* I wake up.

I had my first full-time summer job as a lifeguard at a brand new beach that opened at a local lake. I was getting paid to sit in the sun—perfect! I loved getting golden tan while my hair turned a shade lighter. Between guard duty, I usually joined my friends on the sand volleyball courts. And even though I was a good swimmer, the boss made us swim from dock to dock across the beachfront to keep in shape. My eyes scanned the top of the lake as I swam. It freaked me out not being able to see under the green lake water; wondering what lurked below always made me swim faster.

Guard duty was divided into twenty-minute rotations. I had two fears when I was on duty: 1) not knowing when to go in after someone (some kids liked to pretend they were drowning), and 2) not seeing someone go under. There was always a lot of activity on the beach and in the water. Day camps from all over the city packed the beachfront, and I knew that although they waded out in the water up to their necks, many of the kids couldn't swim. Twenty minutes on the lifeguard stand was a very long time for me to sit still and pay attention. I wore Frogskins, the best sunglasses that I could afford, but the sun was still hard on my eyes. The dark lenses hid my eyes and no one could tell whether my eyes were closed or not. So many times I was tempted to close them for just a second.

One afternoon, the exhaustion from playing volleyball and the heat of the sun became too much for me. I started to feel my body sway a little, so I shifted in my chair to play it off. I had my eyes set on one particular group of boys that concerned me. I watched them go under the water and pop back up, over and over. I yawned. The lowering sun made the top of the water sparkle and hard to see as I strained my already heavy and burning eyes. One boy dove and my eyes closed as if following him under. It felt like only ten seconds had passed before I opened my eyes again. After scanning the water, I couldn't find the boy anywhere. There were so many kids crowding the water, but I was sure he had come back up. Although I felt I was as good of a lifeguard as any, I probably shouldn't have taken on a job with that much responsibility, knowing my struggles.

I continued to have nightmares pretty regularly; good versus evil was a recurring theme. I began recognizing the signs of not only being in a dream, but also when evil was present. Typically, when the lights wouldn't turn on, it was a sure sign of the presence of evil. Other signs of evil included feeling like the air was being sucked out of my lungs, losing my voice, and my body feeling unbearably heavy. Although I couldn't "see" anyone or anything, I knew evil was there. I experimented during these times with what I thought of as "dream powers."

Since I knew when I was dreaming, I believed the rules of waking reality must not apply. Although some nightmares prevented me from flying (because of the feeling of heaviness), I had discovered that I could make things appear like magic. I didn't know why or how it worked, but sometimes it just did. Why was I always in my house when I had these nightmares? I loved my house! I was just an all-American kid with an all-American family. I believed in God and went to church. What about the dreams that carried over after I woke up? Could the witch's blade I still felt after waking up really have hurt me? I wanted to ask someone, but was too afraid of being laughed at.

> *My hands feel sweaty and sore gripping the thick white rope. My legs and feet are wrapped around the rope beneath me as I inch my way up, higher and higher towards the sky. Afraid to look down, I look up toward the blue sky and white clouds. I have no choice but to go up, the alternative is simply not an option. I hear a voice, "Come. Take my hand." Slowly, I look down. I see a handsome man I do not know dressed in a black, tailored suit. He has black hair, not old, but not young. He's standing at the bottom of the rope and his arm is stretched out to me, he is offering me his hand. I know this is no ordinary man. He's standing in the middle of what looks like a scene from the Book of Revelations. Demons of all shapes and sizes with horns, tails, and blood dripping from their mouths surround him. I'm reminded of paintings I've seen of battles of heaven and hell. I take a deep breath, "Our Father, who art in heaven, hallowed be thy name...." I hear a chuckle from the man as he says to me, "God can't help you here." I wake up.*

I sat in my car behind our church and stared at the rectory. I wanted so badly to go inside and talk with the priest. But what would I say? "Hi, I think I'm possessed by evil spirits. They come for me in my dreams." He would look at me like I was weird, then pathetic, and feel sorry for me, maybe even call my parents because he would think I was actually crazy. Sure, I shouldn't have watched Freddy Kruger or countless other horror movies, but this went deeper than being scared by those characters. In my dreams, I felt trapped in sleep while my soul was tortured and my faith was tested. I felt alone and vulnerable, even when I prayed for protection. I couldn't be the only one; lots of people watch scary movies. My frustration built as I realized that walking into that house and asking to speak to the priest was probably not a good idea. I'd figure something out on my own. Guess I never should have made up that dumb chant in my room and invited evil spirits to come and give me special powers. It never worked out well for the characters in the movies either. I drove away.

CHAPTER 2

Sleep Like a Baby

John and I stood in the parking lot of my doctor's office and embraced. "Everything's going to work out just fine. You'll see." He said this with such confidence, even a smile, that I wondered if he was actually happy that I was pregnant. We stood right next to a busy road with people going about their business as usual, not realizing that the two teenagers they passed had just been told their lives were turned up-side-down. I felt like I was in an episode of The Twilight Zone. "You'll get to do everything you've ever planned on doing. I'll make sure of it." For a seventeen-year-old kid fresh out of high school, he sure did sound grown up. We hadn't even been together for a year, but I felt like I could trust him with my life. Well, I suppose I was trusting him with my life, plus another.

John dropped me off at my house to talk with my mom while he went to talk with his father. He really respected his father and looked to him for advice. Before talking to my mom, I sat in my room alone and prayed. "God, I promise to be the absolute best parent I can be. But, I need three things in return: The baby will need to be healthy; he'll need to be happy; and I really, really, really need him to be a good sleeper!" Then, I took a deep breath and called out, "Mom, can you come here, please? I need to talk to you!"

The bright sun is setting, turning the tall prairie grass to a yellow-gold color. The wind blows gently, it appears to be autumn. I am not alone. I raise my hands above my shoulders and rest them on the smooth skin of a toddler's legs. I can feel his fingers grip the sides of my head and his little tennis shoes bounce against my chest as we stroll across the grassy field. I wake up.

    The pregnancy was going really smoothly considering my circumstances. Even though the doctor said I could continue to play volleyball, my coach asked me to quit. I don't blame him for not wanting me to risk getting hurt on his time. And none of the kids at school gave me a hard time; I'd known most of them since kindergarten. Besides, my boyfriend and his friends, although graduated now, were notorious. People knew that if they messed with me, John and his friends would pay them a visit. There were a few judgmental parents, and teachers who were blatantly rude and unwilling to work with me, but others were extremely supportive of my effort to stay in school. One morning, I nodded off while a teacher was talking to me; she just laughed and said it was the pregnancy. Six weeks before my due date, I went on homebound (school maternity leave) when a designated teacher would drop off and pick up my homework. During that time my parents hired a college student to tutor me in math and Spanish; that helped a lot. I taught myself accounting but gave up on chemistry completely. Reading for English class without falling asleep was impossible. The good news was that I could sleep whenever I wanted without getting in trouble!

    I had promised myself and God that I was going to be perfect. I switched over to Pepsi Free caffeine-free soda, gave up chocolate, and kept in shape by walking at the school track in the evenings. Good thing stretch pants and long sweaters were in style—no ugly maternity clothes for this teen! Plus John told me I was beautiful all the time. He was totally loving and supportive, he even wanted to pay for everything himself (doctor's visits, hospital, baby food, etc.), which was really hard for him now that he was living on his own. I knew I loved him before, but now I was falling in love with him. There was a difference. I could see a future with him, even growing our family.

By nine months, my waterbed was not ideal, especially when I started getting leg cramps and couldn't easily get up or reach my feet. John had purchased a pager so I could let him know when it was time if he was at work. This was it! My life as a kid was over. I'd only had seventeen years of childhood (except that my parents made sure I still had a curfew and rules). I would parent mine, and they would parent theirs.

Lying in bed, my stomach squeezed so tight that it hurt. I'd learned how to recognize contractions, so I looked over at the clock radio—10:00 p.m. I drifted off to sleep, but woke again as I felt my stomach muscles tightening. I looked at the clock again, 10:30 p.m. I was supposed to keep time, but couldn't remember what time it was when I last looked. This time I made a mental note and closed my eyes to rest. My stomach contracted again and I looked at the time. *Darn, what time had it been before?* This went on and on. Because I'd kept falling asleep, by morning I had no idea how far apart my contractions were. I called John and suggested we go to the hospital.

Doctors and nurses walked in and out of my room while I labored with John and my mom by my side. My dad played it safe and waited in the hall with John's family. My mom started freaking out, afraid John might see something he wasn't supposed to see. "Mom!" I shrieked with embarrassment. "He's seen my butt before, get over it!" I'm usually a nice young lady, but I was so sleep deprived and wanted the thing out of me. The doctors told me to start pushing, but weren't even paying attention. "Hey!" I yelled. "Turn around!" They did as I commanded, and my little baby boy was out in no time. The doctor laid him in my arms for me to see. Yeah, I knew him. Long and skinny and...redheaded?

I smiled as I looked at him, then felt my arms begin to drop with my eyelids. My eyes popped open wide, "Take him!" The nurse didn't understand my urgency, but she took him right away and I fell fast asleep. After I woke up, a few visitors stopped by. I was still pretty drugged up with pain meds and couldn't hold a conversation. The doctor also came by to check on me. He told me that never in the history of his practice had someone fallen asleep that fast after giving birth. I'd even slept through being stitched up. I just smiled. He didn't know how good of a sleeper I was!

My parents made me do just about everything when it came to Dylan, but I believed that was the best thing they could have done for me. Doesn't every parent simply have to figure it out? They would babysit on occasion if I asked.

He went to John's mom's while I was at school. John (when he got home from work) and his mom took care of Dylan on the weekdays so I could be a regular high school kid and even play sports after school. Because Dylan was such a good sleeper, my parents didn't care if I went out with my friends after he was asleep for the night, around 8 p.m. He did, however, wake up at 7 a.m. and I was the one who had to get up with him regardless of how late I had gotten home the night before or how tired I was in the morning. It wasn't too bad because I just had to stay awake until his morning nap at 10 a.m.—which became *my* morning nap as well. Then he'd take another nap around 1 p.m., and another around 4 p.m. Hmm...he kind of acted like me!

When Dylan was about nine months old, he dropped down to two naps a day and was starting to get into just about everything. One Saturday morning, I simply could not keep up. John's sister, Cindy, caught me in a very embarrassing situation. I had volunteered to babysit her son, Adam, for the morning. Adam was only two months older than Dylan and they played together really well. It was just me and the boys for a few hours. I shut the door to the bedroom and spread out all the toys for them to play. They babbled words here and there, but other than that it was very quiet. As I lay on the floor playing with the babies, my eyelids started to get heavy and I ached to close them. I did a quick scan of the room to make sure there was nothing they could get themselves into that would hurt them. There wasn't anything they could crawl into, and they had plenty of toys. *OK*, I thought to myself. Then I let my eyes close. "Oh my God!" *Oh, no*, I thought, *what did I do?* Cindy started laughing out loud. The babies were both sitting almost on top of me. All three of us had white cream smeared all over our faces, hands, and clothes. The babies had taken the Diaperine pads and painted on each other. And me!

With my parents' generous offer of free babysitting, I was allowed time for teenage freedom. One night my friend, Jeanne, and I went to see the movie *Flatliners*. In the movie, medical students help each other have near-death experiences so they can discover what is on the "other side." As each of the students is dying, they see images of people who have already passed on or things about themselves that need to be resolved in order to cleanse their souls. It's as if their minds are dreaming while their bodies are flatlining, and then once their bodies are restored, their minds snap back into their bodies. I liked those kind of movies, they made me realize just how afraid yet curious I was about the supernatural. Will I know what to do when I die? Where will I go? Is it beautiful? Do I need to cleanse my soul? As I thought about my dreams, I wondered if they were providing direction for me to figure out the answers to these questions.

I decided I'd do my composition class research paper on dreams. Why do we dream what we dream? Although I was afraid of my nightmares, I was also curious to know more. Do they have real meaning? The paper gave me the opportunity to explore some of these burning questions, but as I stared at the "B" on the top of my research paper I thought to myself, *One day I'll write my own book about dreams and sleep. People don't take sleep and dreams seriously.* I was tired of buying "dream dictionaries" that claimed to uncover the hidden meanings in dreams. *Someone like me, who really knows dreaming and does it a lot, needs to write this book.* I believed that it was up to the dreamer to discover the hidden meanings in their own dreams. What one object meant for me couldn't possibly have the same meaning for someone else; we would have had completely different experiences with that same object.

I liked Sigmund Freud as someone who really valued dreams. He spent much of his life trying to understand the meanings behind dreams. Shortly after the publication of *The Interpretation of Dreams*, Freud wrote a letter to a friend. "Do you suppose," he asked, "that someday one will read on a marble tablet on this house: 'Here, on July 24, 1895, the secret of the dream revealed itself to Dr. Sigmund Freud?'" But I didn't agree that all dreams were about hidden desires. I preferred Carl Jung because he analyzed the dream in the present rather than looking to the dreamer's past. I just didn't agree with his theory about archetypes and the collective unconscious. I did agree that dreams represented more than our individual selves, but not in the form of symbols for everyone and for all time. I knew there was so much more to dreams than people understood, and I planned to discover what that was myself. I would need to develop my own theories based on my own experience.

Considering my circumstances as a young mom, I knew my best option for college was starting at the junior college. I definitely didn't think I would be able to continue playing sports. Funny how things work out. I was playing volleyball on the beach at work one afternoon and the coach for the junior college just happened to be there with her team. She approached me later in the day and asked if I would be interested in playing for her team. I was so excited! But there was no way I could juggle my school schedule, Dylan's schedule, volleyball practices and games. Then she offered to pay for my school. I believed that if I worked hard and was a good person, opportunities would come my way. This was not only my chance to make up for missing my junior year of playing, but it would also let me be a kid just a little longer.

The college was less than 10 miles from my house, but I fell asleep at the wheel almost every time I made the drive. After several near misses on the road, I was really starting to worry. Each day I'd stroll into geology class at 8:05 a.m. and slide into a chair at the front row table to show that I wanted to do well and focus, but the teacher didn't seem to understand that I was really trying. He hated it when I popped open a Pepsi and unwrapped my Snickers bar in the middle of class; if only he knew I was doing this to stay awake for him. Not to mention that I risked my life every morning just to get to his class. Thank God my friend Noel sat next to me in almost all of my classes. Her job was to hit me in the back of the head whenever I'd start to drift off.

Just as I had in high school, I looked forward to volleyball every afternoon. My teammates teased me for being last at everything: last to leave the locker room, last when running laps, last off the bus, and last on the court. But I played well on the court, and that's what mattered. I discovered the vitamin store GNC and their all-natural energy pills, so I tried them. I don't think they helped much, but at least I was trying. We often played colleges that were a long drive away, so I'd sleep in the van to and from games. The girls messed with me while I dozed, adding to my growing collection of "Brianna Sleeping Pictures."

College provided me with ongoing opportunities to research sleep and dreams. For my speech class, an informational speech on the science of sleep was the obvious choice. I learned about brain waves, the stages of sleep, and the patterns of the stages our brains go through each night. I learned that rapid eye movement sleep, better known as REM, is this stage when dreams occur, and that our bodies become paralyzed during REM to help prevent us from acting out our dreams. In my research I found that a person spends the majority of their sleep in Stage 2 and reaches REM in about ninety minutes. I had a problem with this.

I had dreamt during naps that I knew were shorter than ninety minutes, so how could it be? What about the time I started dreaming as soon as I closed my eyes? I made posters with graphs of squiggly lines that represented the various stages of sleep and taught the class what I had learned from my research knowing full well it didn't apply to me. In the end, my speech simply informed the audience about the basic sleep patterns. When I started researching the topic, I had been hoping to get some answers about my own sleep habits. Yet again, I didn't find the answers I was looking for.

I was finally assigned a research paper in psychology class! Psychology was one of the few classes that I could actually stay awake in. Of course I took the opportunity to write about dreams. In my paper, "Dreams: Neuroscience vs. Psychoanalysis," I compared Freud's belief in dream interpretation from a person's unacceptable, hidden wishes and fears to a more scientific approach of modern-day neurologists. In Freud's essay "Project for a Scientific Psychology," he attempts to explain dreaming in biological terms based on activity in brain cells to help support his psychoanalytic approach. But modern neurobiologists attacked Freud's dream research as lacking in scientific knowledge of the brain and discounted his explanation by proving his energy sources for neurons in the brain were not, in fact, driven by somatic drives such as sex and aggression. In comparison, two neuroscientists at the time hypothesized that dreams were the result of a random firing of neurons in the lower part of the brain, specifically in the pons. Their theory, called the activation-synthesis hypothesis, stated that these neurons control eye movement, which explain rapid eye movement, and also send messages to the cortex, which then combines these messages with existing knowledge and memories. The cortex simply tries to give meaning to these random signals.

As an expert dreamer and student of modern brain research, I found there to be a little truth in both theories. As crazy as I thought Freud was in his beliefs, I agreed with his psychological approach to dream analysis giving real meaning to the images produced, rather than being seen as random. But, I didn't think psychoanalysis gave the whole picture. Why couldn't dreams incorporate Freud's theory plus all of the new science, which showed that our dreams come approximately every ninety minutes in REM, during which time our bodies are paralyzed and neurons are firing? If researchers couldn't offer an answer that made sense for the whole picture that included modern, biological knowledge plus the analysis of dream images specific to the dreamer, my goal was to figure it out for myself. Maybe one day, there would be a marble tablet on *my* house: "Here, in this house, in 20__, the secret of the dream revealed itself to Dr. Brianna Morrison."

I became more and more nervous when I was alone with Dylan. Our environment was quiet when it was just the two of us; he hardly ever cried. Quiet and calm activated my sleep mode, bringing on what I called a "sleep attack." I could feel the sleepiness coming, but nothing I did would make it go away except sleep. Dylan especially enjoyed bath time, but for me it was the worst. One afternoon, the two of us were in the hall bathroom. The door was shut to keep in the warmth as the tub slowly filled. Dylan sat in his little blue bath chair for stability, but he still had some freedom to grab and play with floating toys. The humidity and sound of running water made my eyes heavy. I sat alongside the tub on the floor next to him and leaned forward to rest my head on the porcelain. I was struggling, but wanted to power through it because he was enjoying himself so much. As I felt my eyes close briefly, I flew into panic mode and my eyes shot open wide. Dylan turned to look at me and smiled. "Sorry, bath time is over sweetie." I turned off the water, swept him up out of his chair, wrapped his hooded towel around him, unplugged the drain, and prayed to God that my sleep nightmare would one day come to an end.

My parents were away on a cruise for their twenty-fifth wedding anniversary when I got a congratulations card from them in the mail. *How strange*, I thought, *congratulations on what?* I guessed they'd sent it hoping I would receive it at the right time. I read the card. I was overwhelmed with excitement, but none of my friends were home and my grandma, who lived in the in-law apartment behind our house, was out, so there was no one available to tell. I was getting engaged! *Well*, I thought, smiling, *my wish of no longer having to sleep alone will finally come true.* The card must have come a day too early because it was John and my 3rd year anniversary and we had a date that night. It had to be when he was going to pop the question. It wasn't like Dylan would have a clue what I was talking about. I'd just have to wait patiently. The night couldn't have been more perfect. John and I went to dinner, then he got us a room at the Ritz at the Country Club Plaza. Leaning against the tall picture window, gazing at the pretty Christmas lights lining the plaza, I almost forgot what was about to happen. Then, I heard his knees crackle behind me, and I smiled. It was finally happening. We were going to be a real family.

The perfect night came to an end the next morning when I had to go to work. At least I got to go to work with a diamond on my finger! I was working part-time at La Petite Academy day care center while going to college. When there was an opening in the babies' room, I could bring Dylan with me while I worked, but I had to pay for him and really didn't make enough money to afford it. I understood then why some moms simply couldn't work. It made no sense for me to watch other people's kids but not make enough to pay for *my* son to be with me. I liked working there, but arriving while the babies were napping was hard for me. The lights were turned off, the babies were asleep—I had to fight to keep my eyes open. I couldn't leave the room, and no one else was there to keep me awake. Playtime with the babies was better, but I still had to be creative to keep myself awake. I'd usually act a little over dramatic and talk much too loudly; the director must've thought I was a nut case. Each and every day my focus was on staying awake. I'd think, *I know what it must feel like to be an alcoholic wondering when and how can I get my next drink. For me, it's when and where can I get my next sleep?*

On October 3, 1992, John, Dylan, and I were officially a family living in one house together. Because we were young, our wedding was packed with relatives and friends from high school. Dylan was the most adorable ring bearer. We didn't go on a honeymoon, but put what money we had towards our first house a few blocks away from John's parents' house. Our new home had a bedroom and bathroom for us, a bedroom and hallway bathroom for Dylan, and an extra bedroom for our office. Although I was sad to leave the house I grew up in, I was hopeful I would be leaving all of those nightmares behind, too. For me, having a bed partner for life wasn't so much about sex (obviously a plus), but the end of my crazy nightmares. Our priest came over to bless our new home and a painted cross that a friend of ours had given us for a wedding gift. John didn't know it then, but to complete our new home, I planned to get a dog! He was more of a cat guy.

> *Standing outside my old bedroom in the long, dark hallway, I feel much smaller than usual. At the end of the hallway, I see my father sitting quietly reading the paper. He doesn't know I'm here. Turning my head back towards the darkness of my room, I see the shadow of a person wearing a hat holding a hatchet high in the air. I reach out toward my father and try to move to him, but an uncontrollable force keeps me from moving. My heart pumps faster. An overwhelming feeling of evil flows through me and the hair on my arms stands straight up. The figure is creeping closer, but I can't scream. I'm paralyzed by fear. The hatchet swings downward.*
> *I wake up.*

The moment I awoke I thought: *This wasn't supposed to happen*. John was in the same bed. I wasn't in my parent's house. I'd even stopped watching scary movies! The dreams had followed me; they even took me back to my old house. Why? These were definitely not random firings of neurons making up a story! This story kept happening over and over. Was my hidden wish fulfillment, as Freud might have suggested, to be murdered, or something disgusting between my dad and I? In this nightmare in the past, my dad had heard me. It was as if the dream had anticipated my actions and adjusted itself. I hadn't had time to come up with an escape plan or dream power. The hatchet came down fast! What the heck was going on here? I didn't wake John, but I slid over closer and made sure at least one part of my body was touching his. Feeling safe again, I fell back asleep.

My mom had surgery again. A tumor on her liver had been coming back since they first discovered and removed it when my sister was born. My dad told me the doctor had said everything went well this time. I knew it would; I knew there wasn't anything to worry about. It was kind of strange, but I felt like if I couldn't picture something happening, it wouldn't happen. Not that I thought I was clairvoyant, but it felt akin to that. The same was true if I thought about something too much or had a flash in my mind of something happening—it would happen. This scared me because I hadn't been able to picture or dream of Dylan as an older boy. Usually, I would have dreams that included people in the near future, but he was not one of them. I wasn't sure what to make of this. Did this mean I wasn't supposed to worry about him because he was fine or was something bad going to happen to him because I couldn't picture him?

Now that both my sister and I had moved out of the house we grew up in, my parents decided to move to a new house in a city nearby. Although I was happy they'd built a new home for themselves, I was sad to be losing *our* home. How would I react if I drove by and saw someone sledding down *my* hill? The new owners had already removed the pool in the backyard and put a doorway from the living room into my grandma's apartment. So many memories were in those walls, and I would never go into that house again! Birthday parties, sleepovers, earaches, swimming, and watching *Friday Fright Night* with Gram had all happened there! I knew every inch of the house that my parents had built. I was having a really hard time letting go. Just as I was moving on to a new stage in my life, my parents were also moving on.

I was officially a psychology and administration of justice student at the University of Missouri, Kansas City (UMKC). Psychology was the natural choice for me. After all, isn't that the major people chose when they were trying to figure out what the hell was wrong with themselves? Things were working out perfectly. John was working at UMKC, and Dylan was going to preschool at a brand new childcare center just off campus. I had met a few new friends. One offered to take notes for me in class when I fell asleep, but his handwriting was impossible to read—it looked like Chinese! I worked part-time at UMKC's Career Services office. I did some research in the career books for sleep-related jobs, but had no luck. The closest matches would require a PhD or MD, but I didn't have the time or money to go to school for that long, and I certainly couldn't stay awake long enough to take the hard classes that would require. If I could just work in the field, I thought, I'd be happy.

As I was driving longer distances, I was also having more frequent near misses on the road. I was so exhausted from juggling school, homework, and being a mother and wife, that keeping my eyes open while driving was almost impossible. Then, it would hit me—no, not a car—sleep! Even walking around campus had become a struggle. I was always yawning, and my eyes would start to close against my will. Once, when I went to visit John, I started to doze and almost fell down the steps to his office. I couldn't keep living like this, I had to get a second opinion. I'd been afraid that another doctor would tell me there was nothing wrong with me, maybe a little anemic, but fine. Now that I was married, had new insurance and a new doctor, I was determined to try again.

Still stunned by two close calls while driving to the doctor's office, I began tearing up the minute I saw the doctor enter the room. Concerned, she asked, "What can I do to help you?" I completely lost it. "Please don't tell me nothing's wrong with me! If you don't help me, I'm going to end up killing myself or someone else! Just getting here was a potentially deadly mission. All I want to do is sleep, but it's going to end up killing me if I can't control it!" She just grinned. "It's OK, honey. I know what's wrong with you. We need to get you to a sleep lab."

CHAPTER 3

Put it to Rest

My life would be changed forever. I brought my pillow, a bag full of homework, and wore sweat pants and a T-shirt to sleep in. I was so excited for the sleep study that I actually worried I wouldn't be able to fall asleep. I walked by a control room with glass windows where sleep technicians dressed in scrubs worked behind computers. One technician walked me down a hallway with bedrooms on either side until we came to the one I would sleep in. Although I was in a hospital, the room felt cozy and not at all sterile. The technician explained that he'd attach wires to my legs, heart, head, and face and stretchy belts around my waist, then monitor my sleep. At this point, he could have done whatever he wanted to me; I was just happy to have someone recognize and validate my plea for help.

The doctors were testing for narcolepsy—I knew it! According to the brochure I read, the main symptom of narcolepsy is excessive daytime sleepiness (EDS). Sleepiness can come on as "sleep attacks" and it's almost impossible to stay awake when it comes on. Funny how I always described my sleepiness as being a sleep attack; I didn't even know there was such a thing. The technician gave me an Epworth Sleepiness Scale (ESS) questionnaire to fill out to determine my level of sleepiness, a big factor in narcolepsy. I answered "no" to all the questions that had to do with cataplexy, a sudden loss of muscle use that can make you drop something you're holding, buckle at the knees, or even collapse completely to the floor during an extreme emotional outburst such as anger or laughter. I'd had my fair share of tantrums, and I laughed plenty, but never experienced cataplexy.

Sleep paralysis, the inability to move upon falling asleep or waking up from sleep, and hypnagogic/hypnopompic hallucinations, dreamlike images that you see upon falling asleep or waking up, are also symptoms of narcolepsy. To those questions, I answered a definite "yes." Thank God they didn't ask me to explain my dreams or go into the details of my experiences—I was sure the witch with the knife and the chanting would have freaked them out. I felt very proud of myself as I listened to the technician. I knew exactly what he was talking about.

I slept beautifully that night, and nightmare free. After passing the first overnight polysomnography (PSG) test to rule out any sleep disordered breathing problems, the next step was to nap through the day. They called this a multiple sleep latency test (MSLT). I was so excited because this would be the first time in my life that I could sleep the day away and not get in trouble for it. Doctor's orders! To diagnose narcolepsy, they would look for REM sleep during the twenty-minute naps. The tech woke me up pretty early in the morning, but said I would be able to go back to sleep in a couple of hours. He came into the room every two hours and tucked me in. Well, that's what I called it. He was actually checking wires and plugging me back in for monitoring. The day's routine was eat, sleep, and watch *I Love Lucy* (definitely laughed during this show), sleep, do homework, sleep, eat, watch *I Love Lucy*, sleep.... The day went by really fast. After the fourth nap, the tech told me that I was "one sleepy young lady," and I would not have to finish the final nap.

This experience marked an important turning point in my life. Finally, I not only had a name for my problem, but I also had a treatment. The doctor explained that there was no cure for narcolepsy, but I could use amphetamines on a daily basis to help control my sleepiness. I was given Ritalin. This test made it official, my life would never be the same again! I wanted to run out and tell the world, "I'm *not* lazy! I actually worked harder at everything just to keep up!" I couldn't wait to go back to my high school and educate the teachers and nurses so this never happens to another kid again. No one should have to live life, every hour of every day, struggling just to stay awake!

I'm lying in bed staring at the ceiling. My eyes start to wander around the bedroom. What's wrong with my legs? I can't move them. Oh no, I'm in one of "those" types of sleep again. I guess I'll just have to wait it out. In the meantime, I should test out what I can and can't do. On the count of three I'm going to lift my arm. One, two, three! Hmmm ... nothing. Can I see? Yep. Slightly dark, but I can see my dresser and the end of the bed. Nothing else going on but waiting. Feeling is coming now. Not the kind of tingly hurt that your muscles feel when they wake up. I'm beginning to feel the all-over body release of sleep that binds me to the bed. I wake up.

This sleep paralysis thing was really freaky. But at least I knew what it was now! I didn't have hallucinations this time, so I took it as an opportunity to experiment a little to see what I could and couldn't do while paralyzed. I also knew I wouldn't be stuck like that forever. I wondered if being in a coma was similar in this way, being stuck awake in an unresponsive body. Naps were still necessary on occasion. I tried hard to not take too much of my medicine because I still had to sleep at night. The drug I took didn't work that well either. A year after my diagnosis, I thought I was getting a handle on narcolepsy. I recognized sleep paralysis, took my medicine responsibly, and tried to avoid driving during times of sleepiness.

At about 3 a.m. on a Sunday morning, I headed home from a fun night at the Westport bars with Noel. I had felt perfectly awake and energized when we left the bars. After I dropped Noel off, I blasted dance music in the car to help keep myself awake on the drive home. I wasn't drunk, but sleep was starting to tug at me pretty hard. I rolled down the windows to freshen my mind.

Why is that ONE WAY sign over there and pointing the other direction? Crap. I guess I'd better take this exit. Why was I sitting at a red light? I should've been going south down the highway. Ugh... I decided to circle around the outer road to get back on the highway. *Oh no, there's a ONE WAY sign next to the highway! I hope no one notices I'm going the wrong way. I better get off at the next exit before another car comes.* What? Why in the world was I now sitting on Main Street heading towards my old house? I still had two more exits to go! I remembered seeing those ONE WAY signs, but knew they weren't real.

I just had to stay awake for ten more minutes and I'd be home. Once again, I circled around to get back on the highway. *This can't be right, how did I end up going the wrong direction? How embarrassing, a cop better not see me driving the wrong way. He might think I'm drunk or something.*

No, no, no! Tears streamed down my face as I continued across the bridge over the highway towards Main Street and my old house. I didn't want to, but I pulled the car up to a phone booth in front of a convenience store and called John. "Hello?" "Hey, it's me," I said upset, angry, and nervous. "It's four o'clock in the morning!" John replied, sounding pretty worried considering bars closed at three. "What are you doing?" As I rambled on about the weird visuals and time warps I was experiencing while driving, he interrupted me, saying, "Just come home, Brianna." Frustrated, I screamed at the top of my lungs, "I'm trying!" I slammed down the phone and got back in the car, determined to make it home safely. Fortunately, the adrenaline pumping through my body at this point was enough to get me past the exit and home without feeling the pull of sleep.

"So, I'm guessing you two are up and getting ready for church this morning?" John passed me the phone, "Brianna, it's for you." This was the typical Sunday morning phone call my mom liked to tease us with. "Sure, Mom, I'm getting up and will see you there." Going to Sunday mass was a tradition in our family, but John and I had become lazy since we'd been on our own. John grew up Catholic as well and had always gone to mass with his dad. Since staying awake was easier for me now, I tried to meet my parents and Gram at church more regularly. Keeping Dylan entertained was always a challenge. I once walked out of church with him, screamed to the sky at the top of my lungs to let the frustration out, then we quietly walked back in to rejoin mass. I think I saw a few parents smiling to themselves; I imagined they were feeling sorry for me.

I knew it was hard for my mother to let go of her baby girl at such a young age. At least I lived close by. If the universe hadn't altered my original plans, I would have been living far away in a dorm at the University of Missouri. When I thought about it, I really couldn't imagine myself living in a dorm or sorority. Living in this little house with John and Dylan felt right. There was only one thing missing....

I knew it was selfish of me, but against John's wishes, Dylan and I drove about thirty miles to meet a breeder, and I bought a Dalmatian! Dylan named him Pongo after the dog in *101 Dalmatians*, of course. I'd always had a dog growing up, so it felt like a natural part of any family. Dogs made a home complete. Besides, John got us a cat named Figaro. I told myself that I was an adult and could do what I wanted in my own house, not to mention it was Mother's Day. Between my stress managing sleep and schoolwork, John's stress at his job and wanting a higher salary, and Dylan's constant need for attention creating trouble for him at school, I figured a fun puppy was just what we needed to take the edge off.

I'd never had to deal with a loved one dying, except when my Grandmother on my dad's side died when I was in fourth grade. I knew her, but not well. As a college requirement, I had to take a class called Death and Dying. I found there was a lot to learn about death and dying that would be good to know before it hit me or someone I loved. My mom volunteered to go with me on a tour of a funeral home for an observation writing assignment. We followed the funeral director through the "showrooms" of caskets. The experience was similar to buying a new car. "This is our basic model with minimal comfort," the salesman explained. The least expensive casket was plain, metal, and not appealing to the eye. Then, we moved to a room of more expensive caskets with beautiful stained wood and lush cushions lining the inside. My mom talked privately with the director while I wandered around by myself and took notes from my observations. Strange how much of an interest my mom took, I thought. She explained on the way home that the experience made her think more about what she wanted when her time came, and she was going to make some arrangements, just to be prepared.

Death and dying were far more interesting than I'd anticipated. What we may think is crazy in the way other cultures deal with death may not be as crazy as our own custom of embalming and displaying corpses. I mean, really, how we flush all the blood out of a body, remove the organs, and replace them with blow up plastic pieces and artificial fluids is pretty gruesome. I also learned about euthanasia. In the beginning, I thought the professor was saying "youth in Asia"(!) I thought, *Are they starving or something? How is this relevant?* As it turned out, I already had experience with euthanasia when my parents decided to put our dogs to sleep when they became very ill.

As a Christian, I was a firm believer in thou shall not kill, so I didn't believe it was right to put humans "to sleep" simply because they were terminally ill. I believed God had a plan for everyone, so who were we to mess with that plan?

But, I didn't know if God had a plan for animals. Since they couldn't tell us what hurt or what the problem was, I understood the idea of "mercy killing." It's so hard to watch anyone suffer. For our final paper, we had to choose and write a care plan for a terminally ill patient. Because I didn't know anyone who'd been terminally ill, I had to research what was available. I chose to write my paper on hospice care.

I'd learned to use the World Wide Web at the school's computer lab. John had told me about it a year earlier when he'd learned about it and built UMKC's first Website for the International Student Affairs office where he worked. I didn't quite understand it then because he was trying to explain it in terms of HTML language, and I tuned out. But when I started using the Internet, I thought it was amazing! Of course, I immediately researched sleep, anything I could find on it. I ended up arguing with some random person in a chat room (not a real room, I learned, but a place on the computer where people could type to each other instantly and have conversations about various topics). He had made a comment about how narcoleptics should consider not having babies because they could pass the gene down to their kids.

Wow. I let him have it, especially because chat rooms were anonymous. How dare he say such a thing! If he believed what he said, that meant he thought a life like mine wasn't worth living! Sure, my life was difficult, but whose wasn't? Actually, once I'd made my argument, I realized my life *was* pretty awesome. I played hard as a kid, played sports, had lots of friends, went to parties, vacationed with family, and I was very healthy. I had a husband, a healthy little boy, a house, a dog, and a cat. I told him that I—a narcoleptic—was a student sitting in UMKC's computer lab and graduating with a double major in the spring. My life as a narcoleptic was pretty darn good, and I wouldn't change a thing!

What I didn't tell him was, "Thank God I now have medication to help me." It was much easier to feel good about my accomplishments now that the hard part was over. Well, not "over" by any means, but at least I was no longer at risk of killing myself or others on the streets. When it came to narcoleptics, one thing about driving was true: an undiagnosed narcoleptic was a dangerous narcoleptic. Once I had a label and treatment, I was no longer a threat on the streets. I would get really angry when people talked about taking away our driving privileges. I had a perfect driving record! Besides, adults make choices every day regarding their ability to function behind the wheel of a car. What about people who take pain medication or enter a bar? People get sleepy and cause accidents all the time. In fact, my chemistry teacher said researchers believe a worker who fell asleep on the job caused the explosion at Chernobyl. Don't get me wrong, I believed driving with narcolepsy, like many other conditions, could be dangerous. But, I also believed that with treatment, the choice to drive or not should be left to the individual.

Sitting in the back of one of my Administration of Justice (AOJ) classes with my head resting on my arm, I listened to the teacher talk about stereotyping and discrimination against people with epilepsy. "I have that same problem, but I have narcolepsy," I'd heard a girl say from the front row. My head popped up and I looked around to see who had said that. Like a groupie waiting outside a concert for my favorite singer, I practically attacked her after class with questions. I wanted to hug her like she was my new best friend! I had never noticed her before, but we actually had quite a few classes together. "My mom also has narcolepsy and was sort of KU Med's guinea pig for a while, so she knew to keep a look out for me," she explained.

Unlike me, my new friend Stacy had cataplexy. "I don't have it often and it's not severe, but it has happened a few times. I felt totally humiliated." She went on to tell me how her tongue, being a muscle, stopped working when she was testifying on the stand in a courtroom. Her emotions, at an all-time high, had triggered a cataplexy attack. A hand or arm muscle was one thing, but not being able to speak properly in front of a group of people and not being able to say why must have been horrifying.

I felt like I'd found my soulmate, my twin... we both had narcolepsy (she also had cataplexy); we were the same age; we were both AOJ majors (I was also psych); we were both pregnant as teenagers (she had a daughter, I a son); and we were the same height and weight (her skin was black, mine was white). *This was amazing,* I thought! Stacy leaned on me for support during those sleepy times in class when her medicine wasn't working well. I knew she wasn't lazy. Worse than being perceived as lazy, however, she was also dealing with racial discrimination.

Most amphetamines used to treat narcolepsy are classified as a controlled substance, therefore illegal without a doctor's written prescription. A person is only allowed a thirty-day supply at a time. "The pharmacist refused to fill my prescription because it is a controlled substance." Although she never actually referenced "race," Stacy firmly believed that her being black had everything to do with the pharmacist questioning her business of obtaining the drug. "The anger and frustration built up to where I was going to explode. It triggered a cataplexy attack and all kinds of muscles stopped working." Witnessing the cataplectic attack but not knowing what it was, the pharmacist had called the police. Her story filled me with sadness and anger as well. Had he known the effects of the condition he was providing medication for and not made assumptions of illicit drug use, the pharmacist could have prevented such a horrible experience.

I thanked God every day that I didn't have to experience the horrors of cataplexy. I'm sure being a white woman in a white community had its benefits, but I'm also pretty sure that there will come a day when I'm turned away empty handed from a pharmacy. I could never go back to the way things were. I'd rather buy amphetamines off the street than go back to the nightmare that life was when I was sleepy.

Experimental Psychology was at night; it also happened to be one of my longest classes because of the lab. We were packed tight in small, old-fashioned wooden desks in a little outbuilding on campus. I wasn't typically claustrophobic or anxious, but the circumstances made the room feel like it was crushing in on me. All I could think about was how to escape. I don't know why I picked the desk furthest from the door in the back, because the combination of a heavy sweater, darkness and rain, heat from the register next to my feet, and a quiet classroom was a recipe for disaster. My eyes were so heavy and hot they hurt. I had already made a huge disruption trying to navigate through desks and backpacks on the floor to use the bathroom. I couldn't concentrate on anything but my escape plan. I needed to get up and move around before my head nods made me look like I was possessed! I felt like crying. My brain hurt. I had to shut my eyes or get out. The teacher didn't know I had narcolepsy, and none of the students in this class were friends of mine. What would I have said? "Excuse me, I have narcolepsy and you're boring me, so against my will, I'm going to sleep now." *This is never going to end,* I thought as I left the building.

My expectations had been that school and family life were to become easier, not harder. Besides the narcolepsy, something wasn't right with me—I was a total bitch! I hated everything, especially food. I had gone from weighing one hundred twenty pounds to one hundred and three. Thanks to a fast metabolism, I'd always been the kind of person who ate all the time and would get grouchy if I didn't. But now, just the thought of eating made me feel nauseous. John usually invited friends over when the Chiefs played on Sunday afternoons; now I'd lock myself in the office to avoid seeing anyone. I couldn't help feeling so irritated all the time. Between my behavior, John's dissatisfaction with his job and increasing weight, and the typical stresses marriage, kids, and a mortgage have on a young couple, John said the words: "I want a divorce." "No!" I screamed. "You wanted all of this! I'm not going to leave my parents and change my name just for you to quit!" But I knew he was right, something had to change. Everyone hated me, John wanted to leave me, I still couldn't stay awake, I looked awful, and I couldn't take it anymore!

Thank God students got up to ten free visits to a counselor, so I didn't hesitate to make an appointment. As with my last doctor's appointment, I started bawling the minute I stepped foot into his office. "I hate food, everyone, and everything!" I cried as I looked at the doctor, yearning for a solution. I told him how hard I'd been trying to keep up with school, work, marriage, raising a kid—life. In addition to all that, I was up to nine 10 mg pills of Ritalin a day and still couldn't stay awake, none of my clothes fit, and I was a total bitch to everyone. He took a deep breath and said, "Have you considered that maybe it's your medication that's causing all these feelings and extra problems?" Silence—wow. It hadn't occurred to me that medication could affect my mood and behavior. "Can the medication really do all of this?" I immediately began to feel relief. "It is possible, yes," he said. My whole body felt lighter (and I don't mean more weight loss). Everything was going to be just fine. I knew what to do, and I would fix it. "Thank you so much for your help!" I said. I left feeling confident and with a second wind.

College graduation couldn't have come any faster. I must have lay in bed for three days straight after all the ceremony and party excitement calmed down. I felt so much relief, not only from the end of classes, but also by my decision to change medication. One simple change in drug choice restored my appetite and changed my mood, which allowed John and I to restore our relationship. I thought back to the hell I'd put myself through and all I had accomplished in those past four years, and it made me cry good tears and bad. Finals were so rough, but I did what I had to do: I took full advantage of my amphetamines and pulled an all-nighter to finish an assignment. At 10 p.m. (after a night class), I started a paper on the death penalty that was due the next morning. Some people need a pot of coffee, but for me it took lots of amphetamines. I decided it was best not to tell my Drug Policies teacher that I had abused my controlled substance. But hey, I got an A!

Understanding and predicting behavior in people can be pretty useful in life, so I didn't feel a degree in psychology was a total waste of time. Dylan had something going on in that brain of his that could use a shrink, and I was determined to help him. Every day in kindergarten he'd bring home a note from his teacher saying that he had difficulty staying on task. After getting in trouble at school almost every day in the month of October, I told him he couldn't go trick-or-treating. His response: "That's OK, I'll have fun handing out the candy!" And, he did. I knew he was a handful, but I thought maybe he was just bored. Honestly, I thought he was very intelligent for his age. I knew the staff at his private, Catholic school believed that I didn't know what I was doing as a parent simply because I was young. The counselor there told me, "Dylan just doesn't know the meaning of consequence." I had tried several of the methods of discipline suggested in my child psychology book. "No, you don't understand," I tried to explain, "he simply doesn't care!"

"Why can't you just not talk and be good for a change?" I often asked Dylan. "I don't know. I can't help it!" At first, I blew this off feeling like it was simply an excuse, then his words struck me as sounding very familiar. It was time to take Dylan to see a psychologist. "We didn't have to finish the tests because we already know," explained the psychologist. This, again, sounded very familiar. "He's borderline gifted, but ADHD is holding him back." Attention-deficit/hyperactivity disorder has three main components: 1) Inattention—trouble staying focused and on task, 2) Hyperactivity—constantly feeling restless and talking too much at inappropriate times, and 3) Impulsivity—interrupting constantly and not thinking before acting. Not only did Dylan have severe ADHD, but he also had oppositional defiant disorder (ODD), which is characterized by defiant and disobedient behavior to authority figures. To me, ODD sounded like a personality type, like his father's. John had always fought "the Man" when it came to school and didn't have much respect for the law until he decided to play by the rules for Dylan and my sake.

Believe it or not, Dylan would also need to be on amphetamines! I thought it was curious how amphetamines worked with hyperactive kids. While the amphetamines helped me "focus" rather than fall asleep, they helped Dylan focus and stay on task to keep his mind from wandering in five different directions. As far as his need to challenge authority, amphetamines were the only solution, unless he were to continue with psychotherapy. I got a tremendously gratifying feeling from recognizing his need for help, and preventing him from going all those extra years without a diagnosis like I had. Life simply wouldn't allow me to sleep when I wanted to or Dylan to pay attention whenever he felt like it. To keep up, my son and I would need to be on drugs for the rest of our lives.

I found the perfect website with any and all the answers I was looking for: Stanford Center for Narcolepsy! There I discovered that trial studies were going on for a new drug called Modafinil. It acts like an amphetamine, but isn't, so it wouldn't be considered a controlled substance. The website showed videos of narcoleptic dogs with cataplexy! So sad, really, but hilarious to watch the videos of puppies trying to run to their treats, only to fall a few inches short because of paralysis. Then, when they started to come to, they'd carefully stretch out their necks and slowly nibble on their bones. I told John that when it was approved in the US, he needed to buy stock in the company. "Why?" he asked. My advice was simple: "A lot of people are going to want to use it." This was probably the one and only stock tip I would ever have.

There was a section on research with a call for subjects to participate by sending in blood samples. With my psychology background, I felt that I had to participate in this research study. I just needed to get my parents to donate their blood. The test results were in! The research team sent a letter saying that the Stanford Center for Narcolepsy had been testing people with narcolepsy and their family members to see if they carry the DQB1-0602 gene. According to the letter, if the person had the gene and did not currently suffer from narcolepsy, it did not mean they would develop it. As it turned out, my dad had the gene! Knowing his need to saw wood at 7 a.m. on a Sunday morning, I knew it was possible that he could have the gene but not the disorder. My mom, on the other hand, did not have the gene. In her words, "Ha! I'm finally not responsible for somebody's problem!" I, of course, had the genetic marker passed down from my father. I didn't ask my sister to participate, but there was no mistaking it—no one in my family had narcolepsy but me.

I didn't know how my parents felt about me being diagnosed with narcolepsy. Neither one had talked with me much about the diagnosis. I wondered if my mom felt bad about not getting me help when I had asked for it so many years earlier. I know I would have if it were me. I struggled with wanting them to feel bad about not taking me more seriously when I told them I needed help and not wanting them to feel bad because they had never even heard of such a condition and couldn't see just how hard everything was for me. Now that I felt a little more at ease with my diagnosis and the reason behind it, I needed to pay attention to the medical problems my mother was facing. I had been so focused on myself that I didn't realize just how serious her condition had become. I suppose she didn't want anyone to worry, she was considerate like that. She let me feel the large lump on her belly, but just smiled a little and said it was "uncomfortable." I didn't worry too much because the doctors had always reduced the size in the past. Besides, they would do more tests in a few months.

Hindsight is 20/20. You may not know it at the time, but looking back later, you'll say, "Of course, I get it!" and some things were finally starting to make sense. I had applied for but wasn't accepted into a Master of Social Work (MSW) program. I was upset because I believed I was a perfect candidate, yet had no idea how I was going to pay for it and, on top of that, was required to work a whole year without pay. Then, a month later, I found out that I not only got into the Master of Public Administration (MPA) program at UMKC, but also got an internship that paid for all of it. I could even work from home only fifteen hours a week, a narcoleptic's dream! There's a plan for everyone; just because you don't know what it is, it doesn't mean there isn't one. I was supposed to be with John, that's why God gave us Dylan. Without Dylan, neither of us had drive for a greater purpose. Maybe Dylan was hyperactive because God wanted me to be active with my child—but I could've definitely come up with alternatives that would have been far easier! As for my narcolepsy, John liked to joke, "That's how you got pregnant!" I was still trying to understand if there was a meaning to it all. Why so sleepy all the time? Why me?

CHAPTER 4

Sweet Dreams

The most bizarre dog encounter took place in my living room. While John was at work and Dylan in school, I was cleaning the house as usual. The warm, afternoon breeze filtered through the open mesh of the front storm door. Rounding the corner to the living room, I was shocked to see a large dog sitting on the front porch, peering in at me. Afraid that Pongo would notice and run for the door, I quickly sent him down the steps to the garage and shut the door behind him. I was a dog lover, so curiously, I headed to the front door. The dog was still sitting there like a salesman waiting patiently to make his pitch. "Hey buddy," I said through the door, "what are you doing out there?" He slowly rose to all fours and looked up at me. I guessed he was some type of boxer mix with short brown and black fur and a really large head. I'm not afraid of big dogs; in fact, the bigger the better. Then, I noticed his face. He didn't appear to be aggressive, but the sight of his lopsided eye, large bulge on his head, and bloody, yellow ooze not only made me feel a bit repulsed, but also leery. I couldn't just shut the door on him! I had to do something.

Broke, I couldn't take him to the vet. So, not knowing what I was thinking, I opened the door. I had pretty strict rules regarding what I allowed on my living room furniture: no food and no dogs. In walked this mysterious dog who headed straight for the couch, jumped up on the cushions, then curled into a ball and fell fast asleep. Still standing at the front door, I was speechless.

He didn't sniff around the house or go to the kitchen looking for food. He didn't head to the garage door smelling Pongo or even acknowledge me. It was as if he spotted my couch through the front door and was on a mission to get there and take a nap. Motionless, his head was snug between his arms and pulled-up legs, his tail wrapped tight. I walked closer to the couch and stared at him for a while.

The door that led down to the garage was just to my right, but I didn't hear a peep from Pongo. Surely, he had to know that there was a strange dog in the house, asleep on our couch of all places. I decided to let this stranger in my house sleep. He wasn't harming anyone, and he probably just needed some rest. After cleaning up the kitchen, I called John at work. I needed to tell somebody this was happening because it didn't seem real. He, of course, told me I was crazy to let the dog in and agreed it was pretty strange. The dog started to wake up, so I hung up the phone, filled a bowl with Pongo's food and put it, along with some water, on the front porch. While I held the storm door open, the dog jumped off the couch and trotted out the front door to eat and drink. I never saw the dog again.

The whole time he had been in the house I felt weirdly curious. I still wonder if maybe it hadn't happened. After he left, Pongo did walk over and smell the couch, but that was it. So many things could have gone wrong by letting a large, injured dog into my home. Had it been a man, strange and slightly injured, I most likely would not have opened my door. Sad and pathetic, but true. I don't think anyone would have blamed me for being afraid, especially since my house was surrounded by plenty of better options for him to have gotten help. It mainly freaked me out because I wondered if it was a test of some sort. I believed that God tested our character periodically to make decisions about our fate. Could this have been one of those times?

Dylan was so excited that he was finally going to have a little brother or sister. It was probably not the best timing because I was in graduate school and had to go off my medication, but would there ever be a good time to go off medication? I wasn't sure just how excited John was because he was always stressed about not having enough money, and we were still working on bettering our relationship. But I didn't want to wait anymore. He had his boy, and I wanted my girl! My baby bump showed much faster this time, probably because I was eating more. Being tired had me searching the kitchen for anything that contained carbs and/or sugar. Caffeine was a nonissue this time;

the doctor said I could have one can of pop a day. I had pregnancy workout videos and was totally ready to do this. Having a life other than your own living inside you is the most amazing experience. It's a shame that men don't have a way to understand the bond that develops between a mother and her unborn child.

I was only ten weeks along, but had already heard the heartbeat at my eight-week appointment. My breasts had stopped aching and I'd had an unexplainable feeling of detachment from the baby. Standing in the hot shower with my hands bracing my belly an overwhelming sadness took me by surprise; I sobbed. Feelings of loss and thoughts of losing the life inside me flashed through my mind. It was then that I understood why I hadn't been feeling pregnant lately. My breathing became more difficult and tears mixed with the water running down my face. I couldn't stop thinking about it. Why would I do this to myself? Why would I allow myself to have such negative thoughts? It was irrational, but it felt forced upon me.

I silently mourned while I carried around my dead baby in my belly. If my body didn't naturally pass the fetus within a week, the doctor would take it out. My mom had shared with me that she, too, had had a miscarriage and explained that it's actually fairly common. I figured only the mother carrying the child was affected by the feelings of loss, so I internalized the grief and tried to move on. I asked John to pick me up from the doctor's office because I didn't feel like driving myself. I had just come from my twelve-week appointment with the OB/GYN. Joh was sweet and appeared sad, but I knew it wasn't the same for him as it was for me. I was sure John was similar to most men, and that men were the reason society doesn't consider having a miscarriage as a "death" in the family.

With the start of a new year, I felt ready to get pregnant again. Thankfully, my internship allowed me to stay on, and I was able to make up the two classes I had dropped the following semester. I was about halfway through grad school, but our family needed me full-time first. I'd been volunteering at Dylan's school just to stay in contact with his teachers. He would be turning seven this year and I wanted my daughter; I needed her. My sister, Renee, said she was planning on getting pregnant as well. John wasn't thrilled about having another baby because Dylan was so much work. "What if we had another one just like him, Brianna?" John would say whenever I brought up my excitement about having another child. "We couldn't handle it." John's best friend,

Richard, had recently been diagnosed with having brain tumors and was scheduled to have massive surgery. I knew John was really stressed about his friend, but he couldn't let it affect our life. Besides, I'd already picked out her name—Claire.

The time had come for my mother's tumors to be removed again. As usual, they would test for cancer. My aunts and uncles on my dad's side were with him at the hospital. *Why are they there?* I thought. I didn't remember them being there in the past. I should have offered to go and be with my father, but I wasn't sure I was invited. When he called to let me know the procedure was done, he didn't sound the same on the phone. I couldn't stop thinking about it. I had discovered that when I thought about something for too long, it was because something was different or significant in some way. Maybe it was just in my head. Could it be that I was the one making it different because I was thinking about it too much? Or, was I thinking about it so much because "someone" was telling me that I needed to think about it? After the shower incident, I hated to dwell on anything. At the same time, I had been grateful that I had that quiet moment to myself to cry and process the idea of losing my baby. I believed that God had given me a little "heads up," and it helped me handle the blow of learning the news later. Being given information from a higher power, I believed that I'd found a bit of acceptance—maybe not understanding, but at least acceptance. Just like dreaming of the little boy riding on my shoulders through the field, I found a sense of comfort in the idea of having him in my life.

We are walking together side by side, my mother and I, along the sidewalk pushing baby buggies. These are the old style of strollers that look like small bassinets with fold down canopies above the head, the kind I used to push my dolls in when I was little. I don't see my mom walking next to me, but I know it is her. Looking down at the infants, one in each buggy, I know they can't both be mine because one is only slightly larger than the other. We don't talk. We just walk silently as we look at the babies. They are both girls.
I wake up.

The news that I was pregnant came as such a relief and something nice to talk about with my mom. When we'd found out that her tumors were cancerous, it didn't feel unexpected. I knew something was different this time because it felt somehow different than in the past. Would it be ridiculous of me to think that I had anything to do with her getting cancer simply because I had thought about it for too long? Renee and I sat with mom talking about babies, *our* babies! Hopefully our mom would get to watch both of her daughters have babies. I was skeptical, though, because the doctor said she only had six months to live. How could I be excited about giving new life when I was in the middle of watching my mother die?

"Brianna, tell me again about the dream you had about the babies." My mom always liked hearing about my dreams. This one in particular was a favorite of hers. It gave her hope to believe she would be alive when the babies were born. She looked so sad when I asked if she was interested in watching the babies for us after they were born. I guess I didn't understand the gravity of the situation. I didn't know cancer. I didn't know what was happening. What I did know was that my sister and I, for the first time in our lives, were friends. We finally had something in common. We were both pregnant, and we were both watching our mother die.

> *The sand squishes between my toes as I watch the cold ocean water rush up onto my feet. I hear seagulls screeching and waves breaking in the background. Florida, I think that's where we are. We must be on vacation. My dad is with me. I don't look at him to see his age, but I know that I'm older. We aren't alone. Someone is here with us. I don't see my mom. She's not here at all. Someone else is. And she, whoever she is, is with my dad.* I wake up.

My belly had gotten much bigger, and I was glowing! I had to take a break from school again, but the teachers were all understanding. Being at home and off medication was the perfect equation to make me fat. Well, the pregnancy had a little to do with it, too, I guess. When tired, I craved food, especially sweets and Mexican food! Eat, sleep, eat, sleep, walk the dog, eat, sleep, work a little, eat, and sleep. That was my schedule. My sister and I took long walks together and really started building a relationship. This was her first pregnancy, her marriage was falling apart, and her mother was dying. I was happy to be there for her.

Mother's Day was not the special day that I'd been blessed with for so many years. The day was spent in a hospital room visiting Mom after her last surgery. I walked around the gift shop looking for the perfect gift to help cheer her up on a day that was supposed to bring her joy. My eyes made contact with the droopy eyes of an adorable Precious Moments stuffed bear. It was large, light brown with a white tummy, and wore a pink plastic tag that read: "Have a Hug." I was a nut for stuffed animals! I'd had quite a few "best friends" in my bed keeping me safe at night. Something inside my head told me that I just had to give it to my mom for Mother's Day.

As I looked at the gifts that lined the wall behind her, I knew this bear was the absolute best. Who wouldn't love such a cuddly bear when feeling scared or in pain? He'd look after my mom.

Suddenly the hospital room began to spin. I hadn't been sick much during pregnancy, especially at four months, but I felt clammy and nauseous, so I quickly left the room. My dad stepped out a few minutes later, walked over to me, and said, "Brianna, we need to talk about what's going to happen next. The doctors say that there isn't anything else they can do for her, so we need a plan. I don't know what to do from here." He'd never come to me for anything before. Proudly, I looked up at him and said, "Dad, I know about hospice."

Visits to my parents' house were difficult. Luckily, I had the free time to spend full days with my mom. John's boss gave him a nice raise so we weren't hurting for money anymore. One thing about Dylan that seemed to make his disruptive behavior more tolerable was that he was a total sweetheart. Mom loved having him around. He was always trying to make her laugh and didn't shy away simply because she was sick. I, on the other hand, struggled with not knowing what to talk about with her. I knew then that she'd never get to see the babies. I thought back to what I'd been through in the last seven years and realized that Dylan wasn't just about bringing John and I together. Giving birth at the age of seventeen, on April 20, 1990, to a little redheaded boy, getting married on October 3, 1992, to John Morrison, and getting treatment for narcolepsy so I could graduate college in May 1995 was all part of a larger plan, someone else's plan. I was so happy to say that my mother was there for it *all*!

I lay beside my mom while she slept and imagined that I had special dream powers, powers that would let me see her dreams. What do people dream about when they know they are dying? On the verge of death, they couldn't possibly dream about the future. Because of the morphine, she slept most of the time. "Brianna!" Mom didn't quite wake up, but she scared the living daylights out of everyone nearby. My heart raced when I heard my name being screamed out in the middle of a dead sleep. She didn't sound fragile either. The tone she used took me back fifteen years, as if I was being yelled at as a child for something I'd done wrong. I was a little freaked out, but also happy that she was dreaming of me.

At four-and-a-half months pregnant, the baby hadn't moved yet. I lay in bed quietly, trying not to disturb John with my sadness and tears. He had enough going on with his best friend's diagnosis of brain tumors and stress of being the sole provider. Good and bad always came together, I knew, but now I greatly appreciated it as I wrapped my arms around my belly to feel grounded as I felt the weight of the world come crashing down on me. I took a slow, deep breath and prayed, "God, please give me something else to think about. I can't stop thinking about not having my mom in my life!"

I thought of a future with my children, and how I planned to give them all the wonderful memories of holiday and birthday parties, vacations, and simple family fun just like the ones my mother provided me with. I believed that my sister and I both became pregnant at this point in time not only to lessen the impact of losing our mother, but also to finally become friends. We would need each other. Suddenly, my thoughts were interrupted. My eyes began to burn and tears rolled down my cheeks. I grabbed John's hand from beside me and placed it on my belly next to mine. As he woke up and looked at me, I smiled at the next little nudge that hit our hands. Everything would be OK.

Girls! Renee and I were having girls! We just hit five months, so we were able to get a sonogram and find out the sex. She may not be able to meet them, but at least our mother would know they were girls. Renee and I told her their names—Claire Ann Morrison was my little one, Emily Jean Johnson was my sister's. My mom held on the best she could. I felt selfish expecting her to continue suffering just so we could have another day with her. I wanted to think that she suffered because *she* wanted another day of life. My mother loved us so much and probably didn't care that we were being selfish, so she endured.

I no longer felt sadness or anger about losing my last pregnancy. I believed that God only "postponed" Claire until the time was right. Maybe that day in the shower was God telling me that although I really wanted a baby, His plan was the one I needed to follow. My sister had always been a bit jealous of the relationship between my mom and me. It would have been too difficult for Renee if Mom had known both of my children but had never met hers. These baby girls were our mother's parting gifts to us, her daughters. I understood now. I found acceptance.

Time spent at my parents' house was heartbreaking. My half-sisters Janice and Julie came into town from California because they'd heard the time was near. Gram lived in the lower level of my parents' house, so she helped with my mom as much as she was able—she was in her mid-eighties, but healthy in body and mind. I knew it broke her heart to watch her child die before her. The day Gram found us girls in the closet dividing up our mother's clothes broke her heart, I'm sure. Mom had given us instructions to do so while she was still alive, in case we had questions, and to leave any matching outfits to Dad for country dancing. "When your dad gets remarried," she explained, "I want him to do everything that we had planned to do." She wanted him to find someone who loved to dance like she did, to buy an RV and travel with in the winter, and to have a partner for the rest of his life.

I understood that my baby could feel any tension I was experiencing during the pregnancy, so I tried hard not to freak out and cry all the time about my mom. I also tried to keep quiet and be cheery so as not to upset John. He was actually much more fragile than I had imagined during stressful times. I was the lucky one who held a beautiful reminder of love and life inside my body to refocus my emotions. Yet on most nights, silent tears rolled down my cheeks. The thought of losing this baby had not entered by mind, but the memory from my earlier loss made me anxious.

I still hadn't had any dreams about her! I'd had at least one or two about Dylan when I was pregnant with him. As always, I turned to God for support. Being careful not to be too greedy, I prayed, "God, please help me through all of this heartache. I love that you've given me Claire, but I'm so scared! I tried just as hard for the last one, and I lost it. I can't lose this one. I'm already losing a mother. Please let me know that everything will be OK. I'm holding on so tight to this little girl. She's the only thing that can help me get through this. Please help me."

> *She's so beautiful! What is this, a school picture? I don't take my eyes off it because I don't know how long I have. My hand grips the 5 x 7 portrait, and I just stare, studying every little detail. Her straight, silky hair is just like mine, but darker in color like John's. Her skin is so smooth, darker in complexion than her brother's. I can tell she gets very tan in the summer. She's a perfect combination of John and me: his coloring, my features. Her eyes are chocolate brown like John and Dylan's. Her hair lays all one length, probably midway down her back with a red ribbon used as a headband. Smaller nose like mine, but not exactly. In this picture, she looks to be about fifth or sixth grade. She looks like me, but is not me. This is my daughter, Claire. I wake up.*

"John! I saw her!" My weird dream outbursts no longer startled him. He rolled over and looked at me, showing I had his attention. He relaxed a bit once he realized I was smiling and actually looked excited. "I saw Claire! She's got straight hair just like mine, yet brown like yours; nose like mine; skin like yours and brown eyes. I was staring at her picture!" The look on his face told me he totally believed me. Ten years with me had shown him that I was always sincere and never lied. Sure, he teased me about being weird and such when it came to sleep, but this was different. I believed that it was at this moment that he really felt like a father to a baby girl. The last pregnancy for him was just a "pregnancy," not a baby. With Dylan, my pregnancy was a turning point in John's life—he was becoming a man; it was a fresh start and gave his life purpose. For the first time in a long time, we both became excited about our future.

I couldn't wait to tell my mom about her granddaughter. What an amazing gift I was given! I'd heard the saying, "Ask and you shall receive," but I was always afraid of being too selfish. I just wanted to be thoughtful when praying for my own needs. If I asked for too much, I may not get anything at all. I never did ask God for a cure for my sleepiness. I'm not sure why, actually. In times of need, I had asked God to get me home safely when driving or simply get me through a test without falling asleep. I'd still fall asleep during tests, but God came through for me when it mattered most. Seeing Claire's face when I asked for something else to think about was so powerful that it brought tears to my eyes every time I thought about it. My mom may never get to meet her granddaughter, but I could certainly pass this gift along to her.

Having another day to see my mom's face meant the world to me. I took it for granted that she'd be at the house, waiting for me. She looked frail, but still coherent and smiling like always. She didn't look surprised as I told her about my beautiful dream of Claire. Of course she would look like me; I looked just like my mother. I teased her by telling her how John's mom suggested she come back reincarnated as Claire and become *my* daughter this time. She laughed, "Oh, no, honey. I've had a long, happy life. I don't want to come back and do it all again." Sadness overwhelmed me, but I couldn't let her see me cry. "Maybe you could be Claire's guardian angel then." She smiled, "Yes, I could do that."

As I looked at my mom lying in bed in what turned out to be her final week, she looked back at me with embarrassment on her face. "My hair is falling out," she said softly. "I'm so skinny. I look really bad." Her words brought tears to my eyes. "Mom, our bodies are just shells. My body is getting bigger. Yours is getting smaller. We are just held temporarily inside these shells." I tried to sound intelligent and sympathetic at the same time, not sure I'd achieved either. The toilet was only a few feet from her bed, so I offered to help her up to go. But I didn't have the strength to hold my mom up when she started to collapse to the floor. "Dad!" I tried to yell for him, but my voice cracked as my throat closed up. "Dad, come quick! I can't pick her up!" The dead weight of my mom slumped at my feet was too much for me. I couldn't tell if I really didn't have the strength or if my muscles became weak because of the emotional impact of the situation. I'd never felt so helpless in my life.

This was it. I'd never really talked to her about her feelings about death and dying, but I knew her faith in the afterlife was strong. Was there something I was forgetting to say? This was all the time I had left with her. She didn't talk much anymore, so all I could think to do was just assure her Renee and I would be just fine and not to worry about anything. She asked why she was still alive, since she stopped taking food intravenously. The hospice nurse told her that it was the Sprite she was drinking that was keeping her alive. She announced that she would no longer drink it. My time with her was up. There was no more. Anything else I wanted to say would have to be left unsaid. This was good-bye.

Dark, empty, dreamless sleep. Darkness turns into a black hole. Forces pulling, turning, spiraling. Kaleidoscope of colors. Pulling at my soul. Ripping. Nothing. I wake up.

The phone call came the next morning. I didn't have to ask John who it was. He knew that I knew, but he said the words anyway. "She is gone." The funeral felt very mechanical and scripted. My mom had picked out some amazing poems that were hard to listen to without my eyes flooding with tears. Her body was washed, hair curled, make-up done, and she was displayed in a coffin decorated with beautiful flowers. I couldn't help but think about the grotesque process used to make her appear as if she were alive.

Someone had asked one of us sisters to put more lipstick on my mom because she looked a little pale. Of course she's pale, I thought, but because I had the color that my mom liked, I volunteered. I thought I would feel something walking over to her coffin. Yet, as I approached, there was nothing. No feeling that she was just asleep. No feeling that her soul lingered. No bond as her child that I could feel towards the shell of her body that lay before me. I believed she (her soul) was not there. It was just as the poem had read: "Do not stand at my grave and weep. I am not there. I do not sleep. Do not stand at my grave and cry. I am not there. I did not die."

The priest came to my parents' house to visit and share a special letter my mother had written almost a year earlier. She had instructed the priest to keep it until she passed, then share it with the family. The letter was general, but some comments were directed to us as individuals, instructions for things she'd like to have done. She asked for my dad to find someone to marry so he wouldn't be alone. To me she wrote that although I had asked when I was little if, when she died, I could have the new plates and bowls my parents had just bought, I couldn't. "Sorry, honey, but your dad will need those." She always found a way to use humor. Then, her final words, "I truly believe that death is a simple crossing over to something better. And, I *will* see you again."

I took refuge in Claire's baby room from time to time. Thoughts of her kept me strong. I hugged the soft, light brown, "Have a Hug" Precious Moments bear that I'd given my mom in the hospital, then set him gently inside Claire's crib. He had a new home now. A few days after the funeral, we piled into my Dad's old, blue van and drove to a rose garden for a short prayer ceremony and to spread Mom's ashes. On the day she joined me for the funeral home visit for my school project, she had changed her mind about being buried. No one complained about standing in the summer heat while her ashes blew through the air, across our bodies, and settled along the rose beds. We simply stood silently listening to the prayers, afraid to take in a deep breath.

"Hello?" "Hey, Baby." "Mom? Oh my gosh! I can't believe you called! How are you? Is everything OK? Are you alright? Where are you?" "Everything is alright. I just wanted you to know that I'm OK. I have to go now." "No, wait!" Silence. **I wake up.**

Wow. That's all I could think—wow. I had heard her! Not images of her or a dream about her, I'd actually heard her voice in my dream. We'd had an interactive phone conversation in my sleep! It was so short, though. Is there some kind of heaven protocol? Is it like jail where you get your one phone call? Whatever it might be, I was happy I got it! Funny, though, that it came as a phone call. I wondered if anyone else in my family had gotten one. But, I was too scared to ask, because what if they hadn't? I knew I was different when it came to dreams, but this wasn't any ordinary dream. I would wait and see if anyone else mentioned having dreams about Mom. It had been a few weeks since she had died. Then, it struck me … it was her birthday!

When I was eight months pregnant, we decided to put our house on the market. John got another raise and the stock we bought was doing really well, so it was time to move on. My days consisted of sleeping, eating, and walking our dog Pongo. I was glad I had pregnancy to blame for my weight gain because I was gaining a lot more than I had with Dylan. I didn't really have to drive any long distances, so that was good since I was off my meds. Our new house was perfect: Dylan didn't have to go to private school anymore because our new neighborhood had really good schools, Pongo loved his big backyard, and there were plenty of kids Dylan's age in our cul-de-sac. We decorated Claire's room with dolphins, ready for her arrival. John had talked his friend Richard into moving his family into a house right behind ours. Although he still had brain tumors, he attended college and his wife Susan gave birth to their first child.

> *"Hello?" "Hey, Baby." "Mom!" "How are you?" "I'm doing alright." "I have so much to tell you!" "I know, but I have to hang up now." "Wait! Can you call again?" "No, Baby, I can't." There was silence. Waiting.... I wake up.*

I was so confused. I would get random "phone calls" from my mother, but she never had very long to talk. I had so many questions for her and wanted to tell her everything that was going on, but she always had to hang up right away. Was she really not going to call me again? Why couldn't she? I wanted so badly to understand how this all worked. My dreams were open for her to call anytime she wanted. Before I went to sleep at night, I tried to think about how I might go searching for her in my dreams, but I was simply stuck in whatever dream scenario I was put in. There was nowhere for me to "go" to find her.

"Can't you see her?" John and I lay in bed and talked about our new arrival expected at any time. He looked at me funny, "What are you talking about?" I couldn't really explain to him what I meant about "see" her because I didn't mean physically see her. Pointing over toward our bedroom doorway, I smiled and asked again, "Can't you see her? Standing there with her little footie PJ's on; smooth, brown, silky hair, holding her bear and sucking her thumb?" He stared off toward the door and laughed. "Yeah, she'll totally wear footie PJ's. Those are my favorite." I wasn't sure if he really did see the picture in his head the way I did, but the vision of her in my mind was so clear, it was almost like having a memory.

Claire Ann Morrison arrived on October 29, 1997. The delivery went as well as deliveries could go. Dylan was such a proud, big brother. I decided not to breastfeed because I couldn't wait to get back on my medication and didn't plan on feeding amphetamines to my baby girl. Emily Jean Johnson arrived just five days after Claire. Renee needed an emergency C-section, but Emily was healthy. I don't know what it was with my sister, but nothing seemed to go smoothly for her. Emily looked huge next to Claire even though she was five days younger. She had a large, slightly bald head and big, beautiful blue eyes. Dylan may have been God's gift to me for all kinds of unknown reasons, but Claire and Emily were my mother's parting gifts to her daughters.

Renee and I helped Gram move into her own apartment once my dad started dating. She was eighty-five years old and absolutely perfect! She didn't drive anymore, so Renee and I took her wherever she wanted to go. She loved finally having a little independence and being away from the constant reminder of her daughter's death. My dad began seeing Karen, a woman he'd met in a hospice group for widows and widowers. His church held dances for people to mingle. My dad said that he was the only man who danced, so all the ladies liked him. Honestly, I believed my mother had handpicked her for him. Her late husband also died of cancer. She was a nurse and ten years younger (perfect to care for Dad if he ever needed it or to give advice to Renee and me). She had three really nice sons around our age, one even had a toddler and a baby. My dad was a "do-it-yourselfer" and perfect for her sons to turn to if they needed help with anything. Could Karen's late husband have gotten together with Mom and decide the two were a good match? Talk about a match made in heaven....

How could I feel sadness with so much joy around me? My tears were not of sorrow, but of amazement and awe. Yes, I watched my perfect mother wither away until the cancer finally took her. But, I looked back on all of the miracles that had happened (both big and small) and was overwhelmed to the point of simply crying. At the time, I hadn't understood why my life had to change with a teenage pregnancy, but I wouldn't have changed it for the world. Everything else in my life became possible because of John and Dylan. God may have taken my mother early, but He had given so many gifts in return for me to know that there was a very good reason she had to leave, even if I couldn't understand why. I had felt cursed with an endless need for sleep, but I was starting to believe that my ability to dream the way I did was actually a gift.

My dreams were so vivid and detailed, and I could remember almost every one. While most people simply watched themselves as a "character" within their dreams, unaware that they were experiencing an alternate reality, in many of my dreams I was aware of the difference and understood that I was experiencing a dream—I was lucid. I'd gone through some difficult times with narcolepsy, but it also helped me become who I was. People may have thought I was "weird" because I claimed to have spoken to my dead mother, seen my unborn daughter's school-aged picture, or lay paralyzed by REM while fully conscious, sometimes seeing and hearing things others could not. There was so much people didn't understand about sleep, so they were afraid to talk about it. Sleep was "my thing." I was good at it. It was my gift.

CHAPTER 5

Living in a Dream World

In 2001, I went to my first Narcolepsy Network conference. Considering my neurologist had asked me to pick up some information on narcolepsy for him while I was there, I decided it was best that I became my own expert. I'd been repeatedly disappointed in the lack of knowledge doctors had about narcolepsy. I had tried a new drug, Provigil (formerly Modafinil in Europe), and told my doctor it didn't last long enough and gave me headaches at the end of the day. When I told him that sitting in rooms waiting for doctors was the perfect spot for a quick nap, he responded, "Oh, I would have thought that the fluorescent lights would help you stay awake." If my doctor didn't understand that excessive daytime sleepiness (EDS) was not your standard feeling of being tired, how would anyone else? This conference was my opportunity to meet people like me and, hopefully, talk to medical professionals that really knew what was going on.

John, Dylan, his cousin Adam, and my father-in-law, Bart, went with me to the conference in California. They did tourist stuff while I joined the rest of my narcoleptic family. I was in the minority not having cataplexy. Their stories just broke my heart. I don't know how cataplectics do it (life)—I felt so blessed and thankful that I didn't have cataplexy. For one, I didn't think John and I would have survived our marriage. Knowing my son, he would have had me on the floor (falling from either laughter or anger) every chance he could! He was devilish like that. John's ability to make me laugh was one of the reasons I fell in love with him. It was difficult, however, for him to make me laugh out loud. Laughing required energy and, with my constant exhaustion, he'd mostly just get smiles out of me. At the conference, I bought a book called *Narcolepsy: A Funny Disorder that's No Laughing Matter*. The author, Marguerite Jones Utley, has narcolepsy. I found myself laughing at her stories and crying as I realized that I wasn't alone in the experiences and feelings I'd been through.

It turned out that developing a "mom attitude" was a very good thing for me. I had learned to be brave, to be an advocate for those who couldn't advocate for themselves, and even to question authority. Moms learn to do these things for their children. So, using this newfound courage, I approached the microphone that was open for people to ask questions of the panelists. The presenter had just finished explaining his latest research regarding the onset of narcolepsy. He concluded that the average age of onset being in the preteen years was linked to the onset of puberty. I had my personal experience, but I also had a degree in psychology and the ability to pose questions regarding X factors not considered. So I asked, "Could it be that the reported age of symptom onset in the puberty years (middle school) has to do with the learning environment rather than the body's physiology? That the learning style in middle school requires a longer attention span more often and less interaction and hands-on learning than in elementary school? That taking notes and sitting quietly for long periods of time could create the perfect environment for EDS to present itself, and that a drop in grades brings attention to the problem and a need to seek help?" The look on his face was priceless. My goal wasn't to make him look bad, but he did appear to be speechless. It actually made me felt pretty smart, and I had to hide my smile.

I really did think this was true. It made sense to me. I had never had a problem staying awake in art, music, gym, and especially lunch and recess. I waited for his answer. Surprisingly, he admitted that his research didn't involve that type of study and should be considered. This made me feel proud, like I had something intelligent and useful to contribute. I took my seat. The weekend trip had been a success: I met nice people and even began a conversation about nightmares that everyone was eager to join and share their personal experiences; I learned more about the hardships of cataplexy; my family and I did some fun things like go to the marina; and best of all, I felt motivated to go back to my high school to educate the counselor or whoever would listen, so kids would have a chance for diagnosis with early intervention.

Fall arrived and the time had come for my dad to remarry. My sisters and I stood proudly alongside our father while Karen's sons stood tall next to their mother, representing a union of two families. Close friends and family also joined the small, yet beautiful Catholic wedding. I didn't feel as emotional as I thought I would, probably because I knew it was what Mom wanted. As the priest talked, I noticed John slip out the back doors with Claire. She was never a fussy baby, but John, like Dylan, had a very short attention span. Through the glass windows at the back of the church, I could see John holding Claire while he watched the ceremony. When it was over, I had a step-mother and three step-brothers. Dad and Karen needed each other and would be happy together. The marriage felt right and good.

I joined John and Claire, and as we headed to the reception in the church gymnasium he pulled me to the side with a startled look on his face. "Brianna, the strangest thing happened after the ceremony ended. I was standing here holding Claire and she leaned over my shoulder, waved, and said, 'Bye, Bye.' I turned around to see who she was talking to, but there was no one back here but us. I totally got chills because I really think that your mom was standing next to us the whole time." We just stared at each other for a few minutes. I knew that he wasn't comfortable talking about spiritual experiences such as this, so he was definitely telling the truth.

Dylan met Lawrence, his new best friend in second grade. His mother was very patient with Dylan and let him come over after school to play until I got home from work. He had made other friends, but Lawrence, his cousin Adam, and the kids on our street were the only boys he hung around with. However, I did notice that he began getting a lot of phone calls from kids with whom I wasn't familiar. Dylan said they called him to ask about trading Pokémon cards. Since Pokémon cards were not allowed at school and Dylan tended to get obsessed with random things easily, we decided to simply ban the cards at home. In response, he decided to become an expert on all aspects of Pokémon. He even organized a notebook of all the Pokémon characters, which was strange since he was never organized. Apparently, he had become the kid to call if you needed advice on trades. *Hmmm, interesting*, I thought. I wondered if he would become a successful stock market trader one day.

Beyond his social life, I worried about him academically. The Ritalin seemed to be working well, but John didn't like that he was taking it. I knew what a difference medication made for me and saw the difference it made in Dylan. I tested that difference all the time. If he ran out or he forgot to take it in the morning, I wouldn't inform his teacher, and it never failed…

> Dear Mrs. Morrison,
>
> Dylan had a difficult day today. He repeatedly talked out and could not stay on task.
>
> Sincerely,
> Mrs. Miller

I wanted to prove to myself that medicating him was necessary for him to do well in school. I wished someone had intervened for me! I wished my teachers had written notes to my parents saying, "Dear Mrs. Ryan, Brianna had difficulty again today staying awake in class. Has she been feeling ill lately or having trouble at home that would prevent her from sleeping well at night?" Teachers only seemed to involve parents when a child disrupted their classroom. This was my call to provide more education to teachers in the area of sleep disorders. They didn't have to make a diagnosis, but they were first in line to discover symptoms and help bring awareness to parents.

With a nicely put together information packet on narcolepsy, I waited anxiously for the counselor at my old high school. I hadn't told her what the meeting was about when I made the appointment. As soon as she sat down I began, "I want to share with you some information on a sleeping disorder called narcolepsy. It is not very common, but I think teachers should be aware of the disorder so they can help detect it early in their students and bring it to the parents' attention." She looked at me like she was interested, so I went on to explain a little bit about narcolepsy. I wrapped up with my reason for returning to the school, "I was a student here years ago and suffered from narcolepsy unknowingly. I fell asleep during most classes on a daily basis. I did OK with grades, so my parents didn't realize that I was having any issues. Some teachers would get angry or send me to the nurse, while others would simply lecture over me. I really wish someone had taken notice and seen that this wasn't normal, or informed my parents about my struggles in staying attentive during class. That way, I might have been able to get help sooner."

At that, the counselor's expression changed from interested to annoyed. She responded, "So you think it is our fault that you didn't get help? That it's the teacher's responsibility to know something is wrong when even your own parents didn't know?" I was floored by her response and speechless. Why was she so angry? This was not the response I expected at all! I tried to back up the conversation so she would understand that I just wanted to educate teachers and school nurses so that they were aware, but her resentment seemed to cloud her judgment. I was so hurt by the response that I wrapped up our meeting and left. I didn't understand what had happened. I hadn't said anything about blaming anyone! I wanted their help to make sure others didn't experience school the way I did. Sitting in my car outside the school, I didn't feel like crying as much as I felt like punching someone (specifically that woman!). *Oh well*, I thought, *at least I tried.*

"Baby Bear" was his name. Protector of all that is good and defender against all that is evil. With her little fingers gripping his tail and her mouth plugged by her thumb, Claire slept soundly knowing that Baby Bear, her best friend, watched after her. I don't know the day it happened, but Claire had bonded with this bear. I'm sure it was similar to the way I felt about Blankie, able to take pain and fear away when I held it tight. It's amazing the special powers our heart gives these objects. He pretty much went everywhere with Claire. Each day that I saw Claire grip Baby Bear's tail with her fingers while putting her thumb in her mouth, my heart filled with warmth. I, too, had a special bond with Baby Bear, for he was the bear that I had given to my mother.

There was an element of risk, however, when allowing a child to possess a powerful object like Baby Bear. The emotional impact and scar it would leave on her heart if she were to lose him could be greater than the sense of security he originally provided. Fortunately, our family only felt the impact for one week. I couldn't tell you who was more affected during that traumatic week, Claire or me. People pushed by in a rush to purchase last-minute Christmas gifts on a busy weekend. There were also those who simply strolled to enjoy the holiday atmosphere the mall provided. John and I split up so I could shop while he took Claire to find Santa. She waved at me from high on her daddy's shoulders as I spotted them in the back of the toy store where we had agreed to meet up. "Hey, where's the stroller?" I asked John as I reached to pull Claire from his shoulders.

We had an awesome stroller, the kind with big, go anywhere type wheels made for bigger kids. "I left it parked out in front of the store because it was too big to push around in here," he said. *Oh, this isn't good*, I thought. "Uh... there's no stroller out front." I followed him to the front of the store, and he motioned to where he had parked it. My heart sank when I saw the empty space. *Oh, no. Baby Bear!* After unsuccessful attempts to get the mall's security remotely interested in my plea for help, we sadly returned home, not only without the awesome stroller, but also without our beloved Baby Bear.

At two years old, Claire didn't understand the impact of the situation. Or, maybe I was more upset than she was. "Bad people took Baby Bear," Claire repeated as she got settled in her crib to go to sleep. I knew that I had been saying this to her earlier in the day, but didn't want her to go to sleep with such an image in her head. "Well, honey, I think that whoever took our stroller did so because their little boy or girl needed one, and they didn't have enough money to buy one themselves. I don't think they meant to be bad people. They just wanted nice things for their kids and didn't know how else to get the things they felt they needed. We are lucky we have enough money to get another stroller."

She seemed to calm a little and settled down in her crib with her second favorites, Grey Kitty and Brown Kitty Ty Babies. I continued, "Maybe Baby Bear can help the other mom and dad by being a really good friend to their child the way that he has been to you. If that child really needs Baby Bear, then he will be their best Christmas present ever!" Saying these words not only changed the worried look on her face, but I also began to feel better. She didn't know it, but I, too, was struggling with letting go. For all I knew, Baby Bear was covered in pop cans, French fries, and whatever else people had thrown away in the parking lot trashcan.

All hope began to fade during the week-long hunt for a new Baby Bear. Thank God for the Internet! I searched websites for Precious Moments bears every day, particularly the "Have a Hug" bear. I finally learned that the bear I was looking for was a limited edition. As ridiculous as it seemed, I prayed. "God, I know that I'm probably being silly and wasting your time by praying for this, but I feel so empty inside without this bear. I say I'm searching for Claire, but this is also for me. I know finding a new bear won't be the same as having the one I picked out for my mom, and I really do hope the original bear comforts another child. For us, I'd really like help in finding a new bear. Claire's been really brave and sweet by accepting that her bear is gone. Please help us, Amen."

After eight days of searching, I needed to make a decision. Three possible bears that came close in looks displayed on a Precious Moments eBay website. I thought one of these bears would be nice and make Claire happy. I ran downstairs and asked John to come look at my options and give his opinion before I chose. "Isn't this it?" he said as he pointed to the monitor. "What the...?!" I pushed in front of him to get a closer look. "That wasn't there before. That's it!" *No way*, I thought. I know it wasn't there just five minutes before! My heart beat so fast I thought I would pass out. Excited and amazed beyond belief, I knew that bear would be mine. I would pay a million dollars before anyone could outbid me. I just had to wait twenty-four hours. There would be no sleep for me that night, narcoleptic or not. If I had cataplexy, I would have totally hit the floor and loved every minute of it.

I still couldn't get over that I was able to find another Have a Hug bear! Seeing Claire's face light up when she opened the package and said, "I got a *new* Baby Bear!" gave me goose bumps all over. Of course, she knew it wasn't the original, but she loved him just the same. A woman in New York had just "decided" to put her bear on eBay the very night I had given up hope searching for it. No, I didn't believe there was anything random about her decision. Someone (my mom possibly) heard my plea for help. Maybe that woman heard an angel whisper in her ear, *Sell the bear.*

My dad's wife Karen had begun to experience some spiritual mysteries as well. Knowing my mom's silly nature and her love of practical jokes, I was not surprised by Karen's stories. "Wayne, wake up," Karen whispered to my dad late one night while he slept next to her in bed. "The light just flickered." They had a touch lamp in the bedroom that turned on and off at the touch of a hand. "Oh, Karen, it was nothing," Dad replied half asleep. "Go back to sleep." "Wayne," she said with a little more urgency. "The light just flickered again, and the turntable on the stereo just spun around!" While trying to sound comforting, he answered, "Katherine, I mean, Karen, go back to sleep. It's probably just a power surge." Being a retired electrician, he must have thought she would believe him and relax. I didn't know if my dad realized it at the time, but he confessed to Karen later that the night that happened was the anniversary of my mother's death.

My mom loved playing practical jokes and had always gotten a kick out of doing silly things on April Fool's Day. Once she put plastic wrap tightly over the toilet bowl, then put the lid down hoping that I wouldn't notice when I sat down to pee. She didn't get me but was very surprised when she unexpectedly felt hot wetness under *her* legs after sitting down on the toilet on April Fool's morning the following year. I had found the joke to be quite funny, after all. After John and I were first married, she still managed to get me pretty good, and John got a taste of my mom's weird sence of humor. John and I crawled into bed one night and discovered piles of uncooked spaghetti noodles stuffed under the covers at the foot of our bed. I wasn't sure whether she'd run out of practical jokes or what, but that one was simply bizarre.

I praised Karen for being able to sleep in the same bedroom that my mom passed away in. Although they did get all new furniture, I still don't think I would have been able to live in the same house if I were the new wife. Although Karen was Catholic and a firm believer in heaven and the afterlife, experiencing phenomena from the afterlife was still scary to her. "Grandma," my two-year-old niece Aleah said, "who is that lady?" Karen was helping Aleah's older brother get dressed in her bedroom. "You mean the lady in the picture?" she asked. Aleah shook her head no and took Karen by the hand, pulling her into the living room. When she pointed across the room, Karen looked up and saw a faint glow of a light hovering in front of the fireplace. The realization of who might still be hanging around the house made her feel very uneasy. "OK, let's go downstairs." Karen quickly grabbed the kids' hands and led them down the stairs without discussion about who the lady was that Aleah claimed to see. Although frightened, Karen knew that my mother would never do anything on purpose to upset her—a few fun tricks maybe, but never harm or want to scare her away.

We survived the anxiously awaited world shut down as the clocks changed over to Y2K. Some exciting events were already lined up for the year 2000. I knew my professors never believed that I'd actually finish the MPA program, but they'd see me walk across the stage in May. I could not have done it without my best friend, Dexedrine. Provigil just wasn't good enough for me. However, it did make us lots of money in the stock market! In fact, the stock market had done really well for us, so we decided it was time to move over to Kansas. Richard was pretty irritated that we wanted to leave the neighborhood since they had just settled into their house right behind us. But we wouldn't be far away. Although my life had dramatically changed for the better since I'd been able to manage my sleep disorder with medication, John really wanted Dylan to go off his. I'd proven to him time after time that Dylan got in trouble in school when he wasn't on it, but John insisted.

We used the summer to try alternative therapies like neurofeedback and even some ridiculous desensitization method to allergies that a chiropractor came up with. Both failed miserably. Neurofeedback/biofeedback required Dylan to train his own brain using a computer program. Dylan didn't have the attention to focus long enough to do that! We tried to stop feeding him as much as we could from the ten pages of items the chiropractor said Dylan was allergic to. No sugar, wheat, artificial colors or flavors, dairy products, and on and on were allowed in his diet. He became a zombie. Finally, after the chiropractor told me that Dylan was allergic to my blood and wanted him to hold a vile of it while he did an adjustment to "desensitize" him, I told him that we wouldn't waste another minute of our time with him.

As summer came to a close and the new school year began, I quickly became friends with Dylan's new teachers. This was necessary with a son like ours, not to mention the fact that we were always the youngest parents. The better the teachers knew us, the less likely they were to jump to the conclusion that we were bad parents. Dylan was a very lovable boy, but so incredibly exhausting, even for those without narcolepsy. I understood John not wanting Dylan on drugs his whole life, but I knew full well what a difference being able to focus in school could make for a student and their self-esteem. Being the new kid was hard enough without being negatively labeled by the teachers. I loved young, enthusiastic teachers because they were extremely cooperative and willing to try new ideas. We talked about keeping Dylan in the front of the classroom to avoid distractions, giving him a stress ball to squeeze, and various classroom chores to keep him active.

Once Dylan was settled into school and Claire into daycare, it was time for me to enter back into the work force. I'd always try to pay attention to the signs around me when determining if I was on the right path. Sometimes, though, this could be as subtle as a gut feeling. Even in job hunting, I tried to look for signs. While interviewing for a special events coordinator position at a local nonprofit organization, I noticed two things: 1) I really liked the woman interviewing me. I felt like we could work together really well. 2) Every question she asked me about possible special event scenarios correlated with past struggles and lessons I'd learned from previous job situations. Until then, I had believed that these past experiences were mistakes or unfortunate, when in actuality they were opportunities to prepare me for the next step in my life.

It was only day two at my new job when I realized that I was going to have to trust my new boss and tell her I had narcolepsy—my pill bottle hadn't made the switch to the new purse. I'd never told anyone work-related that I had narcolepsy before. Not that I wanted to deceive people, but they'd never even know unless I forgot my pills. I knew this was not the best way to start a new career, but I had no choice; there was no way I could make it through the day or even until lunch without having to put my head down. Plus, a thirty-minute drive home and thirty-minute drive back would not pass for taking a break.

My boss put a stack of paper in front of me and gave instructions to enter names in the computer and write Thank You notes to donors. The lack of stimulating activity gave me no choice. "Can I talk to you about something for a minute?" I asked my boss before she left my office. "Sure, what's up?" She looked at me with all smiles, so although I was nervous I felt comfortable. "I have a sleep disorder called narcolepsy. Are you familiar with it?" At this point, she began to look a little worried. She shook her head no, so I continued, "Well, the main symptom is excessive daytime sleepiness." As her look became more serious, I quickly added, "But I have the sleepiness completely under control with daily medication. So, as long as I take my pills, I'm good to go." Her look turned to relief, and she was smiling again. "However, today I changed purses and left my pill bottle at home." My sheepish look made her give me a little smirk. "OK," she said, "make it back here as quick as you can and get right back to work." I was so excited about how easy that was that I told her I would bring food and work straight through lunch. I never wanted to feel like a burden or need any special accommodations on the job. She never treated me differently or expected less.

Gram had been really sick with pancreatic cancer. It's weird to say, but I actually believed she was happy to have a terminal illness. She had enjoyed her time living in her own apartment among other women her age, but she was ready to be done with this life. My uncle Jack helped Renee and I take care of

Gram along with hospice nurses in her home. The day Jack called to say it was almost time, Dylan and I went to Gram's house to visit. She was ready to leave this world, especially after watching all her siblings die, and even outliving her youngest child. I understood and didn't want to make her feel bad by being selfish for not wanting her to leave, but I felt like I was losing the last mother figure in my life.

Dylan and I joined Gram in her room where she lay quietly on the hospital bed that replaced her regular one. When she saw us, her eyes lit up, but then saddened a little. "Isn't Claire with you?" she asked expectantly. "No, sorry, she's at home napping." I felt sick to my stomach. I knew she loved Dylan, but I also knew that Claire was very special to her. "Dylan! So help me if that thing falls on me," Gram glared at Dylan as he bounced his body against the old mattress leaning against the wall next to her. She sounded as normal and as spunky as ever for someone so close to death. Then she turned to me, "Brianna, I had the most amazing dream last night!" Her eyes were wide and she had the biggest smile. "Katherine was there. She was standing there with a light behind her and holding her arms wide open for me." At that moment, I knew my grandma would be leaving us that night. She was the happiest that I had seen her in a very long time. How could I not be happy for her? Besides, her daughter was waiting with open arms.

I decided to give my uncle private time with his mother, so I told Gram it was time for Dylan and me to leave. What do you say when you know there's no time left? These would be my last words. Or, maybe they wouldn't. My faith had grown exponentially after my mother "called" me from heaven. As if she needed any more convincing after a strict Catholic upbringing, Gram's faith had the golden seal after seeing her deceased daughter's welcoming gesture the night before. She wasn't afraid to die. She was excited to die. As I leaned down to hug her good-bye, she gave me an extra tight squeeze to let me know it would be my last.

Our young family went on to enjoy the holidays through fall and winter just as they were meant to be enjoyed. The new year seemed to kick off with all the same hopes and expectations a new year holds. Then, without much warning, our Dalmatian Pongo started throwing up continuously. I took him to the vet where he stayed the weekend. Pongo was Dylan's buddy. For a dog, having a hyperactive owner must have been awesome! Walking the dog meant Dylan putting on roller blades with leash in hand and saying, "OK, go!"

What ten-year-old cared about possible consequences in that scenario? If he crashed in the grass, all the funnier! Our new home's association had a rule that no dogs were allowed in the pool. I wondered what the story was behind that rule being put in place!

> *What is this thing sitting on the table next to me? I'm in a small room. It's an animal of some type. I can't take my eyes off its big, sad, dark, oval eyes. They remind me of a cartoon picture of large frog eyes. I don't feel scared. I'm not sad. I feel comforted because Grams is holding me. I can't feel her physically, but I feel her warmth and comfort within her embrace. My gaze, however, can't leave these big, beautiful, sad eyes.* I wake up.

"I can't figure it out," I complained to John. I knew the dream was meaningful because it was slow, and I was lucid, so I really spent time taking it all in. Gram's appearance, although she didn't speak to me, felt very real. We simply stood together for a long time while she comforted me. "So, what is it with the frog eyes?" I ask John, knowing I really didn't expect him to try and analyze. John still liked to call me weird, but I was pretty sure he always took me seriously when it came to dreams. My grandma hugging me felt so natural. To anyone else, the frog was just a weird thing that happened in dreams. To me, however, it had meaning.

Pongo wouldn't be coming home as planned. The vet called me from the operating room, "Hello, Mrs. Morrison. I'm sorry to tell you this, but Pongo has cancer everywhere. Should I leave him asleep?" This question totally took me by surprise. Dylan thought we were going to pick him up that afternoon. We hadn't seen Pongo all weekend. I knew that bringing him home terminally ill and vomiting constantly was not the best solution and wouldn't make Dylan feel any better. I tried to think of something that may ease the pain, for everyone. I asked the vet, "Is there any way that you could wake him up a little bit? Not enough so that he got excited to come home, but enough so that he knows we are there? I think it's important that our family has time to say good-bye."

There was no time to waste, so we all took a sad and quiet drive to the vet's office where Pongo was waiting. I had never seen my son so quiet and still before. The vet pushed through the door carrying a large, polka dot bundle wrapped in a donated hand-made quilt, and laid him on the exam table next to me. My throat tightened and my head felt dizzy. There they were, the sad, solid black, dilated "frog eyes" of my beautiful Dalmatian staring up at me. His anesthesia had not worn off completely. Though I was upset, I also felt totally at peace knowing that Gram was right there with me as she had been in my dream, holding me.

> *I walk along our wood floor leaving my bedroom and heading towards the steps that lead upstairs. I stop at the steps and look up to see Pongo sitting on the first landing. I'm so excited to see him! I never thought I would again. "Pong! Hey! Do you need to go potty? Are you hungry? Want a drink?" I'm not sure what I expect to happen, but since these are my usual questions, I asked him anyway. He only sits there and stares at me, then gives a little sigh. "Oh…" I somehow understand. He's OK. He wants me to know that he's OK. Walking towards him, I kneel down on the step just below and wrap my arms around his body. I feel him so perfectly. His body is solid and warm. I feel the short bristles from his black and white fur in my fingers. He doesn't move. I don't speak. He lets me hold him for a little while. I wake up.*

I prayed that I had made the right decision and that Pongo would forgive me if I hadn't. He didn't speak when I saw him again. Of course he didn't, that would have been too weird. That was not a dream "about" Pongo; my dog, my friend, had come to tell me that he was OK. He came so we could have a proper good-bye. I prayed that he had done the same for Dylan.

Those who knew the John who barely graduated high school never would have believed that he was on the Dean's list in college. Deciding to go to college because he wanted to made a huge difference in attitude and effort. I was pretty jealous, however, because he made doing well in school look so easy. For Dylan, school was the same everywhere he went. The teachers loved him as a person, but would rather not have him in their class. Claire, on the other hand, was a breeze. Good thing Claire was so easy because I spent all my energy keeping Dylan in line. For this reason, John and I decided that it was best for me to quit my job. I joined the Parent Teacher Organization (PTO) and volunteered on as many field trips as I could to help ease the burden on the teachers. Being an intelligent kid goes a long way, but the teachers were still exhausted by his constant need for attention.

Dylan's experience in middle school, even with me volunteering at school and joining the PTO board, did not go very smoothly. The teachers were not as patient as they had been in elementary school. Parent-teacher conferences were all the same, "If he'd only apply himself…." I had talked John into letting Dylan go back on his medication, yet I'd catch Dylan lying to me about taking it. He'd say, "Mom, I don't want to have to take drugs the rest of my life. I want to do it on my own." *Well, at least I didn't have to worry about him being a drug user when he was older,* I thought. I guess I could say that I had gotten psychology and administration of justice degrees to help me raise Dylan, but I wasn't sure they were helping.

CHAPTER 6

The American Dream

My thirtieth birthday in Cancun, Mexico, during a drab Mid-west winter would be the best birthday surprise ever! John was full of surprises and always aiming to please. Plus, we all needed it. I rushed out the back sliding door of our resort room to the shore as soon as I dropped my luggage. The cool, white powdered sand puddled between my toes as I stood at the edge of the water looking towards the horizon. With a warm, humid ocean breeze blowing through my hair and turquoise water so clear that I wasn't afraid to wade in for fear of what lurked below, it felt like paradise. The kids found friends their own age to hang out with at the resort while John and I chilled at the pool or on the beach. There were no fights about homework, no stress about work, no carpools or parking lots to sit in and wait for dance class to end, there was just relaxing the body and mind and enjoying a cocktail or two.

The serenity and beauty of Cancun made me not want to sleep. I would wake before dawn each morning to capture breathtaking sunrise photos and walk across the street to the lagoon every evening for sunset. We'd taken a fun excursion where Dylan and I swam with dolphins. Dolphins were much like dogs, I discovered. Looking into their eyes, I could tell they were sizing me up. They were like mystical creatures from ancient times. What did they know about the world that we didn't? Being in the water with them was a magical experience. Entering the freezing cold, lake-green water with lots of fish was the hardest part for me. The dolphins' massive, strong bodies swimming all around us didn't feel scary at all, but riding on the tip of their noses by my feet was tricky. I almost lost my suit!

The waves of ocean water carries me out to sea. I know I'm dreaming. I'm breathing underwater easily. The rush of water on my skin is an eerie feeling because I know I'm not actually wet. Dolphins swim along on all sides, leading me somewhere special. I follow them to a place where something wonderful will happen. I feel very anxious. I stand alone in the sand under a small, round palm-covered hut. I'm not sure exactly what I'm waiting for, but I know to be excited. "Mom!" She enters the hut and walks toward me. She looks beautiful! Her hair is curled and her face is made up. She's wearing bright, Mexican colors with a long, flowing skirt and short-sleeved top. It looks similar to an outfit she may have worn when she and my dad were in a dance group. She's approaching me. Frantically, I search myself to see if I brought any pictures. "Wait," I tell her. "I need to find some pictures of Claire to show you! Mom, she's beautiful." She quietly calms me and says, "It's OK. I know." I relax and understand. She knows Claire. I feel so at peace. Grateful. "I have to go," she says. She smiles. I wake up.

This place is definitely paradise, I thought to myself, lying in bed. She knew Claire! I always thought she might, but now I knew for sure. She watched her do gymnastics like she used to watch me. She came to all of her dance performances, too. Claire was just as I had described: silky, straight brown hair, beautiful tan skin, with a nose similar to mine… a new and improved Brianna, just like she said I had been the new and improved Katherine. My mother hadn't missed Claire growing up, she just wasn't able to be there in person. Of course I told John, he was my best friend (and already thought I was weird).

Dad and Karen were doing great. They had bought an RV to be snowbirds in the winter. Now that both were retired, traveling in the RV would be the next phase of their life together. I knew my mom handpicked Karen! We hadn't had one argument about anything. She even liked country dancing with Dad. They took a trip with Dylan, Claire, and me to Florida. John had recently taken over as owner of the company he worked for, so he didn't feel comfortable leaving. Dad and Karen had a great time with us and decided to start taking their RV to Florida during the winter months. Of course they would be traveling to Florida, this made perfect sense! *Karen* was the woman I couldn't see in my dream standing next to my dad on the Florida sands before my mom died.

The time had come to look at puppies! A friend of ours called and asked if we were ready to be dog owners again because his Belgian Malinois had just had a large litter and he needed to find good homes for them. I had never seen a Belgian Malinois before meeting his. They are shepherds typically used in the military for search and rescue and law enforcement. I had read an article about the breed being a vital part of search and rescue efforts after the Oklahoma City bombing. Apparently, they are so sensitive that volunteers had to hide in the rubble so the dogs would find some "live" bodies and not get depressed and stop working.

How dare John say that he didn't want to get a dog while driving us to go look at puppies! "Can't you see her?" I stared at John and asked with a serious face as the tears started to well up in my eyes. I felt like a little girl arguing with a parent trying to get in the way of something I really wanted. Like before, an image was so clear in my head, but this time it was a large, fawn colored, fluffy shepherd lying in front of the fireplace on our ivory shag rug. Claire yelled from the back seat of the car, "I want her name to be Sara!" *Of course,* I thought, Claire had been naming all her dolls Sara lately. John couldn't take a girl (*two* girls) to go look at puppies and then tell them they couldn't bring one home.

We walked into their small kitchen and there they were, a bundle of furry roly polies huddled in a boxed-in corner, a few searching for a way out. Some were reddish or grey and others fawn colored like the mom. Their ears were still floppy, but would stand straight soon. Belgian Shepherds and German Shepherds have similar features and people often get them confused. Claire pointed to a couple in the corner that were reddish, while John played with

the lone grey one (I knew he wouldn't be able to resist). "I picked one out for you," Tim said, as he handed me the biggest, fluffiest fawn colored pup. "I think her temperament is perfect for you guys." And there she was. Quite a bit smaller than I had imagined, but that was definitely Sara.

The older I got, the more illness and death surrounded me. We had taken Richard and his family to Cancun the year after our first trip there so they could relax in paradise together one last time. I never asked Richard if the trip affected him like it had me the year before. There were times, however, when John and I watched Richard sitting alone on the sand near the water, staring off at the horizon. He knew his time was near, and we hoped he was making peace with himself and God.

One of the perks of owning your own company was the ability to hire your closest friend, no matter how sick and withdrawn they'd become. John and Richard had always worked together and their entrepreneurial minds always fed off each other. Together, they were brilliant. Richard's brain tumors, however, had multiplied, enlarged, and were now cancerous. The office atmosphere had changed from excitement and creativity to stress and trips to doctors' offices. "Richard's medicine has side effects he can't control," John would say, apologizing to clients whenever Richard yelled obscenities at them on the phone. John tried asking Richard to stay home and rest, but he explained, "Going to work gives me purpose and a reason to get up in the morning." So John, being the friend that he was, continued to pick him up for work each day.

Richard passed at thirty-five years old. He had never been a smoker, never even tried drugs or alcohol. He had waited until his wife and kids left for the afternoon before passing on. His sister-in-law, a very emotionally strong and close friend, was there with him. I bet that he, too, knew he was ready to leave this world. I prayed that he had opened up to his wife, Susan, and talked about everything they ever wanted to talk about, and that he didn't leave with any regrets. I also prayed that Susan and their kids see him again in their dreams for their own personal good-byes.

"You can use me for one more day to be with her," I had said while standing in front of the mirror. *What did that mean?* I wondered. I was uncertain what the image of Richard's reflection in the mirror was supposed to mean to me. Standing there and saying those words to him was all I could remember of the dream. I also wondered if John's restless nights had to do with Richard's passing or possibly being visited in his dreams, but I never asked because I knew he didn't like to discuss his dreams or spirituality. He knew he could have talked to me, and that he couldn't have been a better friend to Richard.

With Dylan entering high school, we really needed to rein our son in before something in life slapped him in the face and made him grow up, the way my pregnancy had made me and John grow up. We considered military school, but ended up going with a strict, Jesuit all boys' high school instead. Luckily his test scores were high enough to get in. Structure would be his friend, even with medication. Claire started kindergarten at our Catholic church's school. I loved being able to volunteer at both schools, but Dylan didn't enjoy his thirty-one-year-old mother being a volunteer. For most kids, going there was not only a family tradition, but also a privilege. Dylan, on the other hand, had a huge attitude—we'd already met with the principal regarding his thirteen demerits for talking out within the first few months. Why weren't his meds working? Damn that ADHD!

Besides the stress of children, most married couples fight about two things: sex and money. At the time, money was plentiful. In fact, John was looking to find something to invest in as part of a retirement plan. Unfortunately, fights about sex were also plentiful. Normal issues like wishing you were with someone else or not wanting sex weren't our problems. Our problem was sleep. For a narcoleptic, a warm, quiet bed meant instant highway to dreamland. After being together almost fifteen years, the natural, initial adrenaline dropped significantly. Although John was fully aware of my amazing ability to fall asleep within minutes, dozing off when he was trying to be sexually active was not very complimentary. It hurt his feelings no matter how many times I begged him not to take it personally.

Great sex, on the other hand, also came with problems. I'd been told that people with cataplexy must consider the possible consequences that come with an extreme emotion (orgasm). For a man, such an extreme emotion may trigger a cataplectic attack and not end up so well for his partner lying beneath. She may find herself stuck below the dead weight of her mostly paralyzed, yet satisfied partner. My extreme emotion, on the other hand, would lead to two or three hours of complete energy and alertness. I'd become chatty Cathy. This may seem great and all, but not so great if we had sex just before bed. Telling my husband that we could have sex, but not to make it too good was, in his words, "The best thing you've ever said to me!" I wondered if other narcoleptics without cataplexy had a similar outcome. If only scientists could bottle the chemicals in the brain that caused orgasms. In fact, I bet everyone wished scientists could bottle that!

I attended the Narcolepsy Network's conference in Seattle in the fall. Dr. Mignot, one of the leading narcolepsy researchers in the world, would speak. I had sent him an email a month earlier asking if any research had been done on the effects of sex on sleep with narcoleptics, so when I saw him in the hallway after one of his speeches, I couldn't help but turn bright red in the face. I never imagined I'd actually see him in person when I sent the email! I had told him some pretty personal information, thinking I would be totally anonymous, but could tell by his smirk that he recognized my name on the badge I wore. The good news was that I made a few friends at the conference, and we all got a good laugh out of it. One of the lectures I sat through was about treatment for narcolepsy with Xyrem (otherwise known as "the date rape drug"). After hearing about the study, I could honestly say "I don't get it." How could you have a research study to see if a medication worked when all of the subjects (even control group) were still taking their daily medication to control for EDS? Seeing how I was among the few in the audience still awake during the workshop, I decided to stick with what worked for me.

A conversation with new friends at the conference regarding Dylan's struggles with ADHD led to a woman nearby asking, "Does your son sweat at night or snore?" "Yes, both!" I answered. She went on to explain that sometimes ADHD could be mistaken for the effects of sleep apnea. He may act out at school because he's so tired from disrupted sleep at night. He was definitely the poster child for ADHD, there was no mistaking that, yet how strange that she knew to ask if he sweated or snored at night after only hearing me talk about his ADHD. The next workshop I attended just happened to be "Narcolepsy and Sleep Apnea." The presenter discussed how the two disorders created sleepiness and could sometimes be misdiagnosed. Dylan definitely showed signs of hyperactivity and lack of impulse control, not sleepiness, but I'd definitely take the woman's advice and get him tested. Another trip to the sleep lab!

Once again, the conference with Narcolepsy Network had inspired me to reach out to schools and educate them on sleep disorders. I really wanted to get the word out and educate teachers and nurses within our school district. I used some of the materials and methods suggested by the workshop at the conference and even left voicemails. And once again, they all let me down. I didn't know what to expect, maybe at least a call for further information.

While attending Claire's school open house, I recognized a kindergartener's grandpa; he had been my childhood general practitioner. *This is my chance,* I thought. My chance to tell him what a huge misdiagnosis he had made with me back in eighth grade and how I struggled for years because he didn't know what narcolepsy was! Slowly and nervously I walked up to him. "Hello, Dr. Thompson. Do you remember me?" I thought for sure he would after the number of ear infections I had as well as being a pregnant teen. After a minute he answered, "Yes, you look very familiar to me, but I remember your mother much better, such a lovely woman." *Great,* I thought. This was not the time to mention narcolepsy. I let it go.

That Christmas, we gifted ourselves with family. John had always wanted a large, loving family, so we tried our best to keep close with my sisters and their families in California. Since Claire was young, Santa still made his presence known with bites out of cookies (we left a note at home telling him we were in California) and presents under the tree. Yet I think her best gift of all was the beautiful poem her big brother wrote her. Dylan had been worried that he wouldn't have a gift to give his little sister, so I suggested that he write her a poem. I never knew that his inattentive, ADHD brain could cook up such a beautiful piece of work. I hoped one day she would cherish his words and his love for her the way I did. This was by far, in my mind, the best Christmas gift a brother could give.

> *Woodle,*
> *Queen of gymnastics and of dance,*
> *You are weird like the people in France.*
> *I love you as much as you are weird,*
> *just like daddy loves his tickly beard.*
> *I love to play with you because you are lots of fun,*
> *even though you beat me when we run.*
> *I know you love to get a belly flop,*
> *even though you tell me to stop.*
> *I love it when I hear you laugh,*
> *and the few times when I help you with your math.*
> *You cheer for me at all my games,*

and sometimes call me silly names.
You love to sing all the time,
you should practice being a mime.
You know I love you very much,
especially when I give you a punch.
I love it when you give me pictures,
because you are one of my favorite little sisters.
Now you know how much I love you,
so I hope you like this poem from me to you.

—Dylan

Good thing my little red convertible had only been a lease because Sara was huge! I still had my SUV, so she went everywhere with me. She was like my sidekick, I'd even considered her my third child. Mom and Gram would have loved her! I wanted to do everything right as a dog owner; I just didn't want to have any regrets this time. I hired a dog trainer to help me learn how to train Sara. She was too smart for her own good. I had to learn how to be her "pack leader" (I doubt Pongo considered me his alpha). Our cat Figaro was quite irritated that we'd brought another dog into the house. People had just started noticing her after Pongo was out of the picture. And now, at sixteen years old and sick with cancer, she was pretty grouchy. Cancer seemed to take everyone I love.

John took all our money out of the stock market and invested in a small commercial building close to our home. This was the biggest and craziest thing we'd ever done. I wasn't a risk taker at all, but trusted John completely with all big decisions. Win big, lose big! That's how he rolled. The investment did make sense to me, though. He moved his business into the front half and I acted as landlord and leased out office space in the back half. Making a little go a long way for many years had made me very organized and really good at budgeting. I wasn't sure how it would all work, but I was in.

Life was good, for a while. Weekend nights always began with fun and good intentions, but inevitably ended in tears and separate beds. Richard's death, Dylan's problems with authority and schoolwork, the stress around money, work, and arguments about sex had led to an increase in John's drinking. I tried to keep up by taking more pills to stay awake and party with him, but crawling into bed at three a.m. led directly to sleep no matter how hard I'd try. He, on the other hand, didn't want to go straight to sleep. So we fought.

A trip to the vet's office had always been an undesirable chore, yet after Pongo's death I developed a much stronger sense of distaste for the place. The people there were always nice, but the memories were nothing but sad. Figaro's illness made her shrink down to a fragile, six pound cat. Claire sat next to her best friend, Katie, and cradled Figaro in her arms. They cried silently together as they stroked her fur. I knew it was Figaro's time to go when I caught her hiding in the basement storage room. She'd been such an awesome cat. Despite popular opinion, cats have personalities just like dogs. Figaro had latched on to Claire the day I brought Claire home from the hospital. I'd often find the cat curled up in the crib next to her (I'm sure the cat liked the smell of milk). I was sad that the time had come, but felt blessed that we had sixteen great years with such a loving cat. Back to the exam room we went.

Who was I to make this decision for my beloved pets? Did they know I did this because I loved them? When Claire set Figaro down on the floor, the cat collapsed, breathing softly. The girls caressed her as the tears streamed down their little faces. "Would you like to stay with her while I give her the shots?" the vet asked. I froze. Images of Pongo being carried away from me and taken to die filled my head. I couldn't let the girls watch the cat die. I didn't want to watch her die either! "No, I think it's better if we go."

The car ride home was silent. I knew I had made a mistake, but couldn't take it back. I should have stayed. She was my "Baby Cat!" She was lying on some cold, hard metal table dying, when she could have been in my warm, loving arms. I was so selfish! I had only thought of my own feelings. I needed to be there for my dying cat in her final minutes, but I got scared. I couldn't take it back. I would never make this mistake again. If this ever came up in the future for Sara, I told myself, she would never have to die alone! She would die in my arms.

Dylan didn't quite make it a year without destroying his first car. Insurance companies totally have teenage boys figured out—they're completely reckless! John and I argued about whether Dylan would be a better or worse driver having ADHD. John believed that Dylan would be better because he could do many things at once. I, on the other hand, said that was precisely the problem. He tried to do too many things at once. He wouldn't admit it, but his fender bender must have been from searching for music on his iPod. Thank God no one was hurt. Why wasn't his medicine working? He'd tried so many different kinds. Finally, I told the doctor to put him on Dexedrine like I took. That way I wouldn't have to worry about his appetite, and we could share if one of us ran out.

Dylan's snoring was really starting to worry me. I'd stand outside his room while he slept to listen, and was shocked by the length of silence between breaths. I couldn't consciously hold my breath for that long. So I took the advice of the woman at the NN conference and had Dylan tested for sleep apnea. We first visited an ear, nose, and throat (ENT) doctor. Dylan's facial structure, as well as the size and position of his tongue, tonsils, and soft palate, were all good indicators of potential problems according to the ENT. Based on the examination, Dylan had very large tonsils and his soft palate dropped really low, which could potentially restrict his airway.

Armed with the diagnosis, we went on to the sleep lab for testing. The sleep test was a typical overnight PSG like the one I had taken for narcolepsy. However, as breathing events occur (shallow or stopped breathing for at least ten seconds during sleep), a technician calculates an apnea/hypopnea index (AHI) to determine how many breathing events occur per hour. If the patient meets the criteria for having sleep apnea in the first half of the night, the technician fits the patient with a continuous positive airway pressure (CPAP) mask. By using this, the flow of continuous air pressure splints the airway open and allows free, constant breathing throughout the night.

Knowing how poorly he slept at home, we were not surprised to learn that Dylan had received the CPAP treatment during the first night of testing. They were able to reduce his 30 AHI down to less than 5. The doctor's report went on to say that he was severely sleep deprived and had possible depression or even narcolepsy due to his quick REM cycle upon returning to asleep after treatment. The doctor explained to me that sleep apnea in kids can produce signs of ADHD, but the doctor obviously didn't know my son; he definitely had both issues. It was determined that Dylan needed a CPAP machine to help him breathe at night. We would do that, though I couldn't see him using it all night for the rest of his life. What would he do, take it to college with him? All this information sounded crazy to me. Sleep interfered with *everything*!

Being a landlord was no easy task. Fortunately, the realtor who sold us the building also found tenants to fill the empty office spaces. And I wasn't afraid of diving right into something I'd never done before. John had the difficult task of having to pay for everything. "I'm bored with work," he said. He loved to stay busy. "I need a second business." The mortgage industry was doing well, so he started a mortgage company.

I loved Christmas time and how the nights were lit up with all the colorful Christmas lights, so my dad offered to help me hang lights on the building. It was a single story with a metal roof, so we could do it ourselves, and it gave us an excuse to hang out. After testing out six different plastic clips and Dad saying, "Nope, doesn't face the right way," or "Nope, the clip isn't long enough," I was driving home one evening wracking my brain to find a new idea for how to hang the string of lights on metal that wasn't the little plastic clips… *Ha! I got it!* I thought. I felt like a cartoon character with a light bulb floating above my head. *I'm so incredibly genius! How about a Christmas light clip that's magnetic?*

The thrill of being a building owner quickly wore off after the first couple of years. "Got rent?" was pretty much my only interaction with the tenants. The economy had taken a turn for the worse, and John's mortgage company was struggling. Unfortunately one of the tenants moved out in the middle of the night; I heard she went bankrupt. I felt so helpless! I did everything I could to support him so he could focus on his business, but the support he needed now was additional income. There was Dylan's private school, Claire's dance school, and John couldn't bring home a paycheck until his employees and the building expenses were paid first. Nothing was left over for us. Being a lady of leisure had been fun while it lasted.

John suggested I become a realtor because he could get the buyers pre-approved, then I could sell them homes. I needed to work. A RE/MAX hot air balloon hovered high in the sky one afternoon, and I thought, *Yeah, I could do that.* "As long as you know that I'm horrible at sales, and I don't know how to lie or fabricate the truth," I explained to John as he told me the plan. I knew real estate made sense because I would be able to make my own schedule and be there for all of Claire's activities. So, for the first time since I was a kid, I asked my dad for money to pay for the real estate class.

Based on a recommendation from my old friend, Meg, I joined a RE/MAX agency. Again, I decided not to tell anyone at work or any of my real estate clients that I had narcolepsy. People always made assumptions about me based on what they thought they knew about narcolepsy; I'd found that most people believed that anyone with narcolepsy would fall asleep instantaneously at any given time. If I told someone that I didn't have cataplexy, they would ask what cataplexy was and become more worried. My sleepiness was under control, plus I had a perfect driving record (should I ever have to drive clients around), so I never bothered telling anyone anything. There was no reason to.

"What do you mean we own another house?" I asked John in disbelief. "Remember that girl who used to work for me that went bankrupt? Well, I helped her and her husband buy a house. We set up a lease/purchase contract." My eyes widened, I didn't recall doing this. He went on, "We didn't spend any money. We just used our credit and they've been writing the checks." I was always happy to hear about generous things John did for others, but he usually didn't do anything that wasn't also good business. The first house I tried to sell happened to be the one that had been dumped on us—a trashed house where all the appliances had been stolen! Apparently, they had used us for our good credit before they walked out on the deal when the lease was up. They simply didn't want it anymore when it was time for them to make the purchase.

John had wanted to help a young family get on their feet and had the ability to do just that, and now we had two house payments! How could they do that to him? I noticed they wrote Bible verses at the end of their emails. I really hated hypocrites. What happened to "Thou shall not steal?" I had never even *seen* this house before, and now I was responsible for it. They notified us saying, "We don't want it anymore. We're leaving. And, by the way, the next house payment is due in one week." The winter months would consist of long, lonely nights repainting the inside of the house, cleaning muddy carpets (it looked like their dogs lived there alone for a month), buying new appliances, and trying to sell it as fast as I could.

Upon waking in the morning, my hands lie above my head in the usual fashion, crossed at the top of my pillow. I know this feeling. Sleep paralysis. I am completely conscious, yet I'm stuck here. Someone whispers softly in my ear. Too quiet, I don't know what they're saying. "What?" I say in my mind. "I can't hear you!" The whispering is rushed and urgent, it becomes louder. "I can't hear you!" I say again. I feel the sensation of fingers slipping through mine and the pressure and warmth of hands holding mine. The hands grip tight. I begin to make out the words as they became clear. I hear her. "Mom!" Then, I hear her words. "Don't stop talking to me. I can hear you." My mother is holding my hands and talking to me! I want to hold on for as long as I can. She repeats the phrase a few times, then the sound of her voice fades. Her grip loosens and her fingers slip slowly from my hands. She is gone. My body releases from sleep's hold. I wake up.

I slowly opened my eyes and saw that John was sitting up next to me in bed watching television. He looked over and smiled, "Good morning." I wasn't ready to talk yet, not that he wouldn't believe me, but I had too much emotion to process and was speechless. I lay there quietly, trying to take it all in. Ten years had gone by since she passed, yet I heard my mother's voice and held her hands. That was no dream or hallucination! I did not hear her speak through a phone or talk face-to-face as I had in the Mexico dream. I physically heard her voice in my ear and had been completely awake and aware in my mind. Tears formed as I remembered the warmth of her hands as they slipped into mine, then faded away. I thought, *Did she think I forgot her? I need her now more than ever! I always want her advice, and now I know I can ask. She was here with me. She was listening. Mom, I love you.*

Standing at the mailbox, I was so excited to find out that no one had patented anything like my magnetic clips idea. The research report from the patent law firm was in and applying for a Magnetic Christmas Light Clip patent was a go! If I had asked John, he would have said it was because no one *wanted* magnetic Christmas light clips. Well, I believed otherwise. If I had a need for them, others must also have a need for them. There were all kinds of metal roofs that needed lights strung on them for Christmas or for whatever else. Besides, I wanted to feel like I had accomplished something in my life. I was good at supporting others while they accomplished their goals, but I didn't feel like I had done anything noteworthy. This was something all my own. And, I did think it was a good idea. The problem was that I needed four thousand dollars to pay the law firm to apply for the patent. Walking back to the house thumbing through the mail, I saw something interesting. *No way*, I thought. I was holding a check from an old tax return refund in the amount of four thousand dollars. *Mom*, I thought, *you are awesome!*

Sara and I had finally established who exactly the alpha dog was. For two years I had struggled with her not obeying my commands. She would drag me across the yard simply because she wanted to chase another dog. I couldn't handle her the way I'd been taught, so I called the trainer from the Gentle Dog Training company again. I yelled, "No more gentle!" So we settled on working with a shock collar. I told him that Sara would drag me around the neighborhood like I was a rag doll. The collar worked, and we soon built a great relationship based on love and trust. Although I didn't need the collar for her anymore, I thought about what a great motivational tool it would be to get Dylan to do his homework. "Do your homework!" Shock!

CHAPTER 7

Cry Myself to Sleep

Unlike the majority of the U.S., John and I had never tried marijuana. John, however, could tell within seconds if a person was stoned just by looking in their eyes. The stories he'd told me about growing up with friends who let drugs ruin their future made me want to cry. So when our son walked into the house and John looked into his eyes, I believed I was witnessing the actual breaking of John's heart. Our beautiful story of love and hard work conquering all had come to an end.

"Mom, smoking pot makes my head finally feel clear." Dylan pleaded with me, trying to get me to show sympathy. "But it is illegal! Even if you feel like it makes you calm down and focus, you could be thrown in jail if you're caught using it." I did notice that he seemed more pleasant to be around, but that couldn't matter in this case. Number one, it was illegal. Number two, Dylan couldn't do *anything* in moderation. The year before, we had to ban Runescape, an Internet game, because Dylan became obsessed. We would hear the computer room door screech open at three a.m. each night. Luckily John was good with computers, so he was able to block access to the game from our server. In this case, we didn't have the ability to control Dylan's access to marijuana. His choice to use illegal drugs was completely out of our control.

Dylan and I sit in the back seat of a stranger's car. I don't know how we got here, but it is definitely against our will. The driver is increasing speed and has no intention of slowing down or letting us get out. I tell Dylan that we have to make a jump for it while the car is still going slow. I'm not sure why, but he's arguing with me. I can't make him understand that we have to get out now before it's too late. I really hope he follows my lead because I have no choice. I open the door and tumble out onto the street. After rolling to a stop, I turn and wait for him to follow. Fear freezes my body and my breath. I see the car speeding away with Dylan still in it. "Jump! Please!" I plead, but I know he can't hear me. The car speeds away too fast. The door opens and Dylan lunges out of the door. My head begins to spin and nausea takes over as I watch him roll along the street. The sound of his head hitting the pavement is too much for my heart to take, and my eyes fly open. I wake up.

Lying in bed still feeling sick from my nightmare, I feared for Dylan's future. Was this some sort of premonition? I couldn't think of any steps I could take to change anything, in my dream or in real life. Day and night I worried about him. I understood my dream and it scared me to death. No matter how hard I tried to be a good role model for him, teach him good values, and educate him, he would always do as he wished. Unfortunately, I was not confident that he would make good choices. As the dream suggested, if he didn't act now, it would be too late.

We decided not to make any more payments on the "Raytown house" as we called it, the house so generously left to us. We had too many bills of our own stacked up and trying to keep good credit just wasn't doable anymore. The problem was that the real estate market was about to hit a record low. People would love to rent it, but I just couldn't put myself through being a landlord again. However, time had run out. After attempting a short sale, the deal fell through when the inspector wouldn't approve the roof. As luck would have it, a huge storm passed through that did a lot of damage to roofs in the area. So we let the bank take it. I could have used the word "luck" to explain the four thousand dollar check we received from the insurance company to fix the roof that a large storm just happened to tear up shortly before losing the house to the bank, but believed there was more to it. That same week I received notice that the application for my patent had been approved and was ready for me to receive, but I needed to pay the law firm an additional amount of four thousand dollars. This couldn't have been another coincidence. Sure, we could use the money to pay bills, but I really believed that if I asked and I received, then it was mine to spend as I saw fit. *Thank you, Mom*, I thought. *I knew you'd understand.*

Walking through a park on a beautiful afternoon, I search for Claire and Dylan. The grass is very green. Claire is in a day camp here and says she can't find Dylan anywhere. Dylan must be a camp counselor or something, but I'm not sure. I'm angry with Dylan for leaving Claire alone, but I'm also worried that he's missing. I see him coming up a path from beyond some trees leading from the woods. He's not alone. My heart beats faster and I feel dizzy as I look more closely at Dylan and the stranger. The man with him is in his early to mid-twenties, has a few tattoos, unshaven with a buzz haircut, and is wearing old, ripped up jeans and a T-shirt. Oddly, he walks slightly to the side of Dylan and close behind. Dylan looks disheveled, embarrassed, and down at his oversized, belted jeans. The man makes eye contact with me. With one hand gripping Dylan's shoulder, he slowly turns to show me the small blade in his other hand, holding it close to Dylan's side. The rage of a Mother Bear burns inside me, "Is that all you got?" I say as I stare into his eyes. I look desperately at Dylan hoping he'll look up at me. I want him to know my plan to attack this guy together. We could take him down if he'd only trust me and be brave! His slumped shoulders of shame and guilt tell me that he feels like he deserves whatever is happening to him. There's no fight in him. With a final glare at this drug dealing, child stealing,

demon, I lunge forward and shove Dylan to the side.
I wake up.

Again, I felt sick to my stomach lying in bed thinking about all the possible outcomes of my dream. Would Dylan move and fight back or would he step to the side and watch me fight? Would he or both of us get stabbed or would I be strong enough to overpower this guy and stab him? Did Dylan even care?

Despite the hardships of money, work, and now a drug-using son, Claire and Sara brought great joy to John and my life every day. We still had the usual routine of weekly dance classes, but she added my favorite sport to her activities...volleyball! I volunteered as coach for her recreational team. I absolutely loved it! I was so excited because she not only loved it, but she was also really good. I remembered how God gave me that amazing gift of her picture at about this age, but I worried a little because I wasn't having dreams of her in the future. Did premonition dreams only come as warnings? I'd been dreaming a lot about Dylan and none of them were good. I really wanted to have a dream of Claire in the future, just to know that she would be OK.

John's dad Bart had just lost his wife, Addie, after five years of marriage. John's parents divorced soon after we were married, but being a typical man, Bart didn't want to be alone. Addie came along a few years later and stole Bart's heart. Although she was his third wife, he said she was the love of his life. They traveled the world together and I could tell he was crazy about her. Unfortunately, he was now alone again, with the exception of their dog, Maggie. Worst of all, Addie's death came as a complete surprise. She had not been ill, she simply died in her sleep. I couldn't imagine waking up to find my spouse lying dead next to me without any explanation. I prayed that Addie came to him in his dreams, although he'd probably never say if she did. I wished people would open up more when they experienced encounters with the deceased. Who knew, maybe people would find that this happened to everyone and understand that life did not end with death.

It is evening. I'm standing on pavement looking around at all of the activity that surrounds me. There are carnival rides, games, food vendors, music, and lots of people enjoying themselves. I'm not sure if I'm alone or with someone. I see a familiar face in the distance. I recognize it as that of my niece, Emily, except she is a teenager, not the ten-year-old girl I know. Her eyes are very distinct, so large and blue. What I'm shocked to see is her hair! As a young girl, her hair has always been long, somewhat curly, and dirty blonde in color. Now her hair is shoulder length, straight, and almost black. It looks good on her. She's with a group of teenagers that I don't know. Even though Claire and Emily are like sisters, I don't see Claire with her. I am not sure why, but I don't call out to her to say hello. I just watch her from a distance. I wake up.

Of course, I had to tell the girls about this dream. It was so entirely clear and a perfect future image of my niece. Maybe premonitions didn't always have to be bad or warnings. "No way, Aunt Brianna!" Emily screamed and laughed at me. "I would never dye my hair black! I love having blonde hair!" I just smiled and said, "It will happen, trust me. Don't worry, though, you have lots of time to think about it. I'm not sure exactly what age you were, but probably in your late teens." The girls just giggled and went on their way. I didn't know what to make of the whole carnival thing, but I could totally see her with short, black hair.

Not only was the real estate market at an all-time low, but everything and everyone was affected in one way or another. The businesses leasing space in our building slowly up and left and so did their rent payments. Our personal savings and retirement fund were quickly disappearing while we struggled not to lose our home and the building we had invested all our savings in. Fortunately, we had money set aside for the kids' college fund and vowed never to touch it. That was the one thing about Dylan preparing for the University of Kansas (KU) that made me happy. The private school we'd struggled to keep him in had served its purpose; he had been accepted into KU's School of Engineering. John and I were not excited, though. We knew Dylan was not ready for the real world, the freedom to make his own choices, and the unstructured lifestyle. But we also didn't think we should take this opportunity away from him, we had to let him find his own way. Now, if we could just get through the rest of his senior year.

"Mom, I fucked up." I started hearing these words more and more frequently. According to Dylan, the story was that he and some of his friends were out cruising around and a police officer pulled them over. Because he drove a Jeep, everything in the car was pretty much out in the open, including their marijuana. Of all the boys, Dylan was the one charged with minor in possession. I didn't doubt that the marijuana was his. But, I also believed that he took the blame for all of the boys. He had a warped sense of loyalty that way, trying to please the wrong people in the wrong way. Those kids didn't care about him like we did. Ever since we were his age, we'd done everything for him. We had proven that age wasn't a factor when it came to behaving responsibly for the people you love. Everyone thought he was a polite, nice boy, yet for us, his selfish acts ripped our hearts out. It made us question his love for us.

When we were teenagers, John had bought a two-foot-tall, plastic baby bottle and asked friends and family to empty their change into it for Dylan's college fund. When it reached one thousand dollars, we invested the money and didn't touch it for ten years. The market had not done well, but we were still able to give him the cash as a graduation present. Dylan was extremely gracious about the gift, then passed it on to the lawyer he hired for his minor in possession charge.

> *I can't get up. Too tired. My limbs are all so heavy. I'm just lying here on the busy sidewalk and can't get up. Cars on the street zoom past. The people walking down the sidewalk simply step over me. I'm so embarrassed. They don't care that I'm lying here. I'm not sure if they even notice me. Everyone else just goes about their day, but I'm too tired to get up.* I wake up.

I really hated naps! I did everything in my power not to get so sleepy that I had no choice but to nap. When this did happen, I inevitably dreamed about being sleepy. There was nothing restful about my naps. After falling asleep,

I'd simply try to wake from a crazy dream or continue feeling sleepy while sleeping. What was the point? Did my brain just wish to escape this world and enter another?

My husband was a genius! Working in finance, he'd always believed in having good credit, yet after the Raytown house foreclosed and being on the verge of losing our own house, John had an idea that would ease the financial pain that foreclosure on the building would cause. He convinced the bank that it was in their best interest to buy the building back rather than foreclose. It worked! I loved how smart he was. He always pulled us through. The next obstacle was to figure out how to keep the bank from taking our home.

Dylan and I are on campus together for orientation at KU. New students and their parents are talking or walking around the campus grounds together, excited for the upcoming year. Where's Dylan? My eyes search the crowds and feelings of loneliness and confusion fill my head. Why would Dylan leave me? He didn't tell me where he was going. Too much time has passed and feelings of despair set in. In the distance, I catch a glimpse of his bright red hair and tall, lanky body. I see him with other boys his age, but something's not right. The guys are being rough with him and shoving him around. I can't make out what's going on exactly, so I head toward them. They all disappear around the corner, and I lose them. My heart starts pounding faster out of fear. Something's definitely wrong. I see a campus security guard close by and approach him. "Excuse me, officer. I've lost my son. Can you help me find him?" He smiles at me. "Sure," he says. "How old is he?" I know I'm going to sound ridiculous, but I'm so scared that I don't care. "He's eighteen years old." The officer's look changes to surprise, almost amusement. "I think he's in trouble and someone's going to hurt him if we don't find him soon!" The look on my face convinces the officer that I'm serious and very concerned; he looks at me with compassion and sympathy. I can't tell if he is laughing on the inside at the fact that he is helping to locate a lost eighteen-year-old, but he nicely talks into his radio and begins a search. I wait patiently until the officer motions to me to come talk with him. I can't interpret his facial expression. Is he smirking, feeling sorry for me? I don't understand the signs he's giving me. Finally, he explains that they've found Dylan, but Dylan doesn't wish to be found. I wake up.

This was a warning, I knew. I'd had too many dreams that I couldn't interpret quickly enough to react and really needed to understand this one. I told Dylan because I thought he might be able to help me figure out what the dream meant, then we could prevent whatever bad thing was going to happen. He only laughed and said, "Ha! That's hilarious!" His lighthearted attitude made me angry. "You mean the whole thing was staged? My friends helped me 'disappear'?" I didn't understand why he thought this was funny. Did he not hear me say how scared and sick I felt not knowing where he was? That I thought something really bad had happened to him, yet all he got from the dream was that he left campus on purpose with a group of buddies? At least, that was how he interpreted the dream.

For parents, attending orientation at KU with their child is typically a nerve-wracking, yet exciting and joyful experience. I was nervous on a whole different level. Thankfully there were no crazy surprises or disappearing acts from Dylan except when he asked to skip out on an informational meeting to hang with some new friends. I was relieved when he came back on his own. He had no interest in learning about the School of Engineering or meeting the teachers, even though the speaker said that getting to know them was critical to their success.

After orientation, we said our good-byes, the school year began, and we let go. With Dylan out of the house, we could focus on Claire and she wouldn't have to be around all of the fighting and arguing. We were really hoping that Dylan would prove us wrong by doing well. We'd have to trust that he'd take his Dexedrine responsibly. The doctors said that maturity would help shape his behavior the older he got. He gave up on his CPAP machine, of course. I knew it wouldn't make it to college with him (however, I did feel bad for his roommate). The plan was for him to get a part-time job on campus so he'd have spending money. For first time offenders like my son, the courts offered a diversion program as punishment. If Dylan stayed a "good boy" for a whole year after being caught with marijuana, the charges would be wiped from his file. It was a great money-maker for the county and kept kids out of jail. His diversion officer, who was supposed to randomly test him for drugs for a year, was aware that he took amphetamines for ADHD. The program made me feel a little better about him being on his own, knowing that he would be accountable to someone other than us.

We didn't have much communication with Dylan regarding his progress in school until close to the end of the semester. As it turned out, he never did get the part-time job, so I had no idea what he'd been using for spending money. Christmas break was approaching and he had no choice but to come clean.

Mama,

I have been up all night (again) because I don't know what to do. I so badly want to call Dad and tell him I'm going to be alright and that he has nothing to worry about, but I can't. I'm worried because I'm in so far over my head and I keep saying I want to fix it and get my grades back to where they should be but I'm scared that I won't be able to. It's the worst feeling knowing all I have to do to make you guys happy is to get a 3.0 here and I can't do it. I have been honestly trying this past week and it has made no difference. I don't know what's going to happen but I'm so tired of being such a disappointment to everybody. I want you and dad to have some kind of reason to brag about me for once or for Claire to look up to me because I'm a good brother, not because she doesn't know any better. I guess I'm just looking for some assurance but I can only do so much with that. I have no clue why I can't just be a normal college kid who gets his shit done. I love you and I just wanted to let you know what's going on. It's up to you whether or not you show this to Dad. I'd rather you not because I don't want him to think I'm weak but I will leave that decision up to you. I'm sorry about everything that has been happening lately and no matter how many times I snap at you for trying to help, I still love you guys.

—Dylan

"How many grandfathers does it take to change a light bulb?" Claire asked Bart, teasing him with her new favorite joke. We had moved Bart into our basement for six weeks while he recovered from a broken hip; he'd accidentally fallen attempting to change a light bulb. Therapists came and went each week, while I helped him with meals and small stuff. Because he had diabetes, he was very particular about what he ate and when. Which was fine, but I was getting a bit overwhelmed having to make special meals that fit his diet and be on his schedule. I felt like Bart was relying on me too much and wasn't trying to be self-sufficient enough. Eventually he would need go back home and start doing this stuff for himself.

One night, a friend asked me to go see the new *Twilight* movie with her. I really needed to get out of the house for a while, so I asked John to take care of Bart's dinner. He said he would, but in the back of my mind, I knew he was busy and wouldn't have dinner ready at the time his dad wanted it. Bart had been so good to us through our mess with the building, he even gave us money to help us try and keep it. He deserved all my attention, but on this night I felt selfish. "Bart, I'm leaving for a few hours to see a movie. John will take care of dinner for you." He told me what time he wanted to eat, then I took off.

The icy conditions made the drive home from the movie slow. When my cell phone rang and showed John on the ID, I was suspicious. "Hey, would you pick up the pizza I ordered? It's on your way home and will be ready in ten minutes." I couldn't believe what I was hearing. "John, it's 8:30 and you're just now getting dinner for your dad?" I bet Bart was furious! I knew John would either forget or get busy at work. I should have figured out something else rather than asking him.

The night had brought very cold temperatures and the roads were extremely slick. I got out of the car, walked carefully along the sidewalk towards the pizza shop, and *whoosh*! Both of my feet flew up into the air. With instinct from my younger days of bouncing on the trampoline, I immediately landed in a backdrop position. My thick coat cushioned the fall. *Note to self,* I thought, *do not walk that route coming back to the car.* Unhurt, I walked carefully into the restaurant. I don't know what I was thinking on my way out when ... *whoosh!* Up went the pizza and my feet! Landing, again, in a backdrop and fortunately unhurt, I began laughing. "OK, God, I get it! I'm sorry! I was being selfish." I should not have gone to the movies when I knew John wouldn't get home in time with Bart's dinner. "I was just frustrated, God, but I totally get it now!" I, too, at any time, could end up just like Bart and depend on *his* help. It's not his fault he broke his hip. "I promise to try not to be selfish like that again!"

Sometimes, lessons for spiritual growth and understanding were delivered in the funniest ways. I did believe I could learn life lessons after reflecting on experiences, yet at times I wondered if an angel of some type came up with crazy ideas just to be funny. She would snicker, thinking, *I'll show her who's high and mighty and teach her a lesson or two.* I was pretty certain this was one of those times.

Dylan's return home from Lawrence for winter break was not the typical happy reunion most students received from their parents. He had F's in all his classes and would be on academic probation if he were to return the following semester. His first semester had been a complete waste of money. He could have at least withdrawn from classes so he didn't receive F's! Dylan tossed me a book, *Catcher in the Rye*, and said, "Read this. This will help you understand me." I had heard of the book and was told it was fantastic.

I absolutely hated it! After the first ten pages, I decided I really disliked the kid, Holden. Either the writer or the character was severely ADHD. The kid was an over-privileged, disrespectful jerk who threw opportunities given to him by his parents in the trash. "Everyone else is stupid. Blah, blah, blah…." I just didn't get why people loved this story. Of course, my son identified with this character. He was Holden Caulfield! They both flunked out of school and tried to avoid their parents when coming home for winter break. They both had much younger sisters whom they admired, were dancers, and were much more mature than their brothers. What did he want me to understand? How could this possibly help me help him? Were there that many people in the world that identified with this character? If so, I was scared.

I knew that I was reading this book as an adult and had a different perspective, and that at seventeen my attitude would have been much different. I didn't have the choice to grow up or not. Pregnancy—BAM! I was an adult. I had to be. I was sure many people would argue with me about the literary genius I didn't see, but I couldn't get past my initial, very real emotions. I was the mother of a Holden Caulfield.

"Mom, if you don't let me have a second chance at KU, I'll end up moving to Lawrence anyway." John and I didn't know what to say to this. I knew giving Dylan a second chance would be stupid. But we also knew he was telling the truth about moving to Lawrence if we didn't let him try again. We didn't trust that he'd try any harder at school, but we said yes to a second chance anyway. I wanted to know where my son would be, that he had a roof over his head and a meal plan for food. All I could do was pray.

I finally put down book two of the *Twilight* series and went to bed. Reading without falling asleep had a lot to do with whether or not the content was stimulating. If I was engaged, I read for much longer periods of time. That's probably true for most people. John had been asleep for a while, so I slipped into bed quietly. His breathing was erratic. He must have been dreaming about something intense. I wanted to reach out and soothe him with a touch, but I had tried that in the past and ended up scaring the shit out of him. As I slid further into the blankets to get comfortable, John's whimpering and heavy breathing made me too worried to sleep. I sat up a little and scooted close enough so that he might feel my presence.

Paralyzed by REM, he pushed the air out of his lungs as if trying to scream. The noise that escaped his mouth sounded so bizarre and unnatural that goose bumps caused the hairs on both my arms and the back of my neck to rise. The strength of his scream finally broke through in full force. "John!" I called out to wake him from his nightmare. "Are you OK? You were having a nightmare!" He caught his breath and took a minute to focus. "I don't know what you're talking about. I'm fine." He rolled over pulling the green afghan blanket my grandma had knitted for us over him and went back to sleep. I think it was his adult security blanket.

I walk out the front door of our home and head down the sidewalk. It's the middle of the day, yet I feel so heavy and tired. Maybe I'm headed to the mailbox, but I'm not sure. I've been too scared to look at what's waiting for us in there. Scared and worried to the point of exhaustion and sickness, I lie down in the grass next to the sidewalk. Will they take our house? Are we being sued? I begin to cry. I feel something soft and warm lean up against my belly. Figaro. She's the sweetest cat. I know she's been gone for a while now and know this is a dream, but the fear in my heart is not a dream. I reach out and stroke her soft fur. She makes me feel calm. I don't know if she's telling me that everything will be OK, but for now, I feel safe and relaxed. I wake up.

As much as I could pray for God's intervention when life had me down, I knew I must take it upon myself to work hard and take advantage of opportunities that presented themselves. I loved the story about the guy who's drowning and prays that God will save him. Boats and ships come his way, but he waves them on, believing that God will save him. He eventually drowns, goes to heaven, and asks God, "I prayed to you. Why did you not save me?" God says in return, "I sent you boats and ships and you waved them all away." I strongly believed in prayer and knew I was being looked after, but I also believed that God helped those who helped themselves. Don't ask for the lottery. Ask for opportunities. John had been given a fantastic opportunity to make money by a friend that owned his own business. He jumped at the chance and his first commission paid out enough to save our home and refinance with the plan the mortgage company offered. We were saved.

"Mom, I fucked up." There were those words again! "I'm not at my dorm anymore. I'm living with friends in Lawrence because I was kicked out by KU's three strikes rule." I couldn't speak. I thought he was being tested for drugs randomly by his diversion officer. Why hadn't the school called to tell me my son was now homeless? If Dylan hadn't called me, I would never have known that they kicked him out of his dorm and had taken away his meal plan. It shouldn't matter that he was over eighteen. He was my child and apparently had a drug problem. Shouldn't I have a right to know that my kid had nowhere to live and no food? He could be homeless and starving, but too afraid to tell me. I was so angry at the world that I couldn't see straight. What's the point in having degrees in administration of justice and psychology when I couldn't help my own son?

John and I acted on our suspicions regarding his medication and extra income. Without Dylan's knowledge, we switched his phone line to an old cell phone at our house. Within the first five hours, over fifty text messages poured in: "Hey, man. I need some Molly." "Dude, hook me up with some Dex." "Hi, Dylan. This is Cassie from Oliver. Can I get some Dex from you? Thanks!" On and on and on... the drug requests came pouring in. I had to look up what "Molly" was. There were others, too, that I wasn't familiar with. Of course, I knew what "Dex" was.

Weren't drug users sketchy, scary people that you avoided on the streets? Apparently, they were just regular college kids around campus looking to stay up a little later to study, a high to party a little harder, or to stay awake during classes after partying too hard the night before. Maybe I would have been one of them, too. If I had not been given medication for my sleep disorder and someone offered me drugs to stay awake, I might not have refused. Knowing the criminal justice philosophy of being tough on drug sellers and sympathetic towards drug users, my son would be punished severely for being the go-to guy for everyone else's fix.

"Hello, Officer McKensey. Do you remember when you told me that it was common for a family member to call you and report drug use?" Dylan would hate me. He wouldn't understand why I did it, but I put my son in jail. I was a narc. I'd rather see him go to jail for a weekend for using drugs than get caught selling drugs and serve ten to twenty years in prison. *They're all just stupid kids!* I thought while completely frustrated. So many kids on college campuses use all kinds of drugs, yet mine was the one who would get caught and punished. He was the one trying to fit in, to feel important, and he had found a means to do it with the amphetamines that he wasn't using (yet really needed).

I hated him for this! OK, who was I kidding, I could never "hate" him. But, he was the reason why people like me, the ones that acted responsibly, had a hard time getting the medication we needed. He had to understand that this wasn't a game. *Hopefully,* I thought, *one weekend in jail will scare him enough to save the rest of his life.* Dylan, of course, didn't understand. The officers had not been testing him randomly and Dylan had started using all kinds of drugs. After testing positive, he was arrested and taken to jail for the weekend. Even though KU made him homeless, they did not kick him out of school. So, for three dollars a day, he commuted to and from Lawrence from our home to "attend school." When he finally decided to give up his little charade, he left home.

Hey,

I want all of you to know that I love you very much and my only rationale is that I believe that the only way to help myself get out of my constant fuck-up streak is to throw myself out on my ass and force myself to get my shit together. That is the only way I can explain my thinking about it. I know you think I'm making life extraordinarily difficult on myself but I feel that you have bailed me out enough and I need to be extraordinarily hard on myself in order for me to get my shit together. I'm basically forcing myself to not have any option besides figuring my shit out. I seriously want to know the date and time of Claire's speech so I can see her again and explain things to her myself personally. I love my sister and I don't need her to have any misconceptions about me. I feel like if I can at least explain myself to her, she will be more forgiving in the future. I love all of you and I want you to know that the only reason I'm doing this is because I can't even face myself knowing that I am the major concern in everyone's life.

I love all of you unconditionally,

Dylan M. Morrison

My eighteen-year-old son was lost somewhere in Lawrence, I thought, as I reflected on my past dream. I mean, he *wanted* to be lost and with his friends. There it was, even though he still didn't see it. This was my nightmare come true.

Focusing on Claire's achievements as well as dealing with our financial struggles made Dylan leaving home much easier. He missed Claire's speech. She received an award for her "Kindest Kansas Citian" essay, placing in the top ten in the city. He also missed her final dance recital. Was it just a coincidence that Holden Caulfield also missed his sister's dance recital? Without Dylan around, we could focus on turning things around at home now. John's business was picking up; he could concentrate better and even felt better with Dylan gone. Though he didn't seem to realize that he screamed out in his sleep almost nightly. At least, he didn't talk about it if he did.

I hear the shower turn on and my eyes open. I'm lying on my side, facing the wall towards the bathroom. John is smiling and walking towards me from out of the bathroom. He climbs over me, lowers himself down into the blankets, and presses his body up close from behind. I can feel his warmth as his body forms against mine. He only lies there quietly, holding me. I don't move, but my body begins to heat up and want more of him. I wake up.

At the sound of the shower turning on, my eyes flew open. I lay on my side, staring towards the wall in front of the bathroom. A chill ran through my body when I realized that I was waking up for real this time. I didn't move. I lay quietly, processing what I had just experienced. I could still feel the effects on my body from the warmth and pressure of his. John stepped out of the bathroom, smiled, and walked towards me as he had in my dream. He climbed over me, got under the covers, and gently pulled his body close to mine. I began to giggle. "Well, we're good to go because you already got me warmed up." He was quiet for a minute. "Huh?" Confused, he laughed then asked, "What are you talking about? I just felt like lying here with you for a few minutes before I got into the shower. You looked so warm and cozy." I tried to explain the sleep paralysis episode I'd had and said it must have been "Future John" that got me all worked up. He just sighed and said, "You are so weird."

As summer came to an end and fall was underway, our home began to feel empty. Our financial situation had turned around, which allowed me to quit being a real estate agent. Putting my time and effort towards people who simply "changed their mind" about buying a home or treated me poorly was not worth it anymore. I could focus on Claire's activities and spend time with Sara now that John's business income was under control and expenses were manageable. At the same time, however, the mood in our home had darkened. It had been months since we last heard from Dylan. Claire wouldn't talk about him. I thought she may be conflicted between blaming him and blaming us for her not having a brother anymore. We needed to bring some love into our home. What better way to do that than to get a kitten?

His name was Jeter. Yes, John named him after Derek Jeter, the star of the Yankees. This little black and grey tabby was absolutely fearless! He was the only kitten in the cage that wasn't terrified of our one hundred pound shepherd—he earned himself his new home. We spent endless hours laughing as he attacked Sara and latched on to her fur. She was so gentle not to hurt him, but still managed to use her legs to body slam him to the ground. Pets are like having personal angels. Yes, they pee on your carpet and rip your new silhouette shades, but they are so pure of heart and love you unconditionally. We had a new son in the family, a good son. Thank you, God, for letting us find joy in the simple things in life. Love was all we needed.

"Have you read *The Secret*?" John asked me. I knew where he was going with this. I was starting to show signs of depression. I smiled and answered, "I started reading a little bit, but then realized that I'd always lived my life by 'the secret' without knowing it was a secret." I'd been struggling with knowing where my life was supposed to go from here. I wasn't ready to go back to work full-time because I liked being free to take Claire to all her activities and not worrying about asking for work off if we wanted to go on vacation or something. John could do whatever he wanted whenever he wanted, but needed me to pick up the slack so he could concentrate on making money. So...what was I supposed to do? Fundraising would be extremely difficult during this bad economy. Besides, I wasn't that good at fundraising anyway; you really had to be a people person.

If I could only figure out which direction I wanted my life to go, then I could live by *The Secret*'s teachings. I could visualize myself doing what I wanted to do, putting good, positive vibes into the atmosphere (more or less), and then opportunities would present themselves to me. I just needed to figure out which path was the right path for me.

John and I made plans to have dinner at a friend's house that we hadn't seen in a while. Ron was a very interesting guy and business owner. I remembered that he had said he wanted to get into the sleep lab business. Apparently, it was a growing field in the Kansas City area. Over dinner, Ron talked about his new business venture in the sleep lab industry. This really sparked my interest; anything about sleep did. I asked him if he had any jobs that I could do that didn't require being a doctor or having a lot of experience. He mentioned marketing, which I had some experience with, but he'd already filled that position. Then he said, "Have you heard about the new polysomnograph (PSG) program at Johnson County Community College? It's a two-year program that trains you to be a sleep technician." *Hallelujah!* I could not believe there was a program like that that I didn't know about. I'd always looked for something that had to do with sleep. "But you don't want to work nights. No one likes those hours," he said dismissively. Little did he know that he just presented the solution to my problem. That was exactly what I was going to do. I was going back to school to become a polysomnograph technician (with John's blessing, of course!).

"Go home, Mom," Dylan had said while hugging me in a parking lot in Lawrence in the middle of the night. His words replayed in my mind over and over while I decorated our Christmas tree. Dylan and I didn't communicate often, but he made sure I had his cell number for emergencies. When I called and asked him to meet me, he had agreed to meet in a parking lot in Lawrence. He didn't want me to know where he lived. I'd begged him to come home. "Sara! That one's not yours!" I said as my mind snapped back to the present. Sara believed that a gift bag under the Christmas tree meant the gift was for her. She circled the presents a few times trying to sneak a peek, then shoved her head down into a bag like she was bobbing for apples. She knew she had a new stuffed animal in one of the bags. I decorated the inside of our home like usual, but with half the enthusiasm.

Wine, appetizers, and lots of desserts in the company of good friends were the perfect recipe for a wonderful Christmas party. John and I were enjoying the distraction when I received a call on my cell phone from the angry mother of a boy Dylan had graduated from high school with. "Do you know where my son is?" she asked. "I know he was friends with your son and probably took off somewhere with him!" A little irritated by her accusatory tone I said, "I'm sorry you're upset. I don't know where my own son is and barely speak to him. I'll send him a text and ask for you, but he may or may not reply."

After hanging up with her, I went into my friend's bathroom and sat for a while. My breathing became more rapid and difficult, my chest tightened, my head spun, and my body started to tingle. *This must be what people call an anxiety attack*, I thought. Quietly, I found my purse and walked out the front door. The cold wind on my face was calming as I walked down the sidewalk towards home. "Mom," I said aloud, "please stay with Dylan over Christmas. Be there and help guide him. Keep him safe and bring him home."

I wasn't sure our friends and family understood the grief and stress we were facing with our son, not knowing if he was living on the streets, dead from an overdose, starving, or in jail. Was it that they didn't want to upset us by asking about him? Were they wrapped up in their own issues and so didn't ask about ours? Or, did they think that because he was a nineteen-year-old boy, he was fine on his own? I didn't wish for any parent to have to experience this, but it did make me mad that people didn't seem to understand the gravity of the situation. Why hadn't anyone asked how *we* were? Dylan wasn't hurting. He chose his life! We, on the other hand, cried ourselves to sleep.

CHAPTER 8

Up All Night, Sleep All Day

"You got arrested for stealing socks from Wal-Mart?" I screamed at Dylan in disbelief. *So*, I thought, *this is him living life the "hard way" to straighten himself out? What a terrible strategy for self-improvement.* He managed to text me every now and then to keep me informed of his "progress." I'd told him Claire's volleyball team was playing in Lawrence, so he asked if he could come see me in person. He brought his girlfriend Jennifer. Together they happily ate good, free food off the volleyball team's food table while I lectured them. "You're like two drowning kids trying to hold on to each other, hoping to stay afloat. You won't survive this way! A lifeguard learns to shove a drowning victim off of them if they try to cling on. Only then is the lifeguard able to save them. The way you're going, you will drown each other. Go home and learn to swim! I know you think you need each other, but you have to learn to swim first before you will be any good for each other." Although I felt like this was a great analogy, I knew that neither of them cared what I had to say. I hoped Jennifer was smarter than Dylan and would move back to her parents' home.

"This is not what I meant when I said I wanted a college girl!" John liked to tease me about returning to school. Twenty years later, I walked the halls on campus looking for my chemistry class. What was really weird was that I sometimes passed Dylan in the hallways. I'm not exactly sure the true reason he decided to move home, but Dylan had asked for another chance to be a normal college kid. JCCC barely let him in as a conditional student after flunking out of his KU classes for a second time. The last time we were in school together he was in my belly (and in my chemistry class). He worked down the street from the college and sometimes brought me snacks during my long Sunday class. Claire welcomed Dylan back with open arms. If she had been angry with him, she didn't say. I was hopeful this would work out, but John was not optimistic. He was usually right about Dylan, but I tried to remain hopeful at least.

School was coming along well for me, but I stopped passing Dylan in the halls. I began to see less and less of him in the usual spot until one day I stopped seeing him altogether. I wasn't surprised, just disappointed. I bought a drug testing kit one evening and handed it to him. I didn't know why because I knew what I would find, and I also knew that doing it would cause him to leave us again. I'd tried being in control of his Dexedrine by going with him to his psychiatrist's appointments even though he was old enough to get the prescription himself. I'd explained to the doctor that I needed to be involved, but I didn't want him to know Dylan had been selling his meds. If he was going to be in school, he needed his medication. As expected, the test showed that opiates had become a part of his life.

> *Standing in the hallway between my kitchen and the garage door, I wait. I feel sad, yet nervous and anxious. Dylan slowly walks toward me with a small comforting smile and opens his arms. He towers over me, and I feel childlike. It's not only his size, but he's comforting me as he puts his arms around me and holds me tight. We stand there together for a while. Tears stream down my face. I wake up.*

I didn't know how much more our family could take. Our financial success all depended on John's mental well-being. When the king was happy, all the land was prosperous. When the king was sick... Dylan had been the source of John's motivation in life since the day we found out I was pregnant. That source of motivation ended when our son sat in the garage with five large trash bags filled with his clothes and other belongings, waiting for a ride to take him away. We didn't know to where.

We couldn't tell who Claire was more upset with, Dylan or John and me. We tried to get her to open up, but she'd just start crying and yelling at us for making her talk about it. I hated that Dylan was so selfish and careless with his life after we'd worked so hard to make sure he would have a perfect one. We didn't do things for him, but rather provided opportunities to help him succeed. When he threw those away, he was slapping us in the face. I went in the garage where Dylan was waiting for his ride, kissed him on the forehead, asked him to fix his life and went back inside, not knowing when I would see him again.

Months had gone by when I got a text with only an address. The prefix of the phone number was from Lawrence. "Is this Jennifer?" I wrote back. "Yes," she texted. "Does Dylan need an intervention?" I asked. "Yes, you will need to go around the back of the house and up the stairs to the third floor and knock," she explained. I figured they were together, but I hadn't spoken to Dylan in quite a while. This was a Kansas City address and not in a good part of town. I was scared to tell John because he wouldn't want me to go, but I also knew that he wouldn't go himself. I put Sara in the car with me and went to find my son.

Although I had lived in the KC area my whole life, I was unfamiliar with this neighborhood. It was daytime, so I felt safer than if it had been dark. I parked across the street from the address of a duplex-type building and left Sara in the car. As tough as she could be, I never wanted to put her in harm's way. As Jennifer instructed, I went through the gate to the backyard and up three flights of stairs and knocked on the back door. The winter wind was brisk, I should have worn a hat. I could hear noise and commotion from inside, but no one came to the door. Again, I knocked and waited, shivering from anticipation and nervousness more than from cold. I had no idea what I would find, but I was determined to find my son.

After a good five minutes or so, a young, black man in his early twenties opened the door. He looked at me curiously and asked how he could help me. "I'm looking for my son, Dylan Morrison." His look changed to surprise, he told me to hold on and shut the door. Ten minutes must have passed, but I was not going to leave that porch until I saw Dylan. I had nothing but time. Was he high and passed out on a couch? Was he asleep? It was the middle of the afternoon. Finally, the door opened. Dylan stood alone, grudgingly, I could tell. Again, I knew he didn't want to be found.

"Hey, Mom, come on in. It's cold outside." He stepped back into the kitchen and held his arms open. Slowly, I took a couple steps towards him and fell against his chest, holding him tight. He wrapped his long, warm arms around me. I wasn't sure how long we stood like that or what was going on around us, but as we silently embraced, tears tumbled down my cheeks. There wasn't much to say at this point. I knew he wouldn't come home simply because I asked. Even if he did, then what? Where was his rock bottom? How far did he need to go in order for him to want to seek help?

We slowly pulled away, and I looked around. The kitchen opened up into a great room with couches and a TV. There were a few other young men ranging in age from about eighteen to twenty-five years old sleeping on couches and sitting in chairs. What were they all doing here? Did they have jobs? Had they also dumped their families? There was quite a bit of trash overflowing in the trashcans, and all I could think of to say was, "Guess somebody didn't do their trash chore, huh?" He just laughed as one of the guys approached me smiling, "Hello. My name is Josh. Pleased to meet you." As he stuck out his hand, I turned away and looked towards Dylan. Although he had been surprisingly polite, I didn't want to shake his hand. None of this was OK to me. "No," I said so Josh could hear me. "No, it isn't a pleasure to meet you." Confused, he lowered his hand, shrugged, and walked away.

Dylan understood. As much as he wouldn't change, he also knew how much this hurt me. I didn't stay long. I didn't tell him how I knew where he was, but I was sure he'd figure it out. There was nothing a parent could really do at this point but pray. Pray that their child will make good choices. Pray that they will be safe and that they'll come home before it is too late. As I got back into the car, I saw the young, black man who first greeted me sitting on the front porch. He slowly waved and I wanted to wave back like I would have to anyone, but I had too much anger inside. I only stared a minute then looked down. Tears began to fall again.

My head was pounding on the drive home, so I turned off the music and drove in silence. Sara sensed my sadness and sat quietly in the back. I wondered if the young man out front wished that someone would come looking for him. Did those boys know that Dylan had an amazing family (mother, father, sister, dog, and cat) waiting for his return? Did they know that doing and selling drugs, living in that house full of people (who were also probably doing and selling drugs) instead of living in a college dorm, going to class, and doing normal nineteen-year-old things was Dylan's choice? Then it hit me. Our hug inside the back door at the entrance to his kitchen was the hug in my dreams. It was not *my* kitchen we had embraced in, it was his. He was not coming home.

I was certain dogs and cats talked to each other. Whether it was telepathically or some other way, I knew Sara and Jeter communicated. Jeter went out every night and did whatever cats do (cat club meetings, cat games, kill parties, bug hunts). At six o'clock every morning, Sara waited at the back door for him to return. John would let Jeter in and the two animals would touch noses, greeting each other. I'm sure this was how it happened. Sara: "Hey! What did you do last night? Kill anything? See any coyotes?" Jeter: "No coyotes, but I hung out with a fox. He was pretty cool. I showed off my hunting skills and earned his respect."

They learned from each other as well. Sara had a small bladder and woke me up at least once a night to go outside. First she would figure out which side of the bed I was sleeping on, then she'd sit next to me and wait. She was large enough so that her face was right next to mine. If that didn't wake me, she'd hit the top of the mattress with her paw. That usually did the trick. If Jeter got stuck in the house after we were asleep, he had learned to go to the side of the bed and make scratching noises. Some nights I simply didn't want him to go out, so I ignored the scratching. At those moments, Sara would pop up and hit the mattress for him. I would know they had worked together when Sara lay back down in her spot next to the bed while Jeter came trotting after me towards the front door.

Christmas time had come again and with that came the Christmas parties with friends and family. My own family didn't even acknowledge that Dylan was gone because it had become the norm. What was worse, I put on a happy face to make everyone feel comfortable. Last minute grocery store runs had never bothered me in previous years, yet this particular trip I was sitting in the parking lot thinking, *Now would be a good time for a brown bag.* I was hyperventilating. Where was this coming from? I didn't feel stressed. My heart raced and ears were ringing. "Why was my nose tingling?" Until the strange mix of numbness and tingling in my nose, all the symptoms were pointing towards an anxiety attack. Then a thought hit me. I texted Dylan: "Are you doing cocaine?" A minute passed before he responded: "Uhhh... Nooo...?" I thought maybe my maternal instinct was kicking in, but I supposed it was nothing.

I anticipated a phone call from Dylan on Christmas that didn't come, but his girlfriend called the following day. "Mrs. Morrison? This is Jennifer. Would you be willing to let Dylan come home if I brought him to you? I'm really worried about him and not sure what to do. I think he came close to overdosing the other day, and I'd like to bring him home."

After two months of being home, we'd trusted Dylan to stay behind and take care of the animals. We returned home from a weekend out of town for Claire's volleyball tournament, and the signs that a party had been thrown in our basement were plentiful. What possessed John to pull out the basement refrigerator and look behind it, we'd never know. He said he didn't know what he was looking for, but felt the urge to look, so he did. Unfortunately, he found something of interest. He looked on the Internet to find a picture that matched what he held in his hand. It was Molly, also known as MDMA, the active ingredient in the party drug ecstasy. A parent never gets used to telling their child good-bye. Pretty soon, you feel like simply closing your heart to the one who could at any time tear another hole through the middle of it. That's where John had gotten with Dylan. There were so many holes in his heart that he wanted to shut Dylan out to keep it from breaking.

I didn't used to dread high school class reunions, but the plan for my twenty-year reunion was for Dylan to come with me. I didn't really talk to many of my old friends, and I didn't want anyone to ask about him. Most of all, I was worried about running into an old friend who had stopped talking to me about seven years earlier. I didn't know why she stopped talking to me, and she refused to say. She and I had been best friends since we were five years old! I asked her to tell me what I did wrong and all she said was, "If you don't know, then you aren't the friend I thought you were." Well, I guess I wasn't. I just couldn't understand how it was enough to throw away a twenty-year friendship.

> *I'm not sure where I am. I think this is my old neighborhood. Michelle? I'm dreaming. She's been intruding into my dreams for weeks, but I know I'm dreaming this time. I should try*

to make peace with her in my dream since she won't talk to me in real life. This is better than having to send a letter. As she approaches me, I greet her with a smile. She smiles back. "Hi," I say. She says hi back. "I'm really sorry for whatever it is I have done to you," I say. "I never meant to hurt you. Please forgive me." This feels good. She disappears.
I wake up.

I couldn't get rid of her! Night after night she was in my head. Sometimes I didn't realize it until after I woke up. Other times, I'd recognize her in my dream and confront her, then she'd simply disappear—POOF! I couldn't get her out of my head! I considered writing her a letter to release whatever sort of "bond" there still was between us. Maybe the class reunion had her thinking about me as well and that jump-started a mental connection or something. I decided not to write a letter; I was past the point of wanting to be friends again.

I believe I'm alone until I see someone walking towards me. It's her again! Why is she here? Ugh, she's in my dream again!. Why won't she just leave me alone? I told her I was sorry. I begin to scream at her as she nears, "Get out of my head! We aren't friends anymore!" She's gone. I wake up.

What was I supposed to do? I didn't understand what God's message to me was, but I was sure there had to have been one. I told her that I forgave her. I was trying to be at peace with her in my heart. I'd asked her what I did wrong to give me a chance to say I was sorry, but she wouldn't tell me. What else could I have done? If having her in my dreams was just my subconscious missing her, well, I didn't miss her anymore! Actually, I was getting a bit sick of seeing her.

I'm in a library. I'm not sure which library, but I'm slowly walking along a tall bookcase full of books. I see Michelle walking towards me. She looks as I remember her from our twenties. I'm dreaming and she's back. This is my opportunity to end this ongoing nightly intrusion of hers into my dreams. We don't speak when she approaches me. I decide to do something a bit dramatic this time. I stick out my hand and will a large sword to appear. Slightly amused that it actually worked, I grip the sword in both hands and shove the sword into her chest. She's gone. I wake up.

June 2011

Mama,

I have fucked up in so many ways that I honestly don't know who to turn to anymore. I ruined things with you guys to go be with the girl that I loved, then promptly ruined things with her to hang out with friends who didn't really care about me. Then, I ruined things with the good friends out of that group that actually stuck around to try and help me fix things to the point that no one really wants to help me anymore because I can't even help myself. I no longer have any desire to be in Lawrence, seeing as the only reason I wanted to be here is destroyed because I can't be a big boy and get a real job. And even when I don't have a real job, I can't not spend money in such a way as to lead me into debt that makes me want to kill myself. It is like I have forgotten how to be a decent human being. I do not believe I am addicted to anything other than fucking up opportunities for myself. For a while, I was doing better than I would have anticipated. Then, as usual, I found a way to fuck things up and got robbed by someone I thought was a good friend of mine at the time for a decent amount of money while I was out in California. I have been given plenty of chances to fix it down here but I don't. You can fix an addict, you can't fix being an idiot. I don't know what to do anymore. Half the time I'm too depressed to go look for a job, and when I'm optimistic enough to actually apply at a couple of places, I don't get calls back. Every single problem I have right now is and was caused by my own judgment or a personal error I have made.

I'm not asking for a way out, simply advice. I don't know how to live my life anymore and furthermore, I don't really want to. I didn't think I would have gotten back to where I was but it seems that I have gotten way further down. I love you and I'm sorry I couldn't be stronger for you, Dad, Claire, and everyone else that actually cared enough to play along with all my stupid ideas that I will never follow through with anyway. Please help if you think you can. If not, please let me know as well.

I'm sorry,

Dylan

"Mom, will you come get me?" A couple of months had gone by since I received Dylan's email. There wasn't anything I could do for him except pray that his rock bottom didn't kill him. I knew he was serious when he called because I told him not to call me or even talk about coming home unless he was ready to do something completely drastic. He asked me to come get him right away. "There are some people that want to hurt me if I don't pay them. I'll do anything you want me to do. I'll go to rehab or whatever you want. Just please come get me." He had me at "Mom."

John would not allow Dylan in our house, so on the road to Lawrence I talked my dad into taking him in temporarily. Although he agreed, I was a bit surprised when he talked about the need to lock up valuables and prescriptions. I thought, *This is your grandson, not some criminal.* No way would he steal from his own family. I pulled up to the address in Lawrence Dylan had given me and saw him sitting outside with a few less garbage bags than he had left our house with. That was not good because his clothes were never cheap. Man, he looked rough. "I need to pay this guy two hundred dollars tonight," Dylan said as he got in my car. "What?!" I screamed in disbelief. "You honestly expect *me* to meet a drug dealer and pay him money?" I knew he was serious from the embarrassed and nervous look on his face. Part of me wanted to say, "To hell with him." Another part of me wanted to meet this guy and slit his throat. "Fine. I'll get some money, so tell this guy we're coming to see him."

I don't know *what* I was thinking! At the same time, there was so much rage and anger inside me from years of dealing with those bastards (including my son), that I had no fear. Some guy threatened my son and wanted to meet me, his mother, for payment of drugs? He was either high or had a death wish! Did he not know what Mother Bears were like? Normally, I'd consider myself a bitch—loyal, beautiful, loving, but would become vicious and bite if provoked. When I became a Mother Bear in order to protect my cubs, I was out for blood. I only saw red.

We pulled up to a gas station in South Kansas City and parked alongside the car that Dylan said was the one. I was still dressed in my Yankee's gear that John made me wear to a Royal's game we went to earlier that night. With visor, ponytail and all, there was nothing visibly threatening about me, yet I felt like I could go Steven Seagal on him at any moment. "What's this kid's name?" I asked as I tried to size him up. "Jesse," Dylan mumbled, trying to not look over his shoulder at the car next to us. "Are you kidding? Jesse? As in the Jesse on the show *Breaking Bad* who is just out of high school and trying to be a tough drug dealer?" *Great*, I thought. I actually liked that character.

Dylan shrunk down in his seat while I got out of the car and approached the driver's side window of the car next to me. *My God*, I thought, *he's not much older than Dylan*. Visions from past dreams of drug dealers taking hold of my son flashed in my mind. "So, you think I owe you money, do you?" I asked the kid with tattoos and crew cut hair sitting in the driver's seat. He briefly glanced my direction and answered, "He owes me two hundred dollars." A little laugh escaped me as I responded, "Oh, is that all? Well, hell, Dylan owes me thousands of dollars! What makes you so special that makes him have to pay you first?" I didn't know what this guy expected from me, but the look on his face told me it certainly wasn't this.

The mother in me just took over. I took out the two hundred dollars from my back pocket and held it in front of me. "Sixty dollars goes to fill up my tank for having to drive out to Lawrence and back just so Dylan could pay his little drug dealer tonight." I put it in my back pocket. He didn't look at me, but I noticed his eyes get wide. "A hundred goes to me for what I'll call a delivery fee." At that point, he was speechless and shocked. "And, the remaining forty will go to you. I bet you were counting on this money to get some food to eat tonight. Am I right?" At that point, the kid looked like he was going to scream, and I felt very satisfied as I dropped the two twenties in his lap.

"What did you think I was going to do, hand you over two hundred dollars and beg you not hurt my son?" Then I pulled out a few curse words to add to my toughness. "Listen, you little fucker! Stick your head out of the car and smile at the security camera on the building. Has Dylan ever told you that I put my own son in jail before? If I'm willing to do that, what do you think I'd be willing to do to little fuckers like you? I'm going to send Dylan away for a while. But if I ever see you or hear about you threatening him again, you will be sorry you ever met me."

The drive to my dad's house was quiet. "Give me your phone." Reluctantly, Dylan handed me his phone, and I tossed it out the window onto the highway. "I don't know exactly what I'm going to do with you, Dylan, but you can't come home." He just nodded. "I'm taking you to Grandpa's until I can figure this out." At about ten after midnight we pulled up to my dad's house. Looking at the date on the clock, I smiled to myself. It was August 16th, my mother's birthday. My son came home.

"John, I think I found a place to send Dylan." We'd both been searching online for possible inpatient drug addiction facilities, while our dads took turns housing Dylan. We almost settled on one in Arizona, but it would end up costing almost fifty thousand dollars, and they wouldn't stop him if he wanted to leave. "There's a place in Michigan that costs twenty-five thousand dollars, and they can refund us almost all of the money because they take our health insurance. Everything looks good from what I read online. Plus, I don't think either of our dads want him anymore."

I hated asking John for money that we didn't have to spend, especially when it came to Dylan. We'd spent way too much on lawyers and crap as it was. Grudgingly, John said, "I'm getting a twenty-five thousand dollar commission check next week. If this is what you want to do, take it." I was focused on the fact that they would take our health insurance and send us periodic refund checks as they billed our insurance, so it didn't occur to me just how strange it was that the exact amount we needed for this place was coming the following week.

I felt almost numb and a bit in a daze as Dylan and I were transported from the airport in Michigan to the rehab facility. I barely knew anything about these people, yet I was giving them a check for twenty-five thousand dollars, not to mention my son. What if he walked out of this place and I never saw him again? He would be living on the streets somewhere in Michigan! The admissions officer, a past resident there, was nice and took us on a tour of the facility. *Smoking? What the… are you kidding me?* Seeing large groups of young adults sitting together in a courtyard smoking cigarettes sent any hopes I had of rehab down the drain.

"Excuse me, but what is going on here?" The admissions officer stopped and turned around to look at me. "You call this place a drug addiction rehabilitation center, yet you allow people to smoke one of the most addictive substances on the planet?" He went on to say that he quit smoking while he was here and promised to help Dylan as well, but the facility did allow cigarette smoking. *Fantastic*, I thought, *I just spent what little money we had on last minute plane tickets out there, and I had nowhere else to take Dylan.* This felt wrong. The place was weird, especially their detox method of making kids sit in saunas for hours to make a tar-like substance come out of their bodies. I didn't get it.

"Dylan, listen," I pulled him aside to talk before signing the paperwork. "I'm not sure what to do at this point. I can already tell this place is not right for you, but I have nowhere else for you to go. You can't come home. Your grandpas can't deal with your problems. You really just need to be away from KC for a little while to get your head straight. I don't think you have a drug addiction problem. I think you are addicted to the lifestyle, but I can't figure out why. I don't know why you like being around those people. Do they make you feel important or something?" Dylan just gave me a big hug and said, "I don't know, Mom. I don't know why I keep fucking everything up. I'll be OK here. Go on back to the airport, and I'll see you in about five or six months."

I was in! I was one of thirteen students selected for the next year's associates of science in polysomnography program. I never doubted I would be. How could they not choose me? I was a narcoleptic for crying out loud, not to mention the fact that I already had about one hundred and sixty college credits! The interview was scary, but I was confident it went well. "Don't you dare work your invention somehow into that interview," John said half joking, half not. So, I couldn't help but smile when the interviewer asked something about dexterity and being able to problem solve. It just fit! Besides, I not only solved the problem of needing a light clip to work on a metal roof, but I also received a patent on the invention proving that I followed through on projects.

I knew that one of the three interviewers was aware that I had narcolepsy, but from the looks on their faces when I told them, I could tell he hadn't shared that information with the others. Interviewer: "Why do think that you could handle working a twelve-hour night shift in order to handle such a position as sleep technologist?" Me: "I have narcolepsy, so my day/night sleep schedule is already broken. Because I'm broken, I use amphetamines to tell my body when to be awake and when to allow it to sleep. Instead of taking pills three times a day as usual, I would simply change to three times a night. I don't typically have issues with falling asleep during the day, so I should be just fine sleeping days." It made perfect since to me, in theory, and I believed it did the trick for them. I thought people could learn a lot from me. Narcoleptics didn't have to be a liability, we could be an asset.

On the first day of class, we interviewed the person sitting at the table next to us. Robin Morlock just happened to be the one next to me, and so she became my lab partner. She was about five years older than me and was so interesting! I felt bad that I had a hard time looking her in the eyes. My eyes couldn't help but to shift from her blue eye to the brown eye, to the blue, then to the brown, back and forth. Her eyes weren't the only interesting thing about her. She was a spiritual alchemist and intuitive healer, someone who believes in and studies the blending of science and the sacred for intuitive living. Her job was to "gracefully align you with your life purpose" through "soul journey" classes and others on dreams, angels, dimensions, and Reiki. Robin and I would be spending a lot of time together over the next two years, working twelve hours shifts twice a week at various sleep labs. She talked a lot about spirit guides, the Mayan healing practices and her love of writing. I didn't know that being narcoleptic was that exciting to other people, but she was super interested in me as well. Most people just laughed when I told them and waited to see if I was going to fall on the floor or something.

I felt right at home listening to the teacher talk about the sleep disorders, brain wave patterns, CPAP machines, sleep deprivation symptoms, and even narcolepsy. I knew I was going to have to try really hard not to sound like a know-it-all when it came to narcolepsy, but I did feel like quite the expert. I would need to learn as much about the breathing disorder called sleep apnea as I could because I heard it was the norm in sleep labs. I wan't sure whether I irritated the teacher or not by speaking up, but I had to say something when he talked about research indicating the age of onset for narcolepsy. I politely raised my hand and offered, "Well, I'll tell you guys just like I told that researcher long ago...."

In order to really feel like I was making a contribution to the field of sleep, I decided to attend another Narcolepsy Network conference. Las Vegas was an awesome place to hold a narcolepsy conference! I tried really hard to be social, but it seemed like I was one of the few that actually had any energy. I suppose if I had narcolepsy with cataplexy, I might have had a totally different attitude. I wanted to learn more about cataplexy. I had a special place in my heart for people that had to live with cataplexy because I was always thanking God that I *didn't* have to live with it. How could I have possibly done the things I've done, enjoyed the awesome experiences fully, or even dealt with the serious issues I've had to endure if I were always concerned about whether my brain was stable enough to handle the emotion without collapsing?

There was a particular speaker at this conference who I was excited to hear talk during the workshops, a PhD in psychology and sleep medicine. He called himself the "sleep and dream expert" and his topic was nightmares, so the room was packed. An old man raised his hand to speak, "I used to have beautiful dreams when I was young, but I haven't had a dream in a very long time. I really miss them." He looked so sad and sincere. I wondered if he had been on antidepressants or the new drug Xyrem, and that's why he hadn't been dreaming. I wondered if everyone taking meds for cataplexy stopped dreaming. As scary as my nightmares could be, I would never want to give up dreaming.

"I keep having the same dream about me drowning," said a concerned woman. She went on to tell her tale of nightly battles and asked the "expert" what she was supposed to do. Anxious eyes lay on the doctor as he turned to her and said something to the effect of: Examine your fears and make peace with your nightmares. *What?!* I thought, with a stunned look on my face. We all looked around at each other's expressions of confusion. He went on to tell us that we have something to learn from our "demons" and to develop a relationship through communication because we are safe in our beds. *No, no, no!* I thought. This was not right. My demons were not "relationship" material! I would never climb down a rope that led from heaven and extend my hand to the man surrounded by hellish monsters in an attempt to make peace! When I thought back to the day, as a child, I'd had the brilliant idea to "let evil in" and offer some sort of relationship with it (using my little made-up chant), I remembered feeling as if I had opened the door to hell! Just as someone could open their heart to God and let love in, I'd opened my mind to the possibility of evil spirits, and they'd come running.

I did believe that individuals had a lot to learn about themselves through their dreams. However, there may be some dreams, or rather, nightmares, that were only that—nightmares. Not all dreams had to be teaching moments, and I didn't feel that all dreams were in a safe environment for self-exploration. If my dreams could open a doorway to the spiritual world and let my mother in, then what's to stop unwanted guests from entering my soul's space as well?

"Mom, you have to get me out of here. They're making me stare at ash trays to try to make them move," Dylan whispered to me on the phone. "What are you talking about, Dylan?" Apparently, I'd sent him to a Scientology-based addiction rehab center. I'd heard of Scientology, but didn't know a whole lot about their practices. I did know, however, that they weren't anything like our Catholic upbringing. "Dylan, all I can say is to just take this time away from home to focus on getting your head straight. Of course I don't expect you to believe any of their crap, but you have time away from here and time away from the drug scene." He was quiet for a minute. "Mom, you don't understand. There's a lot of shit going on here that's not good. There are no therapists here! This place is crazy and the staff are all ex-patients. The staff even sell drugs to kids in here and make sex deals with the girls in exchange for drugs!" This got my attention. I felt like a real shitty mother.

"John, I started doing some research, and I'm not feeling very good about where Dylan is." John came into our home office and sat next to me. "Yeah, I've been doing some searching on the Internet as well. There are complaints from all over the country about those facilities and there have even been a couple of deaths." January made it five months since Dylan had been in Michigan. He had tried to leave the facility once, but thankfully one of the staff members went after him. I don't know what we would have done if they'd just let him go. "John, I want you to go get our son! I'm starting to feel sick to my stomach and can't wait until next month." It had been a year and a half since John had seen or talked to Dylan, so I wasn't sure how he'd react. "OK," he said. "I'll catch a flight first thing in the morning."

Lying in bed looking over the edge, I call out for Sara. I feel afraid and need her to be close to me. I see an animal make its way towards me. "You are not Sara," I say as calmly as I can so it doesn't get angry. The animal slowly

looks up at me and grins an all-too-wide smile. The beast is Sara's size, yet has black fur, a large, round head, and a round body. The face resembles the Cheshire Cat in Alice in Wonderland. Quietly, I slide out of bed and make my way toward the living room. I'm no longer in my house, this is the living room of my childhood home. Being here doesn't feel right. I see my mother standing in the living room. She's wearing her favorite cotton, light blue nightgown with white ruffle shoulder straps. Something isn't right. This is not my mother. Demons are toying with me again. I play along to avoid making it angry. "Hello, Mother." The beautiful face turns and smiles. My heart quickens as its grin becomes too wide, exposing several rows of serrated teeth. I need out of here. I need to wake up. I start to sing, "Jesus loves me, yes I know...." The beast dog enters the room. "...for the Bible tells me so," I continue. I see that the TV is on. The characters are singing along with me. No, they aren't really singing along with me. They, along with the two demons in the room, are mocking me. "Jesus hates me, yes I know...." I wake up.

No matter what I did to change these nightmares, whether I prayed or tried to outsmart the demons, I couldn't win. Nothing worked. These demons dragged me back to my childhood home, terrorized and mocked me! I tried to be strong and confident to show them I wasn't the scared child their energy fed from anymore. I wanted to rid them of their power over me so they could no longer take advantage of my vulnerability during sleep.

Although I still battled demons, I noticed that John's nightmares had quieted since Dylan's return. John had never told me what his nightmares were about. "I don't know what you're talking about," was all he'd say when I asked him if he was OK when he woke up screaming. We had a long way to go with Dylan. In the meantime, he and John were inseparable. John planned a huge, three-week family trip to Europe. He said this was the first time in a long time that we'd actually gotten ahead financially, and he wanted to enjoy what he believed would be our last family trip together. He had lost faith in his son and wanted to enjoy what time we had left with him.

I really enjoyed learning about the physiology of sleep. For something we spent a third of our lives doing, it was amazing to me that people didn't talk about it more. I called myself a sleep advocate. Sure, I had an occasional energy drink and took amphetamines every day, but I believed in good, quality sleep. People shouldn't be embarrassed or apologize because they are tired. I found that my amphetamines simply didn't work if I were sleep deprived. Studies showed that when we are sleep deprived, our brains crave foods that are high in fat, sugar, and calories. I continuously craved these foods, but was I, as a narcoleptic, really sleep deprived?

A narcoleptic can never really "catch up" on sleep for any long period of time. I can only get enough sleep to obtain my "normal" level of sleepiness. After learning that our brain utilizes sugar from our blood during REM, I wondered if I actually had low blood sugar in the mornings or if I simply craved carbs from sleep deprivation. Whichever was the case, I started asking myself before reaching into the refrigerator for food, "Would fruits or vegetables cure my hunger?" If the answer was "no," then I knew I was "tired eating" and should take a nap instead.

It was satisfying to be able to go back over my own sleep study reports with an understanding of the language. I could even understand the biofeedback report from Dylan's ADHD testing. In class, we'd been learning all about the 10-20 method for electroencephalogram (EEG) hookups. 10-20 denotes the measurements in centimeters made around the head to detect various sections of the brain. Leads (wires) are attached to these spots on the head. The EEG leads pick up electrical currents in the brain and transfers their frequencies and amplitudes as images on the computer, mapping the currents in wave forms.

I giggled to myself as I thought about the dream I'd had just before waking. In the dream, I sat on the back of a 4-wheeler, riding trails across what looked like a globe. There were paths to follow in straight lines broken up in small increments. From a far distance, I could see that my riding path along the globe resembled a map similar to that of the 10-20 system used to measure a person's head when applying EEG wires. Dreaming plays so many roles in our lives, and I had just proved one of the theories correct. Studies show that people have an increase in REM after learning new information and incorporate that new information into dreams. This dream function serves to reinforce learning. Claire and I had gone to an ATV park with her friend's family the weekend before and rode 4-wheelers on miles and miles of trails in Arkansas. My dream combined the ATV trails with the pattern of 10-20 EEG lead applications for a PSG. I couldn't say that it helped me remember everything for my test, but it definitely meant my brain was trying to absorb the new information.

Robin turned out to be not only an interesting lab partner, but a very good friend. She was genuine and always willing to listen to family problems and even my crazy dreams. As my "Michelle dreams" continued, Robin taught me how to use her Reiki practices to "release" Michelle from my mind. "Picture the cord from your soul to hers and cut it!" she'd said. I really did try, even though I thought it was a bit nutty. Robin and I were both spiritual people, just in different ways.

Robin came over for lunch to do some studying for an exam and asked if I would mind if she used her oracle/angel cards on me just for fun. She fanned the cards out in her hand. "Now think of a question you want answered about something, anything. Without touching the cards, put your hand over them and let yourself feel which one you want and take it," she instructed. I couldn't help but be skeptical, but I did as instructed. Thinking hard, I asked silently, "Is doing this PSG program the right path for me?" I chose a card. Robin turned it over and said, "The card category is Work." She went on to read the brief description in the middle of the card. "It says here, basically, that you are to follow what you are passionate about. What was your question?" I was shocked. I knew these things tended to be general so they could apply to anything, but obviously *sleep* was my passion. I had asked about work, so I was definitely on the right path!

Happy National Sleep Disorders Awareness Week! The celebration begins on the first Sunday in March and ends on daylight saving. Some states have declared the Saturday before we move our clocks forward an hour as Narcolepsy Awareness Day, also known as "Suddenly Sleepy Saturday." To champion the effort, I took it upon myself to educate our local school district on sleep disorders so that school officials and staff could become aware of narcolepsy and sleep apnea in youth. I sent out a letter stating that I was a parent with narcolepsy and had suffered while undiagnosed as a youth. I also stated that I had a son diagnosed with sleep apnea at the age of sixteen and was so excited to be proactive to help others get the help they needed early in life. Then, I waited. Nothing. No follow-up emails from interested teachers or staff. No questions. Nothing. The school officials must not have understood the important role they play in early diagnosis.

I know the media talked a lot about how important it was for youth to get plenty of sleep. With sleep disordered breathing, however, all the bedtime in the world wouldn't fix them! Sleep apnea wasn't just a consequence of being an overweight adult, it could happen in youth, too. Maybe narcolepsy wasn't as rare as people thought, just under diagnosed. I wondered if the boldface word in textbooks had distinguished between narcolepsy with and without cataplexy yet. Cataplexy would be much easier to notice.

The time had come to cut my kid's throat out, literally. OK, maybe not *literally*, but something pretty darn close. For some with sleep apnea, the facial structure alone can be a good indication that breathing is difficult during sleep. Dylan had a small jaw. "Turtle, turtle!" he used to say as he'd pull his chin in really far and pretend he had the long neck of a turtle. His large tonsils and low dropping soft palate made the airway very small when he slept at night. Once his body was paralyzed in REM sleep, his face and neck muscles would relax, creating an even smaller airway. Since he never used his CPAP machine and had no extra weight to lose, I made him undergo surgery. The procedure to take out his tonsils, adenoids, and shorten the soft palate was called uvulopalatopharyngoplasty (UPPP). In essence, I had his throat cut out!

The alarm on the pulse oximeter monitor kept buzzing whenever he'd relax and begin to sleep, so I called the nurse and asked for her to add oxygen. Another alarm would sound each time his heart rate dropped below 60 beats per minute (bpm) and woke him up. Again, I called the nurse. "Could you set the alarm for 40 bpm? The alarm keeps waking him up. Below 60 is fine if he's sleeping." The nurse gave me a funny look and asked, "Are you in medicine?" "No," I smiled. "I just know sleep." I knew he was in a lot of pain, but the benefits would be with him for the rest of his life. The doctor said his tonsils were much larger than he initially thought. The poor guy had stitches all across the back of his throat. His "googler," as he called his uvula, was gone.

The PSG program truly was the perfect choice at the perfect time for me. Being able to help my son at a young age was important because having sleep apnea over a lifetime could lead to so many future problems. While a person may not wake up completely during an episode of apnea (stopped breathing), they become sleep deprived by having hundreds of arousals in the brain per night. Researchers have found that lack of sleep as well as increased cortisol levels in the blood (created by apnea episodes) could exacerbate diabetes by disrupting insulin utilization. This could lead to insulin resistance. Although Dylan's sleepiness was masked by his ADHD, many people with sleep apnea become extremely sleepy due to a lack of deep, stable sleep. This sleep deprivation can cause an increased appetite for unhealthy foods, which could increase the risk of diabetes for people with sleep apnea who don't seek treatment.

Our family felt complete again with my son back in the picture. In so many ways, he and his father were very much alike. Dylan was working with John, so they spent every day together. Dylan was naturally good with people, like his father, so sales came easy. But we were not yet over the wrongs of his past. He had to face the law and wrap up old tickets and outstanding warrants. So again, I called his lawyer. I believed my son was one of his favorite clients. We spent thousands of dollars just to keep him out of jail, so we didn't hold back when spoiling our well-deserving daughter. I was really trying to do the responsible thing by helping my son clean up the mess his life had made and provide an opportunity for his future success. If paying more fines and having him on house arrest were what we needed to do to have our son back, so be it.

"Hey Dylan, I brought you down some snacks," I said as I walked into the basement bedroom where he was staying during house arrest. Sara laid on the bedroom floor, hanging out with him. Sitting on the bed facing me, he looked up from his laptop. I didn't understand the frightened look on his face. A kid about the same age as Dylan stood just inside the doorway against the wall next to the bed. I'd never seen this kid before. "Hey, Mrs. Morrison, I've heard a lot about you." I continued to stare back at Dylan as I answered the kid, "I bet you have. And I'm just as much of a bitch as everyone says I am." He laughed a little uncomfortably.

As I took a step closer and peered over the laptop screen, I saw why Dylan was so pale. He was in the middle of cutting up pills of all sorts of colors. The kid continued to talk to me as if nothing was wrong, but Sara felt the tension in the room and got up slowly. With ears back and head low, she quickly trotted out of the room. Something was about to go down. "New kid, you have three seconds to get out of my house," I said as my whole body trembled.

Thank God adrenaline made me feel strong rather than drop me to the floor paralyzed. Dylan didn't take his eyes off me and didn't say a word.

I didn't know why this new kid wasn't moving, but he obviously didn't understand the gravity of the situation. I was on the verge of walking around the corner to the basement kitchen, grabbing a steak knife, and slitting his throat from ear to ear. *How dare he come into my house with drugs!* I thought. Dylan never did think about consequences before his actions, so his actions didn't surprise me one bit. During this short amount of time, I thought of all the ways I could hurt this boy standing next to me. I could punch him in the throat, poke out his eyes, stab him…. Sara was only protective of me, she was not an aggressive dog. Otherwise, I would let her rip out his throat for me. I started counting to three, the universal mom code for "You better do as I say before I reach the number three or else." He got the picture and left.

I wasn't sure what Dylan would say when I slapped him in the face. I could have slapped him harder, but it felt so unnatural. I have had dreams where I tried to slap someone, but my hand would barely make contact. It was as if I were pushing my hand through water. He didn't say anything. I think for the first time, I actually saw tears.

Dylan had made a ton of money working for John within the last few months. Money could not have been his incentive for selling drugs. It had to be some psychological need to feel important or to fit in. Why did he need to feel important to people who didn't matter? He had turned away so many good friends because they didn't like what he was doing. Why wasn't the love of family enough to be a better person and try harder? Didn't he know that his father and I dedicated almost our entire lives to him? Dylan was our blessing as well as our living nightmare.

After his sentence of house arrest was over, he moved out. I had really wanted this time to be different. We should have been looking at apartments together, buying him pots and pans, helping him move. "Please leave your expensive suits that your dad just bought you here," I said feeling numb as I watched him pack his clothes, again. John kept his distance, but told me to give him the bedroom furniture as well as any extra kitchen items and such. We, of course, wished him well. We never wanted him to fail. Dylan insisted that he wanted to move out, even though we told him he could stay longer and work on getting his head straight before he went out on his own. As always, he didn't listen. "Why are you packing your baby blankets?" I asked as tears started to form. And, as always, there was nothing I could do.

Only one week went by before Dylan stopped showing up for work at John's office. I couldn't say we were surprised. He promised to meet me for mass that Sunday and showed up fifteen minutes late. If it weren't for his height and Crayola red hair, I wouldn't have recognized him. Just a few weeks before, he looked like someone on the cover of *GQ Magazine*. Now, he could have been the picture of a criminal on "America's Most Wanted."

I'm not sure what possessed me to go, but I made an unexpected visit to Dylan's apartment. I'd never been there before, but had the address. We hadn't seen nor heard from him in a month. I listened at the door for a moment and didn't hear anything, so I knocked. Dylan answered the door looking in similar fashion as he did at church. He did not look happy to see me, and I could tell he was extremely nervous. Reluctantly, he invited me in. Another guy stood in his living room, but Dylan didn't introduce him. Glancing around the room, the place looked like shit. The nice, gently used furniture we gave him had a black tar-like substance smeared all over it. Dylan's body language as he stood across from me and next to this guy made my whole body alert. Adrenaline pumped through my veins. Mama Bear was back.

"Get out!" I commanded, glaring at the guy. If I were a dog, it would have sounded like a low, warning growl. He looked a little put out and moved much too slowly for me. Dylan didn't say a word or move, but his behavior seemed oddly familiar. His long, shaggy hair and too baggy jeans along with his sheepish, defeated look created the sense that I had seen this before. I felt that this guy was an immediate threat to my son, even though he was only putting on his shoes. "Move faster!" I kicked his remaining shoe out the front door. He looked towards the door, then turned back around and said, "Hey now, you didn't have to do that." The guy wasn't much bigger than myself, so I shoved both hands against his chest as hard as I could. He tumbled back through the front door and onto the balcony. "Now that's assault right there!" he said trying to look serious. I stormed towards the door yelling, "So call the cops, you little fucker!" then slammed the door shut.

I was really bad at remembering names and faces, but he looked similar to the face I saw in my dream years ago when Dylan stood sheepishly next to a young man holding a knife against his back in a park. He also looked a lot like

the drug dealer, Jesse, I had lectured at his car. Who knew? Maybe they were all the same guy.

The dreaded yet inevitable "one phone call" came. "Mom, I fucked up. I've been arrested." It's really sad to think that I actually felt a little glad. When people would tell me, "He just needs to hit rock bottom first, then he'll make his way back," I used to respond, "No, you don't get it. Dylan just bounces along the bottom. He never makes his way back up." Then, after a while, my response changed: "No, you don't get it. When Dylan hits rock bottom, he'll either end up in prison or dead." In this case, I was just happy that he wasn't dead.

"Just stay there, Dylan. After your lawyer got you off the last time on 'technicalities,' the prosecutor isn't going to let you get away with anything. Start serving time now, so you can get out sooner. There's nothing for you out here except more trouble." I assured him that I'd tie up all loose ends as far as bills and such goes. The last thing an inmate needed when they were finally freed was debt. Apparently, Dylan's so-called friends were wired on three different occasions so police could get him on drug sales with no loopholes to set him free. I knew the prosecutor was ticked off that she had lost her case before. I didn't blame her; he was guilty.

The problem with the law was the same damn thing I had written about twenty years earlier in my drug policies class: Prosecutors were sentencing people who sold drugs to a mandatory minimum sentence of fifteen years in prison. Hard core murderers got less time in prison than that! I definitely thought my son deserved to go to prison, however, providing people with drugs that they asked for and with no violent record should not result in a fifteen-plus year sentence. With Dylan gone, hundreds of "good" college kids would simply find another dealer, another kid with ADHD or other prescriptions or someone else who decides to step up when a college kid asks, "Who can get us some Molly for our frat party tonight?"

I walk among a group of others down the hall of a prison. I'm not sure if we are prisoners or visitors. There are jail cells alongside us full of inmates. Up ahead, I notice Dylan's bright red hair and large brown eyes towering over the other inmates in his cell. As my group walks by, he's the only one who notices me in the crowd. I continue to walk along with the group. A few cells down I see Jesse standing alone in his. He sees me as well. He looks scared. He knows that I will kill him if given the chance. I wake up.

Registered polysomnogram technicians (RPSGT) have to do continuing education. Although I wasn't registered yet, I thought I should take my fifteen-year-old daughter to the "sleepy driver" class. There was so much emphasis on drunk driving prevention, yet people rarely discussed or warned against the dangers of driving while sleepy. Everyone, young and old, has the potential to drive sleepy. People talk about the effects of sleepiness on the body and how it can affect one's driving, but they should also talk about prevention.

In the workshop, the presenter discussed all of the latest technology that cars had to help drivers become aware that they were falling asleep. Some have a sensor that will shake the wheel if the driver didn't use the turn signal and the car crosses the lines on the road. He mentioned other devices as well. What he neglected to do was encourage people to stop driving when they began feeling sleepy. So, of course, I raised my hand. "Don't you think that people know they are getting too tired to drive, but continue to drive anyway? These features on the cars are nice, but drivers basically know they're tired. They just don't want to be late for work, picking up their kids, or to an event, so they drive on."

Society has put such a negative stamp on sleep that a person would still be in trouble or even be laughed at if they said they were late because they were too tired to drive. People *might* give me a pass if I told them I had narcolepsy and was feeling too drowsy to drive, but anyone could be too drowsy to drive. The presenter must have thought that I was being disrespectful by shutting down his discussion of car devices because he didn't look very pleased with me. I did feel better, however, when I noticed heads nodding around the room in agreement.

With narcolepsy, sleep attacks come on fast and it's almost impossible to stay awake until the urge passes. But even with sleep attacks, there are signs that precede them, such as constant yawning. When possible, pull over to a convenient spot and take a little walk around. If someone is with you, ask them to drive. If you're stuck in traffic, try calling someone on the phone for conversation. I used to always raise my hand and ask dumb questions in school just to have interaction if I felt sleepy. I just want everyone, especially my daughter, to know that sleepy driving is dangerous, and that it's important to be proactive to prevent it. Don't rely on your car to inform you that you're driving into oncoming traffic. It may be too late.

During our long nights at the sleep lab, Robin liked to listen to my crazy dream experiences. She even bought me a small journal to keep at my bedside so that I could write them down more consistently. Up until that point, I had only written down dreams that I felt could be put into words or dreams that haunted me. Mainly, I just remembered the ones that were significant or that I couldn't forget. Considering that I had at least three to four dreams per night, writing them all out was too time consuming. I thought it was funny how I couldn't remember people's names, song lyrics, or other things most people took for granted, but I could remember almost all of my dreams. It may be a long-term versus short-term memory thing. If I experienced something, it was stored in my long-term memory. In a sense, I experienced my dreams.

I hear the sound of hair clippers in the distance. John is entering the shower with the hair dryer plugged in and blowing while the water is running. I tell him that he will be electrocuted, but he keeps on trying to blow freshly clipped hair out of the shower. I see a spark from the hair dryer. Angry that he might hurt himself, I start throwing things at him. I throw a shoe and it hits a light fixture on the wall next to the shower. That does it. "Now I have to replace the light bulb," he says angrily and leaves. I am satisfied.

Sitting in the house with some friends, I start feeling scared that something else is nearby. I see it. Floating in the air, a round, smooth, yellow-brown glob is heading toward my room. It is moving soundlessly. I hide quietly as it makes its way into my room searching for something. It slows down in front of the broken light. It somehow consumes the broken light. It floats over to the two other lights and does the same. As it leaves the room, it pauses in front of me. I'm relieved as it begins to move to other regions of the house. There are now kids in the house. I worry that the blob will see them and possibly hurt them. I pull them upstairs and explain that there is a light bulb-eating alien in the house.

I'm walking down a country road looking for something. John takes a different road that goes past a residential neighborhood. I avoid it, believing that I will get in trouble if I take it. An old woman comes out of her farmhouse and accuses me of creating crop circles in her land. I don't see crop circles, only dirt paths. She brings me into her home. There's a young girl about three or four years old inside and she wants my earrings. The ones I'm wearing are too big and expensive, but something tells me that I should give her something. I look through others I have to offer. Katie, Claire's friend, is sitting next to us at a kitchen table and looks to be about four years old also. She asks me what kind of stones they are. Katie turns her nose up at the ones I offer, saying they have too much metal. Since Katie doesn't approve, I find a small bear toy to offer instead and the little girl loves it.

I'm on a bus riding home. My two friends and I sit next to a smoker. One friend asks the other for a cigarette. She says she only keeps a couple with her to get rid of headaches. She takes out a nicotine pill and feeds it to her cat. I try to explain that smoking cigarettes every now and then undoes everything she accomplished by quitting. The man that's smoking next to us tells me I have no place to talk since I have no experience in quitting. I know, however, that I am smarter than them all for never smoking in the first place. **I wake up.**

My first entry in the dream journal was a doozy. It must have consisted of several dreams throughout the night. What a crazy mix of junk in my head! Yes, I did feel that way about smokers. That didn't need interpreting. I didn't know why she was feeding nicotine pills to a cat, though. That was simply strange. Yes, Katie was a little princess and only had the best of everything. I couldn't begin to analyze the alien blob thing, so that part would remain a mystery.

The categories of dreams I experienced and their functions seemed to multiply almost nightly. Some, like talking with my mother, may not even have been a typical dream at all. In fact, I believed spirits use our dream state of REM as an opportunity to communicate with us. Dreams providing valuable information for self-analysis are structured for personal use and do not consist of archetypal or general symbols that could be categorized into dream dictionaries. I understood that, as a whole, people share common values, feelings, and experiences, such as anxiety within a school classroom. However, I believed that dreams represent who we are as individuals, not as a collective whole.

Graduating with my associates degree in applied science-polysomnography couldn't have come at a better time. I needed to focus on figuring out my life before Claire left for college and only John, Sara, Jeter, and I were left at home. I was looking forward to following my passion in sleep education. It seemed to me John had mentally broken free from the heartache Dylan had been causing him for so long. Claire, being a teenager, mainly focused on herself and her friends. I, on the other hand, tried really hard to stay in tune with my emotions so they wouldn't end up masked within dreams. I didn't want to mentally break free from our son, or I'd end up feeling like he was dead. Just like mourning a death, we all handle stress and heartache differently. John and I fought many times about our feelings towards our son and came to an agreement. We would respect each other's feelings and ways in which we handled Dylan's situation. We may not like them, but we would respect them.

I'm in the ocean. There's another person with me, a girl. I'm not sure who she's supposed to be. We are sitting on a raft with no sides. It's more like a grate with open holes in the bottom. I'm holding a small machine that blows air like a

> hair dryer. As we sit calmly on the grate, I point the blower down, causing ripples in the water below us. These ripples are attracting sharks. It's as if I'm inviting them. I'm not scared.

I wake up.

Sara and I loved taking long walks together on beautiful trails surrounded by trees, usually a creek or pond, and lots of wildlife. I'm sure she would be a runner if I were, but instead we strolled for miles. "Do you see, Sara?" I'd say as I pointed through the trees at a tall, brown deer off the path. She'd frantically look, but wouldn't find anything. While on the trails she'd give a passing stranger a quick warning growl if they looked suspicious to her. Men only, of course.

For as big and potentially dangerous as she could be, she was cautious around other dogs. I loved how she trusted me and stepped behind me whenever an aggressive dog approached. Sara had become my best friend. Even after she slept all night, she'd stay by my bedside while I slept all day. I tried Doggie Daycare, but she had a severe case of separation anxiety. She was content to lie by my side, and I felt safe.

> There's been an apocalypse of some sort. Zombies, I think. John and I survive. A man and his pregnant wife come to our door and ask us to let them in. I don't feel good about this, but we let the strangers in our home. The man and his wife try to take over our home and make us leave. He takes out a gun and points it at John's head while threatening me to do what he says. He doesn't know that I have a gun of my own. I take out my gun. I turn the gun toward his wife and lower it to her stomach. "You kill him, and I'll kill the baby."

I wake up.

The dream journal Robin bought me was starting to fill up. In the past, I'd only held on to the memories of dreams that really bothered me, and sometimes wrote out others that took story form and were easily transcribed. In this journal, some entries were just images of places, people, or scenes from a longer story not easily put into words. Waking up in the morning, I could typically recall two or three dream experiences, and each one was very different. Michelle was still in at least two of the dreams, but I didn't mind anymore. We never had confrontation; she was just a small character in a larger story. Even though not all of my dreams were worthy of analysis, I found reading them months later to be quite entertaining. My drawings of these crazy images had me cracking up for hours! Again, I thanked God I didn't have cataplexy.

When reflecting on my dreams, I realized what great value so many might have had at the time I dreamed them, if I had only been able to make sense of their meanings. The visits with passed loved ones were priceless memories I'd never forget. Along with treasured memories came the nightmares—good and bad, yin and yang, you can't have one without the other. Not all nightmares were evil. I knew there was a lot of self-discovery in nightmares. My son was going to prison, so nightmares of him in prison were to be expected. My feelings of anger, violence, and aggression revealed themselves in my nightmares. Were dreams a safe way for me to let loose and prevent me from acting out in daily life? Or, were dreams giving me the opportunity for self-reflection and soul healing? Why not both? There didn't have to be a right or wrong answer.

Using dreams for self-reflection were becoming a valuable tool for healing depression and the heart.

Where do our dreams come from? I couldn't say. However, I had found that using prayer for guidance in life not only brought me signs in the physical world (even in a friend's oracle cards), but also in my dreams. If REM provided an opportunity for guidance and help in waking life, then ask and you shall receive. Guidance and assurance were what I'd asked for to help me get through the next five years. I asked for assurance of Claire's future, but had received a dream of my niece. I eagerly awaited her upcoming teenage years, watching for any significance. Confident that there was help for me from beyond our physical world, I prayed, "Please God, help me look forward to my son's future. Help me have hope for him and us as a family again."

I hear the sound of people coming from the next room. They are heading to the bedroom where I've been sleeping. This is Dylan's bedroom, but not in my house. I believe I'm in Dylan's apartment that he shares with a roommate in St. Louis. I came to visit him by myself and slept in his bedroom. He isn't here. He must be at work. The people in the house make their way to the bedroom, so I get out of bed. I notice that I only have on an extra-large T-shirt. Two women enter the room. One looks to be in her early twenties and very pretty. The other is her mother. I realize the young woman is Dylan's girlfriend. I have not met her. She looks surprised and turns to her mother and asks, "Who is that in his bed?" Her mother looks at me angrily, "Who are you? What are you doing here?" Being such a young mom and sleeping in one of Dylan's T-shirts, they must think he's cheating on her with me! I quickly realize that Dylan must not have told his girlfriend that I was here. I stick out my hand and calmly say, "Hi. I'm Dylan's mother." I wake up.

It was sad to think that my future visit to Dylan was made alone. I understood. Claire would be settled in college somewhere out-of-town and have her own life. John would listen to my Dylan updates, but not open himself up again to have his heart ripped out when Dylan "fucks up" and goes back to jail or worse. I thanked God for the gift of dreams. I didn't believe that the dream of Dylan in the future was of an alternate life. I wasn't sure how far in the future it was, but I knew it was post-prison. Why St. Louis? I didn't know. This was what I needed, just a little reassurance that he would have a life in the future. I treasured my dreams. All my dreams.

What do you say to your child when you know you only have a few hours left with them? I was to deliver my son to the law for the next five years. So many times before I'd been in a courtroom with him and imagined him walking out a different door than I. This time, it would be for real. He was dressed in nice pants and a tie to present himself to the judge. It was just Dylan and me today. John hadn't talked to Dylan since he left our house at the beginning of the year. Dylan had driven out to meet Claire before school the week before to say good-bye.

Walking into the courthouse again felt like some distant nightmare. Breathing became difficult. I was going through the motions of walking, but didn't feel anything. I didn't know what it was like for my son, but I knew he didn't feel the same way. I used to be proud that nothing ever phased him; he just adapted and thrived in whatever environment he was in without fear. Now, I wanted him to be afraid. I wanted him to hate this so bad and to be scared to mess up. "It's time to go in," his lawyer said. I couldn't do it. I couldn't walk into that courtroom knowing that I wouldn't walk out with my son. I wanted to be there with him as long as I could, but I couldn't watch it happen! The tears built until they could no longer be contained. His lawyer saw my face and said he'd go in and give us some time alone. The prosecutor strolled by and I felt like punching her in the face. She had wanted to put him away for twenty years! Didn't she know how hard I'd worked at being his mother for the past twenty-three years? Who was she to take him away from me for the next two decades simply because the law allowed it?

"Dylan, I can't go in there," I said as I squeezed him as tight as I could. My tears stained his nicely pressed shirt. "Why?" he asked, confused. I looked up at him and saw tears streaming down his face as well. "I can say good-bye to you here. I can't do that in there." As I said it, I felt like I was cheating him and being selfish. I guess I was being selfish. It was as if I was putting another beloved animal to sleep, too sad and concerned about my own emotions to watch it happen. You said good-bye, handed them over to the vet, then left. That was selfishness coming through because you didn't want the pain in your heart, even though they were the ones with the permanent pain in theirs. You left them alone to die because you couldn't find the courage to face it with them. Was that what I was doing here? It was only five years. But for a parent, not being able to have your child when you want them, five years could feel like a lifetime.

The holidays got easier and harder at the same time, if that's possible. I'd come to expect less so I wouldn't be disappointed. When I was young, Thanksgiving and Christmas were always magical, and family and friends were always present. As an adult, I tried really hard to give my kids the same wonderful experience that I'd had growing up. When they were young, I cooked for up to twenty-five people on Thanksgiving. Between my step-brothers and their families, John's side of the family, Dad and Karen, and Renee's family, we were able to make the holidays special for everyone. This year, only my dad, Karen, and John's dad Bart would be joining our Thanksgiving dinner. So we went out to eat.

CHAPTER 9

Eat, Sleep & Breathe...

A new year always brought hope for new beginnings. Claire was sixteen years old and had her driver's license, so I felt comfortable beginning my career as a sleep technician. As fate would have it, the same sleep lab where I had been diagnosed with narcolepsy twenty years earlier hired me. I was excited to help make a difference in someone's life the way my sleep disorder diagnosis had made a difference in mine. Thanks to Karen, my sister Julie and I reconnected after not speaking for ten years. I suppose Karen heard the hurt in my heart last Thanksgiving when it was my turn to say what I was thankful for: "Sorry, but I can't think of anything at the present time." I don't know what she said to Julie, but I'll be forever grateful that she took a few moments of her time to reach out and help heal two hurting hearts.

John and I went our separate ways for Easter. He took Claire with him for a fun weekend in San Francisco, while I made a three-and-a-half hour drive to the little town of El Dorado, Kansas. Dylan's birthday fell on Easter this year. John took care of his needs with fun distraction, while I took care of mine with seeing my son. I packed a cooler with three different birthday cakes, one for each day I visited. I made sure I had plenty of amphetamines for the long haul, then took off for my first prison visit. The atmosphere of the prison was very laid back and campus-like, not at all what I had expected. For birthdays, you could have multiple visits during one weekend. We spent three to four

hours together each day in a small cafeteria playing games and making small talk as he devoured every bite of cake.

> *Roses are red, Violets are blue,*
> *I wouldn't be alive today without you.*
> *When clouds are dark and skies are gray,*
> *You brighten my world in countless ways.*
> *I fight and kick and scream and shout,*
> *But my mother's love I've never gone without.*
> *"The time has come," the Walrus said,*
> *"To change my ways or my life I will dread."*
> *For what is life without a reason to persist,*
> *And the love of a family that brought me to exist?*
> *Through time of hardship and faithless drought,*
> *Strong and unconditional support I've never had doubt.*
> *Though in the past I've chosen the Id,*
> *Through a veil of sin, I've ran and hid.*
> *But with "swim, not sink" as my parents' creed,*
> *And steady love to give me the strength I need,*
> *To alter my motives and make true my actions,*
> *And keep those naysayers from satisfaction.*
> *So I keep my head up high, and for better will change my way,*
> *I write you this poem for a happy belated Mother's Day.*
> *For without my family's love, my soul would be dead,*
> *But now it's time to take my ass to bed.*
>
> *I love you all so very much, so write me back and stay in touch.*
> —Dylan Morrison

School was out, summer was here, and work was going great! I was amazed by the number of people whose sleep patterns did not fall in the range of what's considered "normal." People experienced a wide range of sleep disorders that developed from congestive heart failure, obesity, large tonsils and low soft palate, neuromuscular diseases, chronic obstructive pulmonary disease (COPD) and asthma, diabetes, alcoholism and illicit drug use, prescription medications, stress, and so many other conditions, all of which can alter a person's normal sleep cycle. Throughout nights, I witnessed patterns of eye movements as well as an absence of REM by those taking antidepressants. Sleep-related breathing disorders severely hinder REM as paralysis of the muscles makes breathing more difficult. As breathing stops or becomes shallow, the heart and brain are aroused and the body is pushed into a lighter stage of sleep. There are countless theories as to why we have REM, but experts all agree that we need REM to live.

I had a soft spot for sleepy people. The world was full of walking zombies. People didn't realize the torture their bodies were going through, struggling to breathe all night as they slept, but I watched them struggle nightly. When they woke with headaches, they'd fill their bodies with caffeine; trudge through the day grumpy and irritable; seek out donuts, chips, and energy drinks; then dread the bedroom where they'd try and sleep again, only to repeat the process. I hadn't come across any narcoleptics yet; I mainly treated those with sleep apnea. The one-way speakers from each of the rooms filled the control room with an orchestra of snoring. For seven hours, the soft "poohing" (expiratory puffing) to loud rumbling of four to six patients became our background music while we analyzed their brainwaves and breathing patterns every thirty seconds.

"So, you watch people sleep?" people asked. "Yes, but I also 'fix' people," I'd answer. I used the slogan from my first job at the American Lung Association: "When you can't breathe, nothing else matters." While up to fifty pounds of weight crushed their lungs with only their diaphragm to move them, patients gasped and choked half the night as their bodies tried to relax. Quietly, I would sneak into their rooms and place the CPAP mask on their faces. As the air rushed into their lungs, their bodies would relax and leave this world for hours, disappearing into the world of dreams. "I save lives!" I once said with a grin. "I make people dream again."

Hallucinations are a symptom of narcolepsy, yet can occur in those without narcolepsy. They can occur upon falling asleep (hypnagogic) or upon waking (hypnopompic), with or without the sleep paralysis produced by REM, just as sleep paralysis can occur without hallucinations. Sometimes these hallucinations can be terrifying, such as seeing spiders or smokey figures that seem to form from objects in the room. At other times, they can simply play tricks on reality, like seeing ONE WAY signs while driving that aren't really there. Then, there are those that are so incredible, both positive and negative, that the experience seems to change your entire outlook on life.

For people with difficulty breathing during REM because of an obstruction or narrowing of the airway, they might feel as though someone or something is preventing them from breathing. They are left to endure the anxiety of not taking a breath for up to one minute or longer until their brain arouses and sends a signal to the heart and lungs. Named after the famous painting "The Nightmare" by Henry Fuseli (1781) in which an evil being sits on a woman's chest, sleep paralysis is often called "old hag syndrome" and is characterized by the inability to move, the feeling of an evil presence, a feeling of overwhelming weight on the chest, and difficulty breathing.

I'd heard people on TV interviews describe alien visits and probing while lying paralyzed and helpless in bed and thought it sounded very much like the typical sleep paralysis with hallucinations. I can't say that I knew what it was the first few times I'd experienced it either, but was pretty sure I hadn't been probed and studied by aliens. I'd been helpless and couldn't move, and I did feel as though I was being watched or that someone was in the room with me that may or may not be human. I could feel, hear, smell, and even see around my room, but my body was completely paralyzed. These events can be very frightening, yet I wasn't scared anymore. I was intrigued.

> *The bedroom is dark, but I can see the outline of the bed, dresser with TV on it, and shutters on the windows. I'm alone in bed this morning. John must have already left for the gym. There seems to be some sort of window open above my bed. Not an actual window, more like a portal to another dimension like you might see in a sci-fi movie. I can't move. Paralysis again. I see someone staring at me through the window. I see only the head, from the neck up. "Who are you?" I ask him in my mind. I don't feel scared, just angry that he's invading the privacy of my bedroom. He could be thought of as scary with his spiky, thick hair and large, boil-like pimples covering his face. He doesn't speak. "Get out of my room!" I say louder, but still telepathically. As we stare at each other, I begin to feel the paralysis leave my body. I wake up.*

During this time of being half awake and half asleep, I felt like I was in another dimension, yet still in my bedroom in real time. I started to believe that the word *hallucination* wasn't appropriate for all episodes. Seeing a face like that had been a first, and I wasn't sure how to react. Had I caught someone spying on me? I didn't get the feeling that he was evil, but he certainly wasn't heavenly. The face could have resembled Dylan's in some messed-up, sick sort of way. If it was meant to, I'd feel really bad that I yelled at him to go away. What if Dylan had simply been thinking of me? The real mystery behind the experience was trying to figure out how I was able to see when my eyes were supposedly closed from paralysis.

After being admitted to the hospital, Bart's case could have been in an episode of *House*. Not one doctor could figure out what was wrong with him. Or rather, what was more wrong with him than usual. It started with a bad cough, then led to a bladder infection, dizziness, and nausea. The list went on and on. I knew he felt bad the entire time we were in Greece the previous summer, but thought it was the time change messing with his strict diabetic schedule. John decided last minute not to go to Orlando with Claire, her friends, and me and instead stayed to care for his dad. I felt bad that we were still going without him, but there wasn't anything we could do for Bart. John was an amazing son and would do anything for his father. I knew it made him sick to think that his son wouldn't (or couldn't) do the same for him.

"Brianna, the sound that came out of his mouth was the most terrifying thing I'd ever heard in my life." John recounted his visit to the hospital. "I've never been so scared. I'm just glad your dad and Karen happened to be visiting him when it happened, or I would have gone crazy!" John described how he witnessed his father "dying" three different times that afternoon while in the emergency room. I should have been there with him. I was glad to hear that Dad and Karen were both there for John when it happened because both have had experience with their spouse dying. Karen, being a retired nurse at a retirement/nursing home, had witnessed many deaths.

Although he experienced "dying" several times that day, Bart didn't actually die, fortunately. "I saw Addie and Maggie," Bart told me with wide eyes and a grin when I visited him at the hospital the following week. I wasn't sure how long he'd been considered "dead" before the doctors brought him back, but Bart had a near-death spiritual experience that he would cherish for the rest of his life. "I was in the hospital with endocarditis and suddenly I was in a grassy field with a stream running through it. There was a bridge over the stream, and for some reason, I headed towards the bridge. I got to the bridge and my wife and dog were on the other side. I was very happy to see them so I started across the bridge, but Addie kept waving for me to go back. The next thing I know, I'm back in the hospital bed surrounded by my son and doctors. John told me that they were there because my heart had stopped for a couple of minutes. I'm sure this was real and not the effects of medication."

I felt very lucky to know that Bart trusted me enough to share such an intimate story. Just as I'd always wanted people to believe me, he wanted me to believe that his experience was real and possible and brought new meaning to life as he knew it. Bart's life would be difficult with all of his health problems, so I hoped that seeing his late wife Addie and their dog Maggie wouldn't make him want to give up on his life here and surrender to the surreal world in his heaven. For now, he had us.

Something strange was happening to Sara. At night, sometimes I'd hear her licking the floor. She would stick her tongue out while on her side and lick, lick, lick… and sound like she was gulping. There were other strange things such as violent sneezing if she rolled onto her back, so I brought this up to the vet. I had to wait with her outside or she would try to climb into my lap in the waiting room. The vet didn't seem concerned and Sara wouldn't do it in front of him. At night, I was woken by sounds coming from Sara that reminded me of a sleep apnea patient. She didn't snore, but she panted and struggled for breath. Then, her nose began to bleed.

I didn't have a good feeling about this situation, yet didn't have any indication, vision, or dream about what was happening. I prayed and counted on God to at least give me a heads-up when something major was going to happen in my life. I believed my dreams were His way of communicating important information to me, whether I knew it or not. I had not dreamt anything that I could recall being related to Bart's illness and near-death experience. Maybe something from John's dreams made him hesitant about joining us on vacation the weeks before we were to leave while his father wasn't feeling well. I wasn't Nostradamus or an oracle, but I believed that I'd found a way to cope with hardship once I knew it was all part of God's plan. I may not like it or understand it, but it was meant to be.

Sara is trotting in front of me off-leash. Like usual, she keeps a pretty close distance between us. We are a crossing a bridge that spans far across and high above a river. The bridge is sturdy with a paved road and steel cross bars for suspension, yet there are no side railings to prevent anyone from falling into the river below if they get too close. Sara is a very smart dog, but I tell her to be careful anyway. Her path changes and she heads towards the edge. Before I can scream her name, she leaps over the edge. I race to the side of the bridge and desperately search for signs for her in the water below. It's so far down. I see her! She's struggling, but she is swimming and staying barely above the water. There are people in small boats and rafts in the water not far from her. I yell to them, "Someone please help her! She's drowning!" They hear me, thank God. The people below look up at me, then they look over at Sara struggling in the water. Why aren't they doing anything? I wake up.

Two weeks went by and Sara's nose was still bleeding. The only emergency vet office in town had a broken CT scanner for animals, so I took Sara to the closest veterinary clinic in Columbia, Missouri—two hours away. MU's veterinary school was highly respected, and the staff was full of young, motivated veterinary students. Sara tried climbing in my lap as I explained her symptoms to the vet, "At night, the sounds remind me of being at work in the sleep lab and hearing people gasping for breath while they slept. She's so tired all the time, too. I catch her falling asleep sitting up. When I hear her struggle at night, it sounds like she's drowning." As soon as the words left my mouth, the memory came. *She's drowning!* Everyone watched her and knew she was drowning, but no one would help her. The gulping, the struggling for breath.... *Please, God*, I thought, *let someone be able to help her.*

The doctor continued her analysis and scanned Sara's head for abnormalities. She concluded she had a nose tumor that was possibly cancerous. She believed that with radiation therapy, Sara would live for at least another year. Sara was my baby girl, so of course I gave a green light for treatment. I knew there were so many people in the world that didn't have the luxury that I did to say yes. Animal healthcare required payment up front and was expensive. There were people who didn't think pets were worth it, but many of us saw them as family. I believed all dogs go to heaven. I believed they have souls just like people.

With all that had happened in my life, I tried to always thank God for what I was given. I was grateful for my beautiful, healthy, and incredibly smart daughter. I was grateful for a husband who was understanding, trustworthy, respectful, hardworking, and basically everything a girl could wish for in a husband. "Just you and me against the world," he would say when life got tough. I was grateful for a steady supply of amphetamines that helped me keep up with the rest of the world. My drugs were especially important when making the four-hour round trips to Columbia twice a week for four weeks during Sara's radiation treatment. Working one night a week allowed me the time, my husband provided the means, and my pills gave me the energy.

To prevent me from having to drive every day, the veterinary school offered a program where a vet student took your pet home each night and brought them back to the clinic the next day for a small fee. Sara absolutely loved her student! The vet student sent me photos via text of walks they took around campus. Sara looked happy. She wasn't nervous anymore and had become quite the celebrity around the clinic. All the vet students and doctors knew her name, and she even did rotations with the doctors. The people in the waiting room thought I was nuts when I showed up with a giant gift bag for my dog. After weeks of radiation, the fur on the right side of her face began sliding off making a bloody mess, and her eye bulged from the swelling behind it. That didn't stop her from shoving her head straight down into the gift bag and pulling out her new stuffed animal.

"She has a rare bone cancer," the doctor said. "Nose tumors are common in dogs with long snouts, but her cancer is eating through the bone." There was no help for her. I would not have another year with her. The time had come for Sara to say good-bye to all the friends she made during her four weeks at the clinic. John drove to Columbia with me this last time to pick her up.

I brought her favorite laser pointer toy and felt bad when she tried to stick her face in the bag of medications looking for a stuffed animal. Sara's doctor even teared up when I declined additional treatment. "She's been through enough," I said. I wanted to take her home. Sara knew she wouldn't be coming back to the clinic, so when she saw her student vet talking with another family, she lightly pulled on her leash, asking me to walk in that direction. Sara's intelligence amazed me. She didn't interrupt the student with the other family, she just leaned gently against her leg to say a quick good-bye. With tears in her eyes, the student continued to speak with the other family while softly stroking the top of Sara's head. It was time for us to go home.

Taking my mother out of a giant microwave.

One of the hardest chapters for me to read in the book *Amazing Gracie* was the one entitled "Good-bye Gracie." It's the true story of two hometown guys who started a national dog treat company, Three Dog Bakery. They were simply trying to save their Great Dane by baking homemade treats for her. After Gracie lived a long, ten years, they called their vet to come to their home and have Gracie put to sleep. After reading what they did, I knew exactly how Sara would spend her last moments, and it would not be alone on a metal table in a vet office. When her time came, Sara would be in our home and in my arms.

Each night I was so sad as I listened to Sara struggle for breath. Dogs weren't designed to breathe through their mouth when they slept. Sometimes, she would stick her tongue out of her front teeth to create an air passage. During the day, I watched her try to hold her eyes open after being sleep deprived all night. Her cheeks would puff out the sides with each breath. When her eyes closed, her breath would stop. After a few minutes, she would jolt awake with the need to breathe again. It hurt me to know I couldn't simply give her air with a CPAP mask like I did my patients, then watch her happily drift into a deep, dream-filled sleep.

"She can't breathe!" I yelled into the phone to our local vet. "She's so tired, but each time she closes her eyes, she can't breathe." There was nothing they could do. I knew that. I sent a text to Sara's vet student and asked if she would spread the word to the other students encouraging them to invent a dental device for dogs that would keep an airway open for situations like this. She liked the idea and said she'd name it after Sara if there was ever one made.

The end was near for Sara. I prayed for God to help me know when it was time. No one ever wants to see their loved ones suffer, but we also don't want to act too soon. How do we know? The after-effects of the radiation had caused much of the fur on the right side of her face to fall off her skin. Unlike when humans lost their hair from chemotherapy, Sara bled a lot when her fur initially fell out. We put a cone around her neck to keep her from scratching her face. Eventually, she began to show signs of giving up, of being too tired to exert so much effort. She didn't want me wiping aloe on her face, and taking walks was too difficult for her once her legs started swelling. Then it happened. John woke me one morning and told me Sara's nose had started bleeding, but this time from the other side.

I'd hoped God would give me a clear sign in my dreams to let me know when her time had come, but He never did. I prayed so hard and so often asking what I was supposed to do for her. She counted on me to take care of her just as any child would look to their parent. All I knew was that the bleeding meant the cancer had passed through the bone to the other side of her face. I made the call to the vet and asked her to come at three p.m. That way, I'd have plenty of time to change my mind. I knew Sara had more time to live, but it broke my heart to see her so miserable. I didn't think either of us wanted to go through another night. I was so sleep deprived that I felt sick to my stomach. I cried myself to sleep each night as I sent her outside our bedroom door so I could sleep without hearing her gasp for air all night.

Three o'clock was approaching too quickly. How do you spend your last day with your best friend/baby girl/guardian? The weather couldn't have been more gorgeous. It was sunny and 72 degrees with leaves beginning to turn fall colors. Sara and I spent the afternoon in the front yard just sitting together. I didn't talk. I'd wished I could have sat with her into the evening, but I wanted to spare John and Claire the heartache. They had already said their good-byes that morning.

When a car came around the corner, I knew it was the vet. My stomach tightened and pulled at my insides. I had only spoken with her on the phone, but she seemed nice. The woman got out of the car, and I met her on the walk that led to the front porch. Sara sat still, looking off in the distance. She never moved from her spot on the grass in front of the large tree or acknowledged the stranger who had pulled into our drive. I guessed she'd wanted as much time as possible in her spot under the tree on that beautiful, fall afternoon.

"Sara, come here please," I said quietly. She didn't move. I didn't want to rush her. "Sara, it's time to go inside," I said a little louder with cracks in my voice. Still, she didn't turn around. I turned to the vet with tears in my eyes, "She knows! She never ignores me like this." This time the tears began to roll down my cheeks. She knew that I was asking her to come inside to die. Then, out of sheer desperation, I did something awful. "Party time!" I yelled in my most cheerful voice. I only used this phrase in emergencies when I needed her to come running to me; it meant I had lunch meat for her. I regretted it the minute I said it. Sara just turned around slowly and looked at me. "Come on, girl," I said choking back the tears. "It's time to go inside."

I knew I had the power to stop all of this with only my say so, but what then? Was I supposed to let the cancer eat away at her skull? "Lie down, baby." I could let her live and try to enjoy as many more days as possible. "Relax,

Sara, Mommy's got you." I would never get to run my fingers through her thick, warm fur again or feel her nudge my hand when I'm upset or scared. "Stop! She can't breathe!" The vet looked at me reassuringly and said, "She's paralyzed now. All that's left is the shot to stop her heart. Just say when you are ready." Sara's mouth pushed open as the air in her lungs forced through and she struggled for a few more breaths. And with a heavy heart, I said softly, "OK."

A neighbor had agreed to come over and help the vet load Sara's body into her car and take her to be cremated. I would not have had the strength for that. I spent a few minutes alone with Sara, then left out the back door so I wouldn't have to see them carry her away in a body bag on a stretcher and load her in the car. For someone with such an awful job, to me the vet was a saint, an angel of death. The woman's service allowed me to have Sara die in my home and in my arms. I was grateful.

Life went on. Claire went to volleyball practices. John ran his business. I went to work. My sister and Emily came over to give us their condolences. I was a bit surprised that Renee thought that sharing pictures and videos of her two new German Shepherd puppies would make me feel better. She looked so happy as she played the videos of them, and I knew she'd been going through a rough time. Those silly animals did so much for her spirit, so I acted happy for her.

It had been over a week since Sara had passed, but I still didn't feel that she was gone. Each night that I walked into my bedroom and made my way to the far side of the bed in the dark, I'd tiptoe close to the bed to avoid stepping on her. I still felt the need to do this, as if her presence was still in my room each night. Some friends of ours came into town for the weekend and brought their little eight-month-old black-and-white puppy. The dog didn't bark much and liked to wander the house and explore. I saw him on the landing and crawled slowly up the steps to pet him. He turned his head and looked up, then slowly backed away from me when I reached for him. "Don't be afraid," I told him. "That's just Sara. She wants to make sure you know that I'm her mommy."

"Julie, quit scratching the van along the street just to get the grass and hay off the side!" My sister Julie is driving our old solid blue van my parents had when I was young. There are

patches of grass and hay covering the front driver's side of the van. Around and around she drives in a loop. Each time she rounds the corner by me, the van dips sideways and scrapes along the side of the road. A side profile image of Sara's face starts to blend with the image of the van. Her eye is hollow and the side of her face and forehead are bare of fur. I wake up.

As I awoke, the image of the side of Sara's face stuck in my mind. I lay in bed and thought how strange it was that my brain connected the two images. Fifteen years had gone by since my parents owned that van. Why was Julie driving it? I understood that the hay and grass represented fur and the scraping represented Sara trying to scratch off the itchy fur falling from her skin, but why had I blended the two images? Why wouldn't I have just dreamed of a memory of Sara trying to scratch the fur from her face? These were the types of dreams, I believed, that simply pulled images from memory and pieced together a story. However, I could be mistaken and totally have missed the significance it offered.

"I don't understand, Robin, why hasn't Sara come to see me and tell me she's OK?" I asked. Although we didn't work at a sleep lab together anymore, Robin and I met for coffee periodically. She just "got" me. There were few people that I could talk to about my dreams and beliefs who actually understood what I was saying. Honestly, she may have been the only one. Robin sweetly replied, "She will, honey. Maybe there are just some things she needs to do first or maybe she needs to understand that you are ready to let her go." I sighed, knowing that she was right. "I talk to her all the time. I still feel her in the house. I do love the feeling of her being around me, but it is really selfish of me if I'm the one keeping her here. It makes me so sad to think that she's just following me around, not understanding what happened," I said as I tried to hold back the tears.

Robin didn't have any children of her own, but she'd always been a caregiver to the people in her life. And she and her husband had a dog that was like a child to them. "Just relax and let her know that although you will miss her terribly, tell her that you will be OK, and she's OK to go now." Maybe I had been holding on. Maybe I had only been saying the words, but she could see in my heart that I wasn't ready to let her go. "OK," I said sadly, "I'll try."

I hear the scratch on the mattress from the far side of the bed. I know it isn't Jeter because I just let him out an hour earlier. She's here! I sit up in bed so fast looking for her. "Sara! I'm over here!" I hear her trotting around the foot of the bed and over to my side. I know I'm not really "awake" physically, but I'm so excited that she's finally visiting me! As I lean over to see her, I can feel John rolling over to kiss me on the cheek. I don't know if he is really doing this or if it's part of this sleep paralysis experience, but he definitely doesn't know that Sara is here. I pull away from him even though it may upset him. I don't want him to think that I'm being mean or insensitive, but I can't let Sara slip away when I just got her. This is almost like a dream inside a dream or something. He never heard me yell, "Sara, I'm over here!"

As John rolls back to return to sleep, Sara jumps up onto the bed. I slowly roll back down to my pillow. Although she is sitting on my stomach, I feel no weight from her. I'm just lying here, staring up at her face. She seems very excited to be here and so happy. I notice that her face and head look a little worse than the last time I saw her. The left side is losing fur now and her head seems puffy and swollen. She doesn't seem to care, though, so neither do I.

I know what's happening. I'm in sleep paralysis, although this time is different. I am actually interacting with her rather than simply being a witness to what everyone calls hallucinations during these times. This feels too real to be considered a hallucination. In fact, I know this is really happening. My physical eyes are not straining to see, yet I see her clearly. My physical body did not sit up and yell for Sara because it's sleeping quietly next to John, yet "I" did sit up and call for her loudly.

I have so many questions for Sara. I know she can't talk, but that's never stopped me from talking to her before. I stare up at her and ask, "Are you OK? How are you? Are you with Grandma?" With this last question her expression changes to excitement and anxiousness, so I know she thinks I mean Karen. I quickly correct myself, "My mommy. Is my mommy with you?" Now, she just looks confused, so I stop. I am disappointed that she doesn't understand my question. Maybe she hasn't been to heaven yet to meet her. She is staring at me so sweetly.

"You had cancer, Sara. It was going to get really bad. I'm so sorry for what I did. You didn't do anything wrong." Strangely, I see her lips move and hear, "Yeah, tough break kid." The voice is not at all what I expect, even if I thought she could talk. It is a male's voice. It looked like it came from Sara, but I don't think it did. If she was able to speak, she could have answered my questions. I notice she keeps looking over her shoulder as if she's in a hurry. My time is limited. I hear the voice again. It's definitely coming from her. "Julian says it is time to go." She jumps off the bed, trots toward the bedroom door, and disappears into a faint light.

I'm still lying here in bed. I know I can't follow her. I'm stuck in my body, paralyzed. That's OK, I take this time to bask in happiness. I think about how much I miss running my fingers through her fur and what her fur felt like. Images and feelings of running my fingers through her thick, golden fur fill my head, but I'm disturbed. I feel strange moles on her skin that I know shouldn't be there. "No, that's not what it feels like!" I try harder to envision running my fingers over the white soft fur on her pink belly.

Sara suddenly jumps up on the bed again. She lies down and lowers her head next to mine. Again, I don't feel her weight. I wrap my arms around her body and hold her close. I pay close attention to the amazing feeling of her long, soft fur between my fingers. This is right. I don't want her to go. I want so badly for John to know that Sara is with me next to him. "Daddy, I got Sara." He doesn't respond, so I try louder. "Daddy! I got Sara!" Over and over I try to make him hear me, but all I can manage is a little squeak from my mouth. I feel my body begin to wake. Sara disappears. I wake up.

After a few moments of reflection and gathering my thoughts, all I could think was, "Who is Julian?" I felt John moving around and saw the flash of bright light coming from his iPad. Do I tell him what just happened? He might get a bit freaked out. "John? Did you hear me? Just a few minutes ago, did you hear me make a noise?" He looked over his reading glasses, "Yeah why?" I paused. How could I explain this? I could say, "I just hugged our dead dog. Oh, and she talked to me in a man's voice." He was understanding and all, but that may have been a bit much, so I kept it simple. "You know how I sometimes have sleep paralysis in the morning?" He looked at me curiously because I'd told some pretty fantastic stories in the past. "Well, it happened again this morning. While I was in it, I was trying to get your attention." He still didn't say anything but looked interested, so I went on. "I finally had a visit from Sara. I was trying to get your attention to tell you I had her. I wanted you to know that she was here." *Great*, I thought. *I went too far.*

The look on his face went from curious to sad, as if he had so many different emotions that he wasn't sure how he felt, except that he believed me. During the past year or two, he'd really grown fond of Sara. His early morning routine included taking her out to fetch the paper and let the cat in the back door, feeding her, and then she lay on the floor and watched him work out. He didn't talk about it much, but he really missed her, too.

Conversations with my deceased mother, premonitions of the future, a photo of my unborn child, the chance to make amends and find peace after losing a friendship, images and stories for self-analysis, and the ability to say I'm sorry and feel the warmth of passed loved ones—these miracles were the blessings within my curse. Neurologists talk about a narcoleptic's lack of hypocretin/orexin being the cause of our "switch" from REM sleep and wake to be broken. As a result, we end up with a unique REM/wake blend that many others do not experience. Being aware within the confines of sleep opens up a new reality, one that has no boundaries or laws of physics. I believed that this broken chemistry of mine gives me a window into another world, the spiritual world.

CHAPTER 10

Let Sleeping Dogs Lie

"Ah, you're awake," John said as I stirred in bed. He grinned his boyish grin and asked, "Wanna make sex?" I rolled over to face him, but seeing he was too far away for it to have been him, I asked, "Did you just kiss me?" His smile faded a little bit. "I don't know... why?" he asked. I lay there for a moment confused. "No, really," I persisted, "did you just kiss me a few minutes ago?" "No!" he said, disappointed that I was ignoring his intentions. More-so talking to myself, I said, "I felt someone kiss me on the side of my face. That's why I woke up. Huh, that's so weird." John rolled his eyes, lay back down, and mumbled, "No, Brianna, *you're* weird."

I thought I wouldn't like waking up on Christmas morning in a hotel, but as it turned out, it all depended on where I was and in which hotel. With their claim of exceptional service, the Trump Hotel in Waikiki totally lived up to our expectations. The holidays at home would have been difficult with both Sara and Dylan gone, so John decided Christmas in Hawaii would be the perfect solution to end our winter blues. Bart had asked to join us and the vacation served as a great motivational tool for him during rehab. Shopping in Waikiki on Christmas Eve was so much more tolerable than in Kansas City, although I had to admit, nothing beat Christmas in KC!

After Oahu, we spent New Year's week in San Diego with our California family. The rental home was absolutely perfect for all of us to spend time

together. The view from high on the cliffs overlooking the ocean was breathtaking. The large, heated pool and spa were perfect to watch football from, even if it was on our iPads. The Kansas City Chiefs played the San Diego Chargers, so I bought everyone Chiefs shirts for Christmas. There were plenty of bedrooms; however, there were not enough doors that could be closed between Bart and my rooms to drown out the noise of his snoring.

"Bart, you should make an appointment with a sleep lab. Your loud snoring had me dreaming that I was at work last night." "There's nothing wrong with my sleep," he said irritably. "I sleep just fine." I didn't know why he would say this to me of all people. He was fully aware of how much I knew about sleep apnea, and he was the one I had gotten all of my diabetes information from for my report for school. "Bart, you have congestive heart failure, diabetes, and continue to have heart problems. Those are big factors for breathing issues when you sleep. You may not wake up all the way from snoring, but your oxygen desaturations and breathing disruptions throughout the night will make your diabetes and heart condition worse!" There really needed to be more education on sleep. People had no idea how much it affected their everyday living—what they didn't know *could* hurt them.

The question remained: "Who is Julian?" I did believe all dogs went to heaven because I believed they had souls. Why was it that every passed soul that visited me was in a hurry? I wished I understood heaven's rules. This certainly gave new meaning to "ghost protocol." How many times could someone visit? Were visits during sleep paralysis considered different from regular REM dreams? Maybe their time was limited based on how long the dreamer was in the right brainwave state to process it. Just out of curiosity, I googled "Saint Julian biblical names." I knew it was silly to think that my dog had been escorted to heaven by a saint, but why not? She was very intelligent and almost like my guardian angel. She was literally handpicked.

I found a Bible story about a Saint Julian. He was said to have been cursed and would one day murder his wealthy parents. In fear, he left his family at a young age, then later married and had his own home. After years of searching, his parents discovered where he lived and made a surprise visit. While Julian was out, his wife welcomed his parents in and offered them her and Julian's bed to rest in. Julian arrived home later that night and saw a man in bed with whom he assumed was his wife and killed them both. Once he discovered the truth, that the curse had come true, he begged God for forgiveness and repented by setting up many small homes for travelers to rest. One day, a leper came to his home and asked to stay in his bed. Julian did not hesitate and let him right in. The next morning the leper revealed himself as a messenger of God sent as a test, and for the kindness he'd shown others, God absolved him of his sins. Saint Julian is now the patron saint of travelers.

This story made me think back to my encounter with the strange dog with the mangled face. I let him into my home, he slept, ate, then left. Since everything about that day was bizarre, I wondered if it was a test of some sort. Why a dog? I didn't know. Was it a test of my worthiness to have good fortune? Our lives had changed for the better after that, even if it was temporary. Losing my mother was inevitable, but our financial security held for the next ten years as we created a wonderful life for ourselves. I was sure I had failed other tests of faith and worthiness over the years. All I could do was continue to work on being a good and moral person.

After my mother died, people were concerned about me because I didn't appear very sad and never mourned in front of anyone. Everyone had their own ways of coping with death. I felt very in tune with my feelings and tried not suppress things at the subconscious level. This, along with having a high level of faith, allowed me to deal with my sadness in a different manner. I was also quite the introvert. Would the people around me have found it more acceptable if I cried all the time and took antidepressants? I'd never felt the need for antidepressants. I was always tired, but in my case that wasn't a symptom of depression. I also went into REM quickly, a sign of depression for some, but not necessarily for me either. If dreams were our subconscious talking to us, and REM a healing mechanism in our brain, then I was always listening, analyzing, and healing.

"Mom! You'll never believe this!" Claire yelled as she rushed down the stairs with her phone in hand. Emily had Snapchatted a picture of herself to Claire. I can't really say that I was surprised. Her once blonde hair was dyed a very dark brown. Claire held up her phone, "'Remember my mom's dream?' I reminded her.' She said, 'I know, I know. I just wanted something a little different.'" Feeling pleased with myself, I said, "Well, now she just needs to cut it shoulder length to make my premonition 100 percent true." *That dream was so long ago,* I thought to myself. Her change of hair color and approximate age were accurate, however I couldn't help but wonder if I'd missed something more significant that could have been helpful now. Something was going on with Emily. She hadn't talked to John or me in several months. We'd heard that she dropped out of high school and moved out of her mom's house and in with her boyfriend. I hadn't reached out to her or to my sister because it was impossible to help people who didn't want to be helped. I'd learned that the hard way with Dylan.

I'm sitting at a picnic table in my sister's backyard. Someone is sitting across the table from me. There's nothing on the table except a sharpened pencil. My sister's two German Shepherds are sitting on the patio next to the house watching me. They look angry. I can see one of the dogs trot towards me in a manner that feels threatening. Although I don't know her dogs, I don't understand why they would want to hurt me. I don't move. His movements become more aggressive, and I begin to feel his breath and teeth close to the side of my head. I love dogs. I don't want to hurt him. Why is he trying to hurt me? My mind is racing so fast because I know I have to choose. Do I allow him to hurt me or do I choose to hurt him? As if in slow motion, I feel his teeth scrape again my skull. I grab the pencil and jam the sharp end into the side of his neck. I wake up.

The push of my cat's paws against my leg woke me up and kept me from kicking him as I moved above the covers. Jeter was funny like that. He wasn't the kind of cat who curled up against your leg to sleep, instead he liked to stretch out long at the bottom of the bed. I sat up to give him a few quick strokes along his belly to let him know that I knew he was there. As I reached out for him, I saw that he was nowhere on the bed.

If this wasn't a hallucination, then what was it? Did something happen during that brief time of REM/wake blending? It reminded me of the kiss on my cheek I thought John had given me a few weeks earlier. I wondered if my mother had snuck a quick kiss on my cheek during that brief period between sleep and wake, a period of sleep like a twilight or dusk. Or was it like "future John," when I experienced an event during sleep paralysis before it actually happened? Maybe Jeter just hadn't made it into bed yet. Whatever the case, my dream experiences were getting out of control!

More and more often I was discovering weird, unexplainable happenings, premonitions were coming true, and dreams were simply unclassifiable. I knew John had enough on his mind and didn't want to hear any more of the craziness that went on inside my head, so I turned to Robin. After sharing the images and dreams I'd recorded, she invited me to one of her classes on spirit guides. I believed in the concept of spirit guides and guardian angels, especially after hearing them actually speak to me. One had practically saved my life by telling me to *Wake up!* Her teachings, however, didn't satisfy me.

I was looking for truth, or at least some sort of tangible evidence that could justify my experiences as real. I believed that I'd communicated with beings on the other side and had experienced so many unexplainable things that I couldn't settle for anything less. I didn't know that what Robin taught about ancient Mayan beliefs was *not* true, but some concepts didn't help explain my experiences. I knew that what I'd experienced was real to me, but I wanted something that validated my understanding as true so that others simply wouldn't dismiss me as crazy or weird just because they hadn't had the opportunity to experience the phenomena themselves.

Since my brain had become accustomed to being awake late at night, I enjoyed reading fantasy and science fiction books by the fireplace in the cold, winter months on my nights off work. I couldn't shake the feeling that working in a sleep lab wasn't fulfilling me as much as I'd hoped it would. I pulled out a book that Robin had suggested by neurologist Dr. Kevin Nelson, who researched near death experiences. She had told me that sleep paralysis is mentioned briefly and thought I might be interested in his book *The Spiritual Doorway in the Brain*. Robin was like my spiritual muse. Who knows, maybe she was one of my personal spirit guides!

As I began reading, I felt more inspired than I ever had in my life! He had searched for tangible, scientific evidence to support the spiritual encounters people reported having during near-death experiences. As a neurologist, he explored the human brain to find out if and how these otherwise unexplainable spiritual experiences are possible when the body is dying, sometimes already pronounced dead. My father-in-law had this type of NDE firsthand when he encountered his late wife and dog as doctors resuscitated his body. I was curious to find out if Dr. Nelson's brain research supported these extraordinary reports from patients, or if he would simply dismiss their experiences as chemical reactions in the brain as researchers often do.

I discovered that his research on NDE encompassed the very same idea and conclusion that I had come to regarding spiritual experiences in the brain—it was a symptom of the blending of REM and wake. He writes, "So I asked myself: what natural physiological process could have caused her precipitous, total, yet temporary paralysis? Suddenly it struck me: we all experience paralysis many times each night, during that period of our slumber when our eyes move rapidly beneath our lids, as if watching events before us. It is called rapid eye movement stage of sleep, familiar to everyone who studies the brain. We call it the REM state of consciousness." "Yes, yes!" I said out loud while reading alone in front of the fire, "You are totally on to something!" I read on, "I knew that not only did the REM state explain Mrs. Martin's temporary paralysis, it also pointed directly to the light that beckons toward eternity or expresses the divine...." Then, I read the words that I had been waiting for, "REM consciousness and wakefulness blending into each other as death approached could explain many of the major features of near-death experiences."

I couldn't wait. I had to talk to this author! I didn't care that I hadn't read the entire book yet; I emailed him right away. In my mind, his research confirmed my theory of REM being the key to our "spiritual doorway in the brain," as he calls it. REM opens this doorway. Better yet, sleep paralysis mirrors his discoveries of brain function during near-death with the blending of wakeful consciousness upon waking or falling asleep while paralysis from REM takes hold. In the case of near-death, according to Dr. Nelson, REM is switched on because of low blood pressure while the brain is awake and conscious. I believed that people didn't need to be dying for this doorway to be open; it is open every time our brain becomes consciously aware while in the paralysis of REM. Our theories were similar in that REM/wake blending is the key component when having a spiritual encounter.

"I don't like how doctors blow off sleep paralysis experiences as dreamlike," I wrote in an email to him that night. "I am fully awake in my mind. In fact, I've always wondered why I could see during sleep paralysis when I know my muscles are atonic." I described my experience with my mother during a sleep paralysis episode. "I think you're on to something with your analysis of REM...." I continued, "You should have known there was something more going on than just in near-death experiences when you interviewed your narcoleptic friend, Matt." I didn't want to scare him off by writing too much, especially since I had only read the first few chapters. So I ended with, "My narcoleptic 'special power' of insight into the spiritual world is appreciated by me and simply dismissed as 'weird' by my husband."

I wasn't sure what I expected from this busy professor, writer, and practicing neurologist, but I was pleasantly surprised to find an email waiting for me the next morning. He said he was excited by my email, but was currently busy at the Mayo Clinic and needed to respond later. I was so entirely thrilled that I hadn't been blown off or called weird this time. For now, I knew he was interested. That's all I wanted, someone to listen and understand.

The large dog at the end of the leash I am holding is growling at me. "Don't!" I say, giving him a stern look. I don't know this dog. Again, he growls. As he lunges at me, I punch down on the top of his muzzle. He lies down and begins whining. "I said don't!" I wake up.

I knew I was having difficulty with my decision to have Sara put to sleep. Dreams of me hurting dogs were coming up more frequently. In each of these dreams, if I didn't hurt the dog, the dog would hurt me. I came to realize that my decision had more to do with protecting myself from pain than protecting her. I'd wanted to believe that I was protecting her from her pain, not me from mine. Analyzing dreams can be extremely useful, yet very painful to examine. I'd never been one to push my feelings to the back of my mind because I knew they would just resurface over time. I believed my soul looked for healing. We were one and the same, my soul and I. The "I" in everything I did, thought, or felt, in waking reality as well as my dream world, remained the same: me. I wanted healing and forgiveness, yet I was scared of the pain I would face in the process. The spirit world saw my pain and reached out to me with dream images that I could understand; it pushed me towards self-awareness and eventually, healing.

There's an explosion in a plane full of people. The plane crashes into a body of water and is quickly being engulfed by mud. We are in swampland. I don't know if Claire and I were involved with the crash, but I see her unhurt nearby the wreckage. The water and mud are so thick that I am crawling to get close to the wreckage. There are people trapped below the surface that need my help. I shove my hand down into the mud and feel fingertips brush my hand. I grab hold and pull hard, hoping that a whole body is attached. One person emerges from the mud and is safe. I continue reaching and heaving and pull a few more people to safety. I don't know how much time is left before the bodies I pull up will be dead and grotesque. I keep reaching. I wake up.

I noticed a new trend in my dreams. Drowning was still a theme, but now I was helping, or at least trying to help. I had another dream similar to the airplane crashing in swampland, except that we were in the desert. I did not fear for my immediate family, yet there were so many people buried in the sand who needed help. I just kept reaching deep into the sand in hopes of making contact with hands.

I'm on the back deck my dad built at the house I grew up in. It's large and has a bench around the perimeter. It connects our enclosed porch to the back entrance of Gram's apartment. There is a dog on the deck with me. I'm not sure if it's Sara or a German Shepherd, but it has dark markings like a German Shepherd. The deck starts to collapse. Water begins to fill the middle of the deck where the boards have fallen. Oh no, the dog is falling! I cling to the bench on the side of the deck and reach for her. The dog paddles her feet among the broken boards. I keep reaching out to grab her paws while she's struggling to stay afloat. In the distance, I notice an image of my mother. She is waving and smiling. The dog goes under for a second time. I can't reach her. Her nose and paws surface once more before she disappears into the water for good. I wake up.

I lived with a serial killer. His name was Jeter, our precious family cat. Several times a week he would strike poor, unsuspecting, cute and furry victims. Later, after he dismembered them with surgical precision, he would leave the remains on our porch as a gift. I wondered if the bunnies felt pain while being torn apart by Jeter's teeth. Surely God wouldn't allow such a monstrous thing to occur simply because it was the circle of life. Occasionally, I'd find a bunny still intact lying on my porch, only appearing dead. Jeter would wait nearby for the right time to finish the kill. He'd meow at me angrily when I put him inside and scoop up the bunny in my hands (wearing gloves, of course). I'd see the bunny watch me as I carried it away to a safer place. After setting it down and walking away, I'd watch the bunny come to life, get up, and run quickly away.

Had the bunny only faked death? People say animals play dead so predators will ignore them, but when that didn't work and they were being eaten, why wouldn't they try to fight to survive? I've heard of animals being "petrified" when their stalkers attack. Maybe this petrified behavior was simply their brains switching to REM and creating a state of paralysis. During my studies in psychology, I learned of ways in which our brain protects us in extreme circumstances such as having a selective memory or creating split personalities. Why don't humans have a built-in mechanism that protects us from extreme pain?

As I continued reading Dr. Nelson's research in NDEs, a light bulb began to glow above my head again. This wasn't a dim light, this was a neon sign that blinked REM IS THE KEY! Nelson's research concludes that the blending of REM and wake provides the opportunity for unique, powerful experiences during near-death. On the verge of death, our brains flip a switch to REM paralysis. This switch is initiated by a drop in blood pressure. I shared this knowledge with my friend Rachel, and she offered her story: "I remember looking down from high above a hospital bed in a delivery room. A crying man was holding his newborn son, while doctors tended to the mother of the baby who was lying on the bed next to them. I remember feeling very sad for the family below. After a few minutes, I opened my eyes and realized that

I had been the woman on the bed suffering from severe blood loss during childbirth." Once her blood pressure was restored, Rachel had immediately returned to her body. She said she felt at peace during this time of crisis, just as Bart had during his near-death experience.

Dr. Nelson writes, "The link I have made between REM and the near-death experience upsets those who see such experiences as a revelation of afterlife or proof of an underlying web of consciousness or the existence of God. For these people, my work puts near-death experiences uncomfortably close to dreams—in other words, experiences that aren't real." This is where we differ. To me, dreams were real in the sense that I experienced and remembered them. I believed that just because others couldn't see, taste, or smell something, it didn't mean it wasn't "real." Pain, for example, was real. However, not all dreams were the same. I did not consider them all spiritual in content. Where Dr. Nelson and I agreed came from the idea that these spiritual experiences happened while we were in the state of REM, and at the same time, conscious.

> Dr. Nelson,
>
> I believe my theory regarding how the spiritual world connects with us is so similar to yours, except that you don't have to almost die! You just have to be completely paralyzed from REM and conscious at the same time (i.e., sleep paralysis). I believe that when our body is alive and healthy, but paralyzed, and we become conscious, it opens a doorway. We can't leave because we are tied to our bodies. I do believe, however, that spiritual encounters can occur in dreams as well.

> Brianna,
>
> I do think that you are on to something. I believe that REM intrusion offers an amazing portal into the spiritual side of our lives. Often in that transition between conscious states.

> Dr. Nelson,
>
> Our theories of REM being the "spiritual doorway in the brain" are the key. Mine came from being narcoleptic, while yours came from studying near-death experiences. Now people can know that they don't have to be

dying or have narcolepsy to have a connection to the spiritual world. We all have REM, even animals.

Brianna,

I enjoyed reading your note. I am unaware of a good book on the experiences of narcoleptics, how they impact the spiritual world and how they may have influenced history. I think if there is no work out there, your book would have a nice place.

The thought of finally writing a book about dreams gave me an indescribable energy. "What's the purpose of this book?" John asked. *Good question*, I thought. I knew that I didn't want it to be another research paper. Everything I needed to know about dreams was right here in my own head. I wanted people to know what I knew. It wasn't just going to be a book about narcolepsy, but because of my narcolepsy, I'd had more opportunities than the average person to experience the blending of REM and wake. Therefore, I felt that sharing these rare opportunities with the rest of the world was important. Researchers, psychologists, and philosophers offer many theories regarding dreams and their nature. They didn't have to be wrong; I simply believed there was more.

I step outside the front door of my house as the repairman approaches. He has his dog with him. His dog resembles a German Shepherd. I know that Sara is at my side, but that no one will be able to see her. She has already passed away. Sara walks up to the man and smells his hand. I think she is making sure that he is not a threat. He doesn't acknowledge her. He doesn't see her or know that she's with me. Sara does not seem to mind his presence. I know Sara is dead, but I also know that she is here looking out for me. The German Shepherd begins to growl and bark at Sara. Surprised by the dog's reaction, I ask the repairman, "Can you see my dog?" The man makes a weird expression. "Dog? What dog?" I wake up.

I tried to give Claire as many opportunities as possible to talk about Dylan and Sara. John and I worried that she may be holding in too much anger. I was happy to hear her finally open up a little about Sara. "Mom," she said. "I had a dream about Sara the other day." *Finally*, I thought, *someone besides me would talk about being visited.* "That's cool, honey." She went on, "I was walking in the house from the garage with my friends, and Sara came up to me like she normally did. This time, though, I was the only one that could see her. I was so excited to see her, but I noticed no one else did." I was so glad that she opened up like that to me. She knew that I, of all people, wouldn't think she was weird or make her feel weird for telling me.

"You know, that happened to me, too. You may not have realized it at the time, but I believe Sara was in your dream to let you know she was OK and wanted to say good-bye." After saying that, her expression changed a bit. I didn't know how she felt, but I believed my words touched her heart. I didn't think she thought of dreams that way before, that they were significant. I was really happy for her.

Before putting pen to paper, I decided to take once last trip to the bookstore. The spiritual component I was looking for in REM had already been made in Dr. Nelson's work with NDEs, but I wanted to see if there were any other writings that could help pull it all together or to find out if someone had already drawn the same conclusions I had.

With faith in this endeavor, I stood in front of the section on spirituality and self-help books. Just as Robin had asked me to do with her oracle cards, I allowed my hand to be drawn to two books that looked promising. As I thumbed through the pages of each quickly scanning the content, tears began to fill my eyes. "Thanks, Mom," I said quietly. "You are always there to help." I looked back at the titles again and smiled. "Yes, Mom, I remember what you said. 'Keep talking to me because I can hear you.'" In my hands, I held the books *Talking to Heaven: A Medium's Message of Life after Death* by James Van Praagh and *Hello From Heaven!* by Bill and Judy Guggenheim.

I used to laugh when hearing about so-called "mediums" and their ability to talk to ghosts. I suppose that came from watching movies like *Ghost* or *Poltergeist*. Yet, as I read Van Praagh's *Talking to Heaven*, I became intrigued by the similarities between this man and me. He grew up Catholic, yet had questions about his faith. Although he claims to have the gift of clairvoyance, he says that we all have our own psychic ability at some level. This energy, he explains, comes from the soul.

He, too, believes in God and heaven and that our souls are made in the likeness of God. "I personally believe that heaven is the other side of our physical world and is very much like our physical world with similar sights and sounds, although more vivid and colorful." His words sounded not only like Bart's description of his NDE, but very much like a description of dreams. What was the "other side" that he talks about? Was this a dimension alongside our own physical world? Could this other side be visited not only during near-death experiences, but also during REM?

He believes that there are levels of heaven based on one's spiritual growth while on Earth. Those at a higher level can aid and assist those who may not be as aware. His book was written to help people understand his beliefs and answer questions about God and the spiritual world. I felt a connection to his beliefs when I reflected on so many experiences within my own life. I believed that life's lessons, whether we understood them at the time or not, were given to us as a means to provide spiritual growth.

Van Praagh believes that we have spiritual helpers and puts them in three categories. These guardian angels or spirit guides are unique to each of us. The first category, personal guides, help us through life with subtle signs or impressions to give us direction. We just need to pay attention to find our way. They cannot interfere in our life lessons, but stand by to help guide us while we learn. As I reflected on my life's struggles, I recognized the countless signs and guidance I was given, and even the small lessons such as slipping on ice to remind me that I, too, was vulnerable and should gladly help others in need. A little poke here and there was enough for me to understand that I was never alone. There was always someone with me, wanting me to do well in life and grow in spirit.

In the second category, specialized or mastery helpers are spirits that are experts in our line of work. If we are open and receptive, they are drawn to help guide us to be successful. Maybe my spirit helper saw my desire to help those struggling with sleep the way I had and gave a little push beginning with a simple dinner at a friend's house. That dinner led to enrolling in the PSG program and becoming a sleep technician. In the third category, spirit or master teachers are attracted to us during our quest for spiritual enlightenment. I knew that during my lifetime I had struggled with ongoing battles

to be selfless, generous, kind, and forgiving versus selfish, stingy, mean, and resentful. I believed that not only had I experienced hardships to learn humility, but my dreams were given to me to provide lessons as well as encouragement. Maybe in my quest to help others engage dreams in their spirituality, I'd been given an open chair next to Robin during the first day of class.

Van Praagh explains that the spirit world operates on faster energy vibrations than in our physical world. He believes that we have our physical body and our ethereal or spirit body that lies within our physical body. He writes that although the etheric body is "an exact replica of our physical body," the difference is that, "our etheric body's molecules vibrate at a much faster and higher rate than its physical counterpart." He also believes that when our physical body dies and our spirit body is released, it has no disease or fatigue and can move from place to place through thought.

His words caused my mind to race through all the memories, beliefs, and theories I'd collected during my lifetime. Our souls never die. We do not lose ourselves in our dreams or even when we die. Our soul is who we are. Our bodies are our temporary hosts. While in the lucid state of REM, I left my physical body and visited my mother in another dimension. Although Van Praagh offers so much insight regarding the spirit world, he does not offer knowledge of this alternate, mixed state of consciousness.

> *I'm lying on the couch in my hearth room, and I feel a slight vibration in my legs. Strangely, I also hear the vibration. I feel myself slip off the couch and onto the rug in front of the coffee table. I see where I am. I remember lying down to take a nap here. Oh no. It's happening again. I still feel so tired and heavy. Can't move. There's someone standing above me. I think it's Claire, but I can't tell. The person has my feet in their hands and begins to drag me. I can only see up to the neckline, so I can't tell for sure it's her. She's wearing a long, dangling necklace. It has a crystal hanging on a pendant. I don't recognize it. I feel the rug brush against my back as she pulls me across the floor. I'm so heavy and tired. Can't move. I wake up.*

I really hated taking naps! Sleep paralysis almost always accompanied my emergency naps because they were brought on by extraordinary tiredness. Upon waking from the sleep paralysis, my eyes felt fresh and my head felt clear and alert; however, my body didn't feel rested. Plus, I was extremely frustrated—I felt violated, like someone had come into my home and taken advantage of my vulnerability. After collecting my thoughts and shaking off the icky feeling in my body, I would continue my day. But it wasn't long before that feeling of violation returned.

Walking through the kitchen, I noticed a long necklace lying in a neat pile on the edge of the counter. "Claire! Can you come down here for a minute?" I yelled when I heard her in her room upstairs. As she walked into the kitchen, I pointed at the necklace and asked, "Is this yours?" "Yeah, why?" To avoid watching her roll her eyes and call me weird again, I simply responded, "Oh, I just didn't recognize it." There was a crystal pendant hanging from the bottom of the necklace.

Robin told me that she had tried for months to have an out-of-body experience (OBE) after reading a book that explains how to induce one on your own. I supposed being dragged across the floor of my living room while my body remained on the couch would be considered an OBE. She said she finally succeeded when she felt an overwhelming tiredness come on and she lay down to nap. To me, this feeling sounded like a description of a sleep attack. She didn't have just one OBE episode, but eventually three.

Upon lying down to nap, Robin said that she had never felt such heaviness and fatigue in her body during the onset of sleep and felt herself drop off the couch to the floor. She talked about feeling immense vibrations throughout her legs upon entering this sleep state. Being a very spiritual person, Robin was excited to tell me that she saw a hand take hold of her and drag her across the floor while she watched the ceiling and windows move past her. She felt it was necessary to say a quick prayer for protection even though she was eager to see where this would lead. Not only had this "sentient being" touched her, but it grabbed her hard, pulled her through the window and took her on a little joy ride, flying across the globe. She mentioned flying past a man on the street who looked directly at her and asked, "Being born?" As her physical body began to cough, her eyes flew open to find herself lying on the same couch where she had fallen asleep.

I, on the other hand, hadn't felt so excited by my encounter. I wasn't sure that the visitor who grabbed me did so with good intentions. I did love her stories, as well as all the others I had read about OBE. I didn't question their authenticity, especially after having had some of my own crazy experiences. During these experiences, we were not in our physical bodies, yet we saw. We were mentally awake and aware, yet unable to move our physical selves. We, our souls, did not choose to leave our physical bodies. We were pushed, taken, and sometimes even invited.

I was pretty certain that my mom had directed my hand as I reached for *Hello From Heaven!* because *A new field of research—After-Death communication—confirms that life and love are eternal* was written on the front cover. The book touched my heart in so many ways. While reading, I folded the corners of pages that reflected experiences similar to ones I'd had throughout my life: voices speaking messages to me in my mind, sensing the presence of the deceased, dream state visits of passed loved ones (both human and animal) providing comfort during times of hardship, visits from passed loved ones that resemble a phone call, physical phenomena such as lights turning on and off, quick visions or thoughts being put in my mind, physical gifts such as money coming at the perfect time, and visions of the deceased at my bedside.

The authors collected two thousand stories of men, women, and children who had all been contacted in one way or another by deceased loved ones. The stories of those who reported "seeing" passed loved ones at their bedside do not use the term sleep paralysis, possibly due to the lack of education in this hybrid state of sleep. All of the stories, however, made me want to yell, "Yes! I know what you are talking about!" The authors encourage readers not to apologize when sharing their stories by starting with, "You will probably think I'm weird, but...." I totally agreed. We are *not* "weird" or "nuts." We are blessed to have had the experience.

For some reason, asking my father about ADC with my mother was uncomfortable, but I wanted him to understand why I wished to share my story of dreams with others. Karen was more than happy to tell me how my deceased mother loved to tease her by making my toddler nephew laugh and look over Karen's shoulder when she was home alone with him. When I mentioned dreams specifically, Karen shared quite a few premonitions regarding meeting my father, but I was disappointed and sad to hear my dad tell me that he had not dreamt of my mother after her death.

Walking around the kitchen I grew up in, a toddler in a T-shirt and diapers clings to my hip. The child's hair is fine and a very light brown, similar to mine as a child. I look over the breakfast bar and see John lying on the couch reading. I'm trying to figure out how to entertain the toddler. "Hey John, what about those video games on the computer? Didn't Dylan like them at this age?" John tells me they probably won't work with the newer computer programs. Two girls in their young twenties come through the front door. They are here to visit the toddler. I'm not familiar with these girls, but I can tell the toddler recognizes them. One of the girls has dark red hair and brown eyes. As she walks up to me, the toddler turns and gives her a little kiss. I say, "Hey, I didn't know you already had a girlfriend!" I wake up.

Who was this mysterious child? Why were John and I babysitting at my parents' old house? I assumed the toddler was a boy, but I never did say his name. I was not lucid. *How old were we*, I wondered. John didn't look much older.

I'm standing in a backyard. I guess it's my backyard, but I'm not familiar with it. Sara's running around like a crazy, happy dog while she keeps her eyes on the landscapers working in the yard. She doesn't bother them, but makes sure they keep their distance from me. She looks beautiful. She's so healthy and young. She's her goofy self as I watch her trip on her own feet while running down a hill. She walks over to me, wanting me to console her. We go into the house to rest and watch TV. I'm lying on a bed with a small child next to me. I'm not sure of the child's name or sex, but I do know that the child is not Dylan or Claire. There's a large barrel of popcorn close by. "Sara will get us some popcorn," I tell the child. Sara scoops a bunch into her mouth, walks to us, and drops it on the bed. I eat a piece. I wake up.

I didn't check Facebook often, but my patients at the lab were sleeping well, so I decided to catch up on the world around me. A post from Emily made my mouth drop to the floor, as I watched a video showing a teenager going about her daily routine with a cartoon picture of a tiny fetus across her belly. Was this an announcement? A midnight posting of a pregnant teenager? I can't say I was surprised. I guess the post explained why we hadn't heard from her in a few months. The only thing that made sense to me was that this was what she wanted and didn't want us to tell her otherwise, just as Dylan had distanced himself from us to live his life as he chose.

Traveling for club volleyball to watch Claire play was good bonding time for her, John, and me. We stayed busy and distracted in our own little world and tried not to concern ourselves with the hardships of others. As selfish as it may have seemed, we yearned for drama-free living. So the three of us tried to enjoy our weekend adventures of long tournaments with loud whistle blowing and cheering parents. If only club volleyball were drama free…

Lying on my back, I start to feel a strange sensation across my left breast. It feels as though a hand has just lightly brushed across my nipple. My eyes slightly open and notice that John is far on the other side of the bed. We are in the hotel room in Minneapolis. As the feeling begins to happen again, it seems to me like an arm is extending from beside me as if the rest of a body is behind me somehow. I cannot actually see the hand or arm, but the feeling of a gentle hand is stimulating. I recognize this type of experience from others I've had in the past. I'm going to try something new. With my right hand, I gently reach across my body and lay my hand on top of the hand on my breast. I still cannot see the hand, yet I feel something. The feeling under my hand is difficult to explain. There is movement, yet there is nothing tangible. I feel sleep begin to leave my body. I wake up.

I immediately looked to my hand. It was not on my chest where I thought it was. It was lying down by my side as if it had never physically moved at

all. Yet the feeling of stimulation in my breast was still there. There was no sense saying anything to John, he would simply turn it into something sexual. Again, I didn't feel scared or nervous, just more curious when hallucinations and sleep paralysis occurred.

My dreams about Dylan increased dramatically as his birthday approached. His birthday is 4-20, did I mention that? (Not long before, someone told me that date was considered National Pot Smoking Day.) I saw he had a ridiculous looking new mug shot photo on the correctional facility's public website with long, slicked back hair, mustache, and goatee. He was actually smiling in the picture. When I saw it, my emotions went from laughing to crying. He was a man now. The last time I had actually played the role of his mother, he was an eighteen-year-old on his way to college. Now, he was a twenty-five-year-old man in prison. I didn't feel like I'd had a son for the past seven years.

Our visit went well, even though the new, closer facility he moved to in Lansing didn't allow food to be brought in, even for birthdays. Instead, we waited in a long food line with fairly decent food and I let him order whatever he wanted. By the way he ate, you'd think they were starving him. When I asked him about his picture, he explained that he wanted to give me a nicer picture of himself to look at since that's all I had. He did say an old friend with a description similar to the man in a dream I had recently joined him in prison, but I decided I was uninterested in meeting him. Birthdays with my son were not supposed to be like this.

Growing up in the Midwest, tornado drills were a big deal every spring. Although I had never experienced an actual tornado, I had taken cover, camped out in basements, and ran for cover as severe thunderstorms rolled in several times each year. In my dreams, watching funnels of white clouds stream from the sky, the feeling of being sucked as if into a large vacuum, and the deafening sound of wind terrorized me while I tried to hold on for safety. These recurring nightmares of tornados were not limited to the house I grew up in. Even if I did become lucid during these nightmares, the only possible thing to do was to hold on and ride out the storm.

CHAPTER 11

Dream On

"Why do you want to write this book? What do you hope to get from it?" This question kept coming back to me because over the years the answer had changed and the reasons had grown. In my youth, I felt plagued by sleep and dreams, but also unique in my ability to remember most all of them. Before understanding the meaning of lucidity, I had experienced lucid dreaming. I had flown like Superman while feeling the wind in my hair and examined the beautiful colors in fields covered with flowers, but I'd also felt the pain and fear inflicted by a recurring evil presence. I wanted others to know about the crazy adventures and terrorizing hauntings that I experienced at night when I closed my eyes.

In early adulthood, I was amazed by the lack of information available and sheer guesses made by experts in the field about what was going on with me. I begged and hunted for answers from doctors and literature, yet found none. There were others just like me, I soon discovered. We all searched for truth. The narcoleptics, the constant dreamers, turned to each other for support and understanding not only regarding our condition, but also our dreams. Dream dictionaries, archetypes, random firing of neurons, and even what we had for dinner were not the explanations we needed to help us understand this other life we led at night (and sometimes during the day).

As an adult, I became an advocate for sleep through education and working in the field of sleep medicine. In a world that sees excessive sleep as a form of laziness, I strove to educate others of all the benefits of "good" sleep. Sleep wasn't something that should be done when one had the time. Sleep was as important as eating and drinking. People were educated about their bodies and some even understood their physiology, but many did not know how their bodies functioned once they closed their eyes. In my quest to find wakefulness during the day, I learned about other sleep disorders that affected my own family members as well as hundreds of thousands of people worldwide. I hoped to spread an interest in and understanding of the important role quality sleep plays in everyone's life, as well as the spiritual and emotional impact of dreams.

I open my eyes to see Jeter snuggled up close to my chest as I lay facing the window. It is morning and John has already left for work. There's a small dog lying quietly on the other side of the bed from me. As I notice it, the dog gets up and walks towards me. I don't see it as clearly as I do Jeter. In fact, I can only see an outline of the dog. It is translucent. As it moves, its body ripples like clear gel, similar to the being in the movie The Abyss. I can't move. I don't wish to. He gently lowers his body next to mine and rests his head gently against the side of my face. Why doesn't Jeter notice the dog? Aren't animals supposed to sense spirits? The dog begins to lightly lick the side of my face. It is a strange sensation. "Un, Uh," I grunt. Or at least I think it comes out audibly. The dog stops. He begins licking my face again, but faster. I gently brush my hand against his face. At least, I think I use my physical hand. He stops and moves back to the other side of the bed and lies down. I stare at the clear, gel-like dog for a while. I'm not sure if I'm supposed to know it or if it's a future dog of mine. It has floppy ears, similar to Pongo. It is a young dog. Maybe Chief, my puppy Dalmatian that died when I was nineteen? I begin to feel my body wake. The dog disappears. I wake up.

In graduate school, I read a book called Zapp! The Lightning of Empowerment. Written as a science-fiction story, the book is about an employee who is able to "see" physical signs in the form of lightning when people become empowered to do their job. He can also see people in colors depending on their mood or as trolls based on their disposition. The main character is able to view regular workplace activities, but from a different dimension. Only he can see and hear things from this other dimension, but he can also see and hear things that are there in real time. For me, sleep paralysis worked in much the same way. I felt as though I was in another dimension, yet looked in on my world in real time. Could this other dimension be the spiritual world exposed?

> *I open my eyes to find myself in bed during the early morning hours. Claire is lying asleep on the other side of our bed because John is out of town. There is something else in the room with us. As nervous as I am, I'm paralyzed in REM and can only hope that this sentient being is friendly. It's very close to my head and quietly sitting seemingly weightless not far above my pillow. I can see that its muscular body is human shaped, but don't believe it has human skin. Long, translucent wings extend from its back, similar to an insect's. It crouches lower and looks down at me, then our eyes meet. I can't take my eyes off its large, dark eyes. We are like two curious creatures from different worlds studying each other. Its face is oval shaped with a small slit for a mouth. I remain calm, but really, what can I do? I am paralyzed.*
>
> *It moves slowly up and over my head until, standing by the side of the bed it faces me. Its closeness and unexpected action feels threatening, so I gather my strength to physically sit up and face it. I can't move at first, but the hold of paralysis begins to release and I manage to sit up. I demand, "Get out!" I watch as the winged being disappears and the world around me becomes clear again. I wake up.*

I looked over at Claire sleeping soundly and wondered if she would have noticed anything different had she woken up. Who was this winged being? How long had it been watching me? Should I have tried to communicate with it? Its freedom to move around me when I could not move felt very intimidating. I just couldn't tell if it meant me any harm, so I told it to leave.

Is REM the key that opens the doorway to the spiritual world? More specifically, is the blending of wake and REM our connection to the spiritual world? If so, then what exactly is it about this sleep state that makes this possible? To decide this, I first needed to determine what part of REM makes it a doorway.

On a polysomnograph (PSG), the sleep stage of REM can be seen as a patient having rapid eye movements, muscle atonia (paralysis), and low amplitude mixed brain wave frequencies. The low amplitude and fast frequencies of the brainwaves closely resemble those in wake, yet there are some distinct characteristics in the architecture of the waves that make them different. During this stage, the brain alternates between tonic (no eye movements) and phasic (fast eye movements and muscle twitches) REM. The heart rate becomes irregular and the breathing rate can increase and be irregular as well. There are theories as to why we have rapid eye movements, muscle twitches and erratic breathing patterns; I believe it has much to do with how the brain responds to the visual stimuli in dreams.

While in REM, our senses are basically cut off from the physical world, however the sensory, visual, and auditory regions of the brain are still very active. We, our souls, are no longer in control of or have use for our physical selves outside of maintaining a live body until we return to wake. We lie in wait to explore another world.

Van Praagh talks about our ethereal energy during sleep and believes that we enter the spirit world through dreams. He believes that people communicate with the spirit world while dreaming and do so each night. He states, however, that we are more impressionable because dreams do not involve rational thought and we are not consciously aware. Van Praagh only touches on the subject of seeing passed loved ones at one's bedside at night by stating that if a person is not "mentally blocked" they could see them. I believe the REM state of sleep offers the ability to communicate with passed loved ones by dissociating us from our physical selves through paralysis, while at the same time providing us with fast enough brain frequencies to accept and interpret the spiritual energy described by Van Praagh.

Dr. Nelson's research shows that there is an increase in the brain's energy level caused by the transition from non-lucid to lucid dreaming. He states, "[T]he resonant energy between the thalamus and cortex increases and resembles wakefulness. This is the same rhythm, with a tempo of four times a second, that may bind sensations and thoughts from distant parts of the brain into the wholeness of conscious perception." This increased energy level during lucid dreaming is considered part of Dr. Nelson's definition of REM/wake blending and falls in the borderlands of consciousness. He also concludes that there are extreme similarities between the reports of those with near-death experiences and those with lucid dreams.

> *Europe is so beautiful. John, Claire and I are visiting Paris. I don't know who's giving me the information or how, but I've just been informed that I have six hours to live! It is like a game or something. What am I to do with my six hours? Go home to family, I decide. I can't take a regular airplane because that will take seven to eight hours. If I'm going to die, I'll just spend what money I have and get a private jet. "John, Come on! Hurry." We are walking fast, but Bart joins us and is so slow. I know he's sick and can't walk fast, but it makes me angry that he's slowing me down. I quickly walk past an elderly woman who looks unsteady on her feet.*
>
> *I'm going to die soon and need to hurry. Now Bart wants to stop in one of the cathedrals. He says he wants to go to confession. I really don't have the time for this. Doesn't he understand the rules of my life? I have six hours! I don't have time for this! "OK, Bart, we can stop in one." Bart makes his way into the beautiful cathedral and joins the priest in the confessional. I walk around the pews inside and see lines of people waiting for their turn with other priests. I lean up against a side wall and cross my arms; I look anxious and in a hurry. I see a man three people back in a line for confession look up and make eye contact with me. "You look like you are in a hurry. Would you like to cut in front of me and confess*

*your sins?" The rush of awareness strikes me hard. I gasp as
I remember my journey up to this point in my dream—an
elderly woman who could have used my help, but I was too
much in a hurry to stop, my impatience with Bart as he tried
to keep up with me to be with me on my journey home....
The man in my dream and I stare at each other as he watches
the understanding unfold in my mind, and he begins to fade.
I wake up.*

I believe that some of our most important spiritual contacts are made while we are at a conscious level in REM. Becoming lucid while dreaming can make impressions on our spirituality that last a lifetime, just as NDE's can. These same "visions" of passed loved ones can very well be seen during a state of sleep paralysis. Just as Van Praagh explains a medium's abilities to communicate with the afterlife, I believe a spirit can take advantage of the opportunity to present itself at the time when our brain can interpret it. In other words, a spirit can appear to us during the blending of REM and wake.

When lucid, I drew on my faith and beliefs to determine whether or not what I was experiencing was spiritually significant, or in other words, real. Although it may seem impossible to others, talking face-to-face with my deceased mother while dreaming was real to me. I was lucid. I also viewed seeing and communicating with my deceased animals as real interactions. Again, I was lucid. My faith gave me the freedom to believe that spirits have the ability to communicate with the living. These were the types of dreams that suggested unearthly spiritual encounter. Unfortunately, not all spiritual encounters were beautiful or came from angels.

*I am back in my old house standing in my bedroom. Robin
is with me. "Something isn't right, Robin. I'm dreaming
and think something evil is here." I am happy she is here.
She makes me feel safe. "Don't worry," she says. "I'll stay
with you." Strange writing and symbols appear all over the
bedroom walls. Robin can't see them, so I tell her what I
see as it's happening. We take hold of each other, then start*

levitating. We float out of the bedroom and turn down the hallway. My sister comes out of the hallway bathroom, but acts like nothing is wrong or unusual. This makes me mad, and I realize that she's just a pawn in this game. We pause for a moment while I say, "At what point, Renee, were you going to acknowledge that I'm levitating? Don't act like this is normal! I know what's going on!" Renee stares at me a moment, then she says she can take me back to "him" in my room if she wants to.

I guess the devil is in my room or something. Robin and I continue on through the living room to the kitchen. I see some strangers there as well as my dad. I don't believe these are good people, and my dad is probably a fake like my sister. I leave Robin and start obnoxiously messing with the other people because I know this is supposed to be a nightmare. I am lucid and don't want nightmares anymore. When I reach my dad, I don't feel a connection or love, so I start slapping him lightly in the face and saying, "Hey, Dad, is this want you wanted to see? Having fun yet?" I wake up.

Although I laughed at myself upon waking, the dream left an uneasy feeling in the back of my mind. Had I gone too far? Had I stirred up trouble with something I didn't have any business messing around with? Still, I felt satisfied with my ability to control my own environment. I texted Robin and told her that she was with me in my nightmare and that we both levitated around my old house telling off potential demons, making sure they knew who was boss while in *my* dream. Robin texted back, "lol. I have been studying levitation lately and have a book with steps on how to successfully levitate!" I assured her that I was fairly certain my "father" wasn't really my father, yet it still felt weird slapping him in the face.

For each dreamer, there are clues that can trigger the recognition of being in a dream. Over time, I have gained knowledge of familiar recurring dreams and some indicators for nightmares. The absence of light when flipping a light switch is the main trigger for lucidity in my nightmares. In the past, logic kicked in to make the determination that floorboards just didn't open into holes when running through a house or that a picture was in fact an image of a daughter not yet born. While running, I realized that my shins felt no pain as they normally would in waking life, indicating a dream and not reality. These experiences support Van Praagh's claim that our ethereal self is an exact copy of our physical self, but without pain or illness. Lucid dreaming is not unique to narcoleptics. I believe most people have experienced this in their lifetime. Some even have methods to become better at lucid dreaming and incorporate it into their religious or spiritual practices.

I'd become aware that not knowing answers for a test, locker combinations, schedules, or the room number for my next class indicated dreaming. "Ha! Sorry, teacher, but I'm not doing your stupid test!" I'd said to the man behind the desk. Of course, the feelings of anxiety from being unprepared were always in the dream initially, but satisfaction and relief would come after I realized the feelings were unnecessary and relaxation would take hold. One could argue that these feelings of anxiety were there for reasons that I was suppressing and just took the form of school and tests. Yet, after becoming lucid, those feelings would subside and the dream would change. If nurturing my soul was important and lucidity provided an immediate opportunity, then why not just acknowledge the message, change the dream, and move on to more restful sleep? If the feelings persisted, they took another dream form, at which time I could analyze and address my waking life issues.

How strange that when we wake too soon, we often slip right back into the nightmare where it left off. We think we've escaped from drowning or survived being murdered only to find ourselves back in the same waters or trying to outrun our killer. With dreams being a big part of my life, I feel responsible for their outcomes. Dreams are so vivid and emotional that the impact can affect me for days. Quickly slipping back into a dream while lucid can be like rewinding a movie and having an alternate ending. The characters are all there, the scene is still right, yet if lucid I feel more in control. I get to say something sassy or chop the head off a villain instead of watching others be slaughtered. I have found that this type of lucid dreaming is very light and doesn't last very long. But it's true, the experience of reentering a nightmare can be horrifying. Dreams can't always be changed. We can drown repeatedly upon falling back to sleep. In my experience, changing my sleeping position can help change the dream.

Becoming lucid does not necessarily help me wake upon command. "One, two, three, wake up!" never seems to work. This could be due to the ninety-minute REM cycle. I have tried many methods to induce wake at times when I feel the need to escape, only to find myself waking into another dream, something I soon discover through lucidity. For example, I jumped off a building to induce wake from the shock of dying only to create a sensation like fainting (a deeper sleep). Our bodies can feel physical distress and pain in dreams just as they do in wake. The regions in the brain that control our senses are very active and respond to internal rather than external stimuli when we're dreaming. Our physical bodies undergo necessary chemical reactions such as insulin utilization during sleep, so waking for the sake of waking may not be good for the body. For those with obstructive sleep apnea, the struggle for breath alone will arouse the sleeper to a lighter stage of sleep. Their struggle revolves around obtaining and maintaining REM.

For a while now, I've been struggling with what to do with myself, my thoughts, and my actions while in a state of lucidity. I know our dreams serve a purpose, whether it's to allow our brains to process information for memory storage, for self-analysis for growth, to receive messages and premonitions, or to problem-solve and, upon reflection, discover solutions. Our brains are designed with preset chemical pathways during REM that do not include the prefrontal region that produces logic and reasoning, yet logic and reasoning can still occur during REM. What then? In the movie Inception, when the characters in a dream discover that the dreamer is lucid, they become hostile toward the dreamer.

Although I'd explored scenery, battled demons, told off teachers who, far after graduation, wanted to give me a test I wasn't prepared for, and even communicated with deceased loved ones, I'd never been sure that I was acting in my own best interest when I took control of my dreams. I would always take advantage of the beautiful, spiritual gifts lucid dreaming provided during interactions with the deceased or moments of emotional healing. But when I interfered for the sake of taking control, was I disrupting the natural balance between sleep and wake and overstepping a boundary between mortality and immortality? As I continued to ponder these questions in hopes of giving guidance to others, my dreams began suggesting answers.

> *I am standing in a living room or great room. I don't know exactly where because I'm concentrating on the headless body in front of me—it is my body. I want to know if I have control and can make it do the things I want it to. "Move your left arm." The left arm moves. "Move your right arm." The right arm moves. I don't feel freaked out that the body is headless because I must be the head that's staring at the body. A man appears at the start of the hallway across the room. He looks angry with me and I sense evil. "Just wait until I decide to fuck it all up for you," he says, glaring at me. Two large, ferocious dogs appear across the room and charge towards me. I run for the front door of the house and barely escape in time. I can't tell if I'm floating or out in the street, but I recognize the front door from my childhood home. The door is open, but the storm door is shut and holding back the two large barking dogs. Claire stands motionless next to the dogs and stares at me. I yell up to her, "Whatever you do, don't open that door!" I wake up.*

The more I questioned the existence of a spiritual realm within this hybrid state of sleep when our minds are supposed to be safe and we are only a passive character in our dreams, the more new and bizarre experiences I started to have. Questioning whether or not I should interfere with my dreams during lucidity created a stream of intense message-filled dreams. Bottom line... the message was to butt out.

> *I'm riding in a cop car with a man who seems familiar to me, so I must know him. It is a fancy, fast car, and he's showing me a new feature. There's a baby strapped in a body harness on the front dashboard where the glove compartment is. The man says that talking over the loud speaker using his radio is a method of healing the baby. Two friends, a teenage guy and girl, and I are now out on the town. I tell them we're going to steal the new cop car and not to be worried because*

it's just a dream and doesn't matter anyway. I see the baby is still strapped in, but I begin driving really fast and reckless. The baby is crying as I lose control and crash at the bottom of a hill. The three of us get out of the car unhurt and aren't far from the man's house who the car belongs to. I'm not worried, it is just a dream.

The man runs over to the car, "Where's the baby?" he screams. "The baby is fine. This isn't real!" I say nonchalantly, yet starting to feel unsure. He pulls the baby out so carefully and looks concerned. I feel bad. "Let me take the baby," I say, and hold out my arms. He looks at me like I'm crazy and storms off towards his house. I follow him, trying to explain that they are just characters and that I'll never see them again anyway. He turns around and stares at me as he shuts his front door. The look on his face is so sad and disappointed that I wonder why this dream is different from every other. This is my dream! It's just a dream, I keep reminding myself. My two friends walk with me quietly. The guy gives me a kiss on the cheek and tells me everything will be all right. He reminds me of Dylan. I wake up.

I woke with tears in my eyes and then started crying harder. I had no idea why this dream caused me so much inner turmoil. For almost half an hour after waking, I couldn't figure out why it had affected me so much. Who were these characters in my dream? And why did I care what they thought of me and my actions? Maybe I was worried that I had crossed a line and went too far where I didn't belong. I had felt sadness when the man was disappointed in me. Why did it matter? How many different lives did I have? I realized I was not lucid during the dream, but was dreaming I was having a lucid dream.

I'm in the passenger seat of Renee's SUV reading my textbook for school. We pull into the driveway of her home; we are returning from a weekend camping trip. I live with her as a roommate. I notice the landscaping in the front of the house and feel disappointed that the cactuses I planted aren't looking very good. We must be in a state like California or Arizona. I'm in my early twenties, she is about four years older. "Why did you let the cactuses die, Renee? I worked really hard on those, and they're not cheap." She only rolls her eyes and pulls the car around to the back of the house and parks right outside the garage. "You know," I say, "I can always move back in with Mom and Dad. I'm here to help you out." "Oh right," she says as she gets out of the car with some bags in her arms, "then you wouldn't be able to have all your boyfriends over."

Renee gathers some items, walks through the garage, and into the house. I grab a few things from the car and put them away on shelves in the garage. There's a side door opposite me that leads up a few stairs to the front side yard. I see a man take the steps down and reach for the handle of the door in an attempt to enter the garage. The man is a stranger, and my instincts tell me his intentions are not good. I quickly rush to the door to make sure it is locked. It is too late. I feel the handle turn. "Renee! Call 9-1-1, now!" I'm scared that she will come back into the garage to check on me instead of making the call like I asked. By then, I feel it will be too late. I wake up.

Dylan, I felt, was in a good state of mind and had hope for his future. My negative dreams of him had subsided. I knew my relationship with my sister, on the other hand, needed attention. I'd never experienced such a dream where we had our same personalities, yet there was no knowledge of our past or present realities. Another place, another time, another life, yet we were the same sisters. Strange how there was background knowledge built into this alternate life within the dream. I knew I was her roommate. I knew that I had planted the cacti. I was among the characters in the dream, not lucid. Was this

dream teaching me something? Or was this simply another way I expressed my frustration in wanting her to simply trust me?

Each time I tried to neatly package and define dreams in an effort to help educate others, new dream experiences took place that simply did not fit. I actually loved that dreams and hybrid mixtures of wake and REM could not be contained and categorized. I only wished that others could experience the thrill that came from having this alternate reality with open eyes. During a recent dream, I had vented my frustrations and anger about the way characters in one dream treated me compared to the characters within the next dream. In another dream, I recognized characters from a dream many years ago, but they appeared years older. "Hi, do you remember me?" I'd said to them while standing in line for the bathroom within the dream. I couldn't say that I had answers as to why I recognized dream characters as if we'd had a relationship in the past or what the significance was. I only knew that I did.

> *After seeing a group of horses fighting, the woman and I break the group apart. That was no way to go. We decide to take one by itself to be burned. "Lie down and be still," we say. The horse obeys, and I look upon it with great sadness as it stares back at me with complete trust. The woman with me seems to be following a routine, but is patient when I let her take control. I notice a neon sign in the background with the numbers 3, 2, 1, some sort of count down. As the fire is set beneath the horse, it just lay there still, watching me. I don't want to watch it burn. I walk away slowly and hold a book in front of my face to shield my eyes from the burning horse. I don't stop the count down, but I know I can. I wake up.*

After a series of nightmares concerning my decision to lay Sara to rest (or, in blatant terms, kill my dog), I found they subsided over time with lots of prayer and recognition of my internal struggles. Upon reviewing my experiences and reliving the emotions associated with the difficult choice to end Sara's life, the nightmares returned. I wished for forgiveness in ending my best friend's life. I couldn't say that my guilt would ever fully be alleviated, but I appreciated my dreams for helping me understand and work on healing my inner turmoil.

The blending of sleep and wake is just that—blending. Our brains do not always follow the rules using the "REM on" and "REM off" switch. The lack of hypocretin in narcoleptics to control the transition is similar to a faulty light switch. This switch sometimes becomes stuck in the middle while the light flickers. Dr. Nelson discusses sleep paralysis based on his interviews with patients. The descriptions are typical and include paralysis, the feeling that someone else is in the room, visual hallucinations, and being terrified. He reports, "…people find themselves lying awake yet unable to move anything except their eyes."

"John, were my eyes open during the times I'd woken up and told you I had been in sleep paralysis?" Considering the crazy experiences I'd had while lying next to him, I thought he may have had the answer. "No, you were asleep. Why?" he asked, but looked like he probably shouldn't have. "Because I could totally see!" I exclaimed with too much excitement. "At first, I wondered if my eyes were open, but remembered that I shouldn't be able to open my eyes because the muscles are supposed to be paralyzed. When I do actually "wake up," I think that my eyes open at that time. It's really hard to tell." John's typical "you're so weird" look appeared, but he replied by saying, "Maybe you just think you see your bedroom when you have sleep paralysis because you are familiar with it." I knew this wasn't true, so I tried to state my case, "But I don't only see my bedroom. I've recognized hotel rooms, even though we may have been in three different ones in one month. And, I know when you are next to me."

I believe that in sleep paralysis one's eyes do not have to be physically open to see. Our eyes have the ability to move during REM paralysis, but our eyelids are part of a muscle group that is also paralyzed. I believe that we "see" during this time with our ethereal eyes (our soul). It is this belief that makes an episode of sleep paralysis similar to a near-death experience. During NDEs, patients have reported seeing and hearing activities from high above the operating table that are true and accurate while doctors desperately worked to resuscitate their body. According to Dr. Nelson, it is during this time that the patient's brain has slipped into the paralysis state of REM while remaining in wakeful consciousness. This type of OBE is similar to reports of

OBEs during sleep paralysis. Why, then, would it not be possible for a person in sleep paralysis to also be able to "see" with their eyes closed?

My curiosity was killing me! Sleep paralysis happened so randomly and infrequently that I couldn't simply video myself to find an answer. So, I posed the question on a Facebook chat room open only to other narcoleptics. "When you experience sleep paralysis, do you believe that your eyes are open or closed?" I told the members that I was trying to clarify some thoughts I had regarding this question for a book I was writing. The answers came in quickly: "Mine are definitely open." "I think mine were closed." "I'm not really sure." There were several of each of these answers, but then one answer really made me smile: "Why does it matter?" This question was the perfect way for me to push people to think about the spiritual nature of our experiences that we took for granted.

I wanted these people to begin thinking about their experiences not as frightening or annoying, but as mystifying and possibly spiritual in nature. So I responded, "How are you able to see upon waking when you are in total paralysis? Sure, your eyes can move around (REM), but aren't your eyelids also a muscle group that remain paralyzed? And what about those of you who claim to have OBEs during sleep paralysis? If your physical body is left lying on the bed, how are you able to see around your room as you float to the ceiling or are pulled towards the opposite wall? For several minutes I waited, watching expectantly for responses to appear. Finally, one respondent typed, "I can't wait to read your book."

> *Adding insult to injury, I not only dream that Pongo and Sara are still alive, but now there is a frisbee lying on my chest? I can't believe I'm in sleep paralysis now. I wonder if it was the power of suggestion from last night. "John," I lean over to grab his arm and snuggle closer, "I keep having nightmares."*

A noise from outside the bedroom startled me, making me realize that John was already up and out of bed, doing his morning routine. I looked next to me and saw that John was not there; I had not leaned over to grab his arm.

What's this? A leash? A prong collar and leash, like the kind I used on Pongo, is lying on my chest. John will see this and know that I'm not making this stuff up. Since he can't hear me because I'm in sleep paralysis, then at least he'll see the leash. I pick up the leash and set it next to me on his side of the bed. I hear the noise from our alarm system chime as John opens the front door to let the cat in like he does each morning. My eyes shift to the bedroom door and, seeing a faint light from the hallway, I hear John's voice, "Hey Buddy, where've you been?" OK, so I must be awake now. "John?" I don't think I'm saying it loud enough. "John!?" The words don't come out as loud as I want them to, but at least I'm saying them, so I should be awake.

As I stare at the bedroom door, I feel the release of the paralysis. I wake up.

The chime of the front door sounds as John opens it to let Jeter in. "Hey Buddy, where've you been?"

I felt I had my answer now. The answer was both. I believed that a person's eyes could be open or closed during sleep paralysis. In and out of sleep I fought, trying to make sense of the morning. I thought I was calling out for John, yet in a quiet voice like I would use upon waking. Obviously he was too far away to hear me, but that was when I heard him open the door for Jeter the first time. How, then, could I have been awake? One thing I was sure of, my paralysis was finally released while my eyes were open staring at the bedroom door.

Since I could not have used my physical eyes to see during the time I leaned over to reach for John's arm, the answer must be that sleep paralysis can occur with eyes open or eyes closed. My struggles between wake and sleep could have caused a teetering effect between the usual balance of REM/wake blending that's typical during sleep paralysis. My eyes could have opened during a brief moment of wake, then I fell back into hypnogogic REM paralysis while my eyes were open. I sure did regret not setting up a video camera!

I often hear the word "cord" used to describe the bond between the body and soul. Van Praagh believes that when we die, our soul is released from our physical body. It makes sense to believe that upon near-death, the cord to our physical body weakens, then is strengthened and tightly wound as we snap back to our physical self when our body is restored. My friend Rachel had described her near-death experience as a floating sensation, causing her to rise above her own body. Both her and Bart described "snapping back" awake in their bodies once the doctors had their blood pressure under control. I believe that when our bodies are healthy during REM/wake blending in sleep paralysis, the cord remains strong and intact and keeps us close.

Of all the NDEs and OBEs that I had heard, not one had mentioned being in control of their destination. "My physical body does not sit up, but *I* sit up and call for her. I'm lying here still in bed. I know I can't follow her. I'm stuck here in my body, paralyzed." When I sat up without my physical body, I did so with my soul. However, I did not have the sense that I could go any further. As Sara left my room, I knew she was not going into the living room or kitchen. She was going somewhere that neither I, nor any other living being, was allowed without an invitation.

Dr. Nelson's research team interviewed those who reported having an NDE and found they had also experienced periods of REM intrusion (such as sleep paralysis) at some point in their lives. They weren't necessarily narcoleptic, but they did have a possible predisposition toward REM/wake imbalance, leading to a significantly greater chance of spiritual encounter in the event of an NDE. So it made complete sense when Rachel shared her amazing, yet terrifying encounter in what we typically call a ghost story.

Many years ago, she and her husband lived in an old, historic home in Shorewood, Wisconsin. On several occasions, an apparition of a woman whose picture was still hung in the old house visited Rachel from time to time at her bedside at night. Although she acknowledged the ghost, she tried hard to ignore it. During these brief encounters, she never felt particularly threatened until a peculiar experience one afternoon.

Extremely exhausted by pregnancy, daily chores, and caring for her toddler and baby, she laid down alongside her children in her bed to nap. She woke suddenly to find the apparition hovering over her sleeping toddler. The sight of it focusing on the boy was so threatening that Rachel sat up and yelled, "Oh no you don't! You've crossed the line, lady!" The ghostly woman floating above turned her head slowly, made eye contact with Rachel, then said goodbye and vanished.

The real estate agent and prospective buyers were embarrassed to find themselves walking into the bedroom of the sleeping owner and her children. The noise of their entry startled her awake and her eyes flew open. "I'm so sorry. I didn't know you were home since no one answered the phone," the realtor apologized as Rachel sat up breathing heavily and looking around confused. The buyers ended up purchasing the old house, and Rachel never encountered the ghostly woman again. Her personal experience is just another example in support of Dr. Nelson's findings of the connection between spirituality and medical science.

The time is right for the world to take interest in, or at least give more thought to the role dreams play in our lives. For thousands of years, people from all disciplines have offered their insights and research, but lately people in the medical field have finally stepped up to the plate. In early 2016, I came across an article in the *New York Times* entitled "A New Vision for Dreams of the Dying." New research is being conducted on the therapeutic role of dreams and visions of those who are in the final stages before death. Palliative care doctors and nurses are seeing a growing phenomena of dreams and visions of passed loved ones reported by those in hospice that reassure and comfort them regarding their upcoming journey. These dreams are usually followed shortly by the patients' deaths.

Just as my grandmother had expressed her excitement after seeing her deceased daughter, my mother, with arms open and welcoming her to heaven the night before her death, the patients being studied at Hospice Buffalo share their dreams and visions with doctors and family members. There are no reports of people with narcolepsy, yet a teenager with Ewing's Sarcoma on the verge of death reported "seeing" her beloved dead dog alongside her bed and feeling as though he was letting her know not to be scared. There are also patients whose dreams may be interpreted as disturbing, such as reliving suppressed memories from time spent as a soldier. These nightmares, however, can also be viewed as atonement or a means to ask forgiveness (from God or from oneself).

As I read the article, I felt an overwhelming satisfaction in my efforts to "normalize" what is typically seen as delirium or wish fulfillment. The families of these patients needed to understand that the meaningful dreams and visions their loved ones shared with them were gifts during the final weeks, days, or hours of life and should be welcomed, not feared. The work of these medical doctors and nurses is extremely important to the patients' wellbeing as well as that of their family members during this time of uncertainty and/or faith in the afterlife. Dr. Quill, one of the team of researchers, states, "The huge challenge of this work is to help patients feel more normal and less alone during this unusual experience of dying. The more we can articulate that people do have vivid dreams and visions, the more we can be helpful."

If these dreams are intended to aid the dying by lessening patients' fears and healing their souls through forgiveness or atonement, then the real challenge for hospice professionals will be learning how to balance medication that is needed for pain versus medication used simply for sedation. The authors of *Hello From Heaven!* not only provide direct accounts of ADCs, but also stories from those who have been contacted by spirits in order to pass messages on to friends and neighbors. Conveying messages from the deceased to a friend or family member can be a blessing, yet one has to wonder, *why not just visit them personally?*

As a sleep technician, I have seen many patients sleep through the night without producing much or any REM sleep at all. They are people who either have severe obstructive sleep apnea (OSA) or are on prescription antidepressant medications (SSRIs), both of which can prevent a person from entering REM during sleep. People with OSA have difficulty remaining in REM due to paralysis that makes breathing difficult. SSRIs as well as some other medications are known to suppress REM. Many people seek prescription antidepressant medications when dealing with the tragic loss of a friend or family member to prevent excessive sleep during the day and help ease their sleep at night. Narcoleptics with cataplexy use these same medications to prevent cataplectic attacks during the day. It is possible that the bodies of those who did not receive ADC messages directly weren't supplying adequate REM for communication. I am not a doctor and do not recommend going off any prescription drugs without the approval of a physician, I am merely making observations and drawing conclusions based on my own beliefs and experience.

Depressed individuals are known to have a shorter REM latency (they fall into REM more quickly than usual). In my opinion, this additional time a body gives someone with depression in REM is therapeutic, not only physically, but also for the healing of our soul. If REM sleep is suppressed with medication or prevented by severe OSA, a person will experience REM rebound once REM sleep is restored. Although nightmares from a traumatic experience are definitely undesirable, suppressing one's dreams may only be prolonging the inevitable.

"Have you seen the new documentary on sleep paralysis called The Nightmare on Netflix?" my newly hired editor asked. I absolutely loved opening the eyes and interest of people who had never been exposed to such concepts as sleep paralysis and hypnagogic and hypnopompic hallucinations. The more I talked with the uninitiated, I found that most were familiar with the concepts and may have even had their own experiences, they just never knew they had a name or that they were a real thing. Of course, it was Robin who suggested KN Literary for an editor and my initial interviewer with the publishing company talked with me for an hour regarding years with her own battles of sleep paralysis and hallucinations. Unfortunately, she had experienced unwanted and frightening episodes like the people in the documentary had, and just as the title infers.

"Spiritually broken," "feeling of evil presence," "Shadow Man," "vibration," "making you feel afraid," "wanting you to feel afraid," are just some of the phrases the eight individuals interviewed in The Nightmare use to describe their experiences during sleep paralysis. These people do not have narcolepsy, but experience sleep paralysis with hallucinations that, to them, have been life altering. As I sat by myself watching the documentary (John and Claire said it was too freaky for them to watch), my emotions went from curious to scared, skeptical to sad. The longer I watched these average, everyday people share their personal, crazy stories of spiritual encounters, the more I realized how similar they were to me in their actions, feelings, ideas, and experiences.

The documentary reenacts the sleep paralysis episodes using actors lying in bed, sometimes motionless, sometimes shaking as if vibrating, but always with eyes open watching a scary scene play out around them. The director tries to capture the intensity behind the episodes with scenes of dark figures in hats, alien looking creatures, or expressions of horror from the actors. I wondered if the actors had their eyes open to demonstrate that the people being portrayed could see during this time or if they really believed their eyes were open. I recognized the "shadow man" (though mine had a hatchet), and the alien creature was similar except that mine had wings. A couple of the characters draw pictures of their encounters and one looks eerily similar to the boil-faced man I had seen hovering above my bed looking down at me through what I assumed was another dimension. Goose bumps spread up my arms and neck as a young man recounts a dream of answering a phone call, "Hello? I can't hear you." A chilling voice replies, "Let me in!"

All those interviewed report having watched scary movies when they were young, so they were exposed to the possibility of an evil existence. Not all are religious, but they all admit to calling upon Jesus or praying when they feel threatened by a demonic presence. "I think it has to do with the spiritual realm," one woman explains. She goes on to say the she believes the evil presence she feels in the room with her really "wants" her and all she can do is pray, even though she isn't religious. "Having fear only feeds it," one man says as he analyzes his encounters. Although much of the documentary focuses on the evil nature of sleep paralysis, I was pleased to hear a woman describe a warm and comforting sensation as the presence in her room slips into bed behind her and whispers in her ear. She believes it is her deceased mother. "I can tell the difference," she explains, between feeling a good sensation and an evil sensation in the room. Another woman feels that her "soul has to heal" before the frightening experiences can come to an end. She has since moved on to a better place in her life.

After listening to the interviews, I saw how tortured and conflicted the subjects were by wanting others to understand without thinking they were crazy. "For a few seconds," one man states, "I can see something that others cannot see." He describes how he is determined to figure out what's happening and becomes consumed by it. I completely understood these feelings and hoped that their participation in the documentary helped them move on, even if they could never fully understand what they had endured. I did believe they would see a change over time, whether from correcting a sleep disorder or finding peace and happiness in their lives so that this evil presence would no longer be drawn to them.

I woke feeling extremely proud of my ability to bring about light within a darkened room when I sensed an evil presence. In the nightmare I tried a "dream power" to create a light of my own. The light began at the floor and slowly rose to reveal a dark figure in the shape of a man. As the light reached the top of his legs, the presence became angry and the room turned black. I woke up. The following week, another opportunity came to bring light to a darkened room where evil lurked within my nightmare. "Let there be light!" I exclaimed proudly with my hands held high in the air, yet no light came. I felt ashamed when I awoke.

"Robin, you must be busy in the spirit world because your name scared off who or whatever had hold of me during an OBE." Robin always appreciated my straightforward, yet funny and random text messages. "I remembered what we talked about and told whatever was at my bedside to pull as I locked my fingers around its neck. I know it was an animal of some kind. I really wanted it to be Sara, but I don't think it was. It pulled me off the side of the bed and down to the foot. When I said I couldn't wait to tell you about this, I heard your name said as a question, and I popped back into bed and opened my eyes!" Robin was definitely someone who I could trust not to call me crazy, and I wanted to share the strange encounter with someone to help me wrap my head around it. She responded, "Amazing! I have had some busy activity on the dream planes, sounds like you have too!"

Although Robin does not have narcolepsy, she has definitely had experiences that incorporate REM/wake blending. After the recent loss of her beloved dog, she was extremely excited to share her unforgettable morning when she felt the comforting compression of blankets against her legs after crying herself to sleep the night before. Although texting wasn't the optimal way to communicate an experience such as sleep paralysis, I followed up writing, "I was teetering in and out of sleep and wanted it to be Sara. I reached out and grabbed something, pulled it in and hugged it. Funny 'cause I have no idea what I was hugging." I hadn't thought about there being any possible consequence for my actions until I read Robin's response: "I guess we need to be careful on the astral plane."

That morning, I had heard a thump on the side of my bed and was so excited at the thought of seeing Sara again that I woke up completely and not within the confines of sleep paralysis. I'd been disappointed and upset believing that Sara could possibly be waiting for me in that dimension where sleep and wake coexist that I stared at the wall and begged sleep to take me, hoping to make contact with a loved one I had lost.

I cannot say what lurks in these borderlands we enter when our brain frequencies run high and we become consciously aware. I knew good and evil existed in both this world and the next, yet as the paralysis took hold, I had been willing to reach out to an unknown presence, grasp it, and allow it to take me. Could I have gone farther with my fingers latched around its neck? Did I snap back to my body because my "cord" had reached its limit? I know that I didn't physically reach out in the dark, yet I did reach. Maybe I had become too comfortable believing that I lay safe in my bed.

> *Some friends and I are on vacation in London, visiting the barbershop on Fleet Street where Sweeney Todd brutally sliced up his victims. After seeing the landmark, we sit on the patio just outside the barbershop to eat lunch. We laugh about all the different ways he could have killed his victims. "If I were a cannibal, I'd feed you this hamburger and say, 'If you're looking for your sister, she's right there between the buns!'" My friends laugh with me and tell me how disgusting I am. I start to have an uneasy feeling that makes me very uncomfortable with our surroundings. Everything looks peaceful on this beautiful, sunny afternoon, but an evil presence is in the air. I want to escape this dream quickly before it gets worse. I try to wake up, but feel a pull to keep me here. I'm struggling with something or someone.*
> *I wake up.*

I looked over at John and saw him sleeping peacefully. It was still pretty early in the morning, and I was exhausted. Why did my coworker have to mention Sweeney Todd at work the other night? It's weird that I had a dream about it because I hadn't even seen the movie. Snuggling back under the covers, I closed my eyes.

> **"You want to taste flesh?"** *My tongue is shoved to the back of my throat as three large fingers jam into my mouth.* **"Bite down on this!"**

*I'm writing this poem
for my darling Mother.
The author, of course,
is your husband's daughter's brother.
I hope that these verses
brighten up your days
as you have brightened mine
in so many ways.
My mother is beautiful and sweet like the flowers
and loves to take naps for hours and hours.
My mother is not only pretty, but smart
and when she is counted on, will always do her part.
A mother so loving and caring and wise
I think of you often when I look towards the skies.
For your spirit is free like a bird or the moon
and don't give up hope, I'll see you real soon.
So here is your poem, I gave it a shot,
while thinking of you on my tiny cot.*

Love always,

Your son

Afterword: Sleep on It

When we go to sleep at night, we undress our souls by leaving our physical bodies behind. They are no longer needed in the "dream world." Our host bodies lie motionless and in autopilot while we dream, waiting for our soul's return. Some are guided away for brief periods of time by spirit guides. Others are taken to a dream world where valuable lessons are learned. We are educated if we only wish to pay attention and analyze. Information from the day or week is arranged, organized and sorted for storage in memory. Emotions that are ignored are given to us in picture stories that are easier to absorb so we are not overwhelmed.

Let dreams come. Confront your demons in your dreams as well as in waking life, for the energies of passed souls are among us, day and night. Our spirit helpers/guardian angels provide valuable lessons to help guide us through life on earth. Seek spiritual healing by acknowledging your wishes and desires, fears and sins, through the analysis of dreams. Our souls lie within the energy fueling our physical body and are constantly shaped and molded in preparation for release upon death. We all have a connection with those in the spirit world, and through sleep we open a direct line of communication apart from our physical world.

People with narcolepsy, those who are dying or come close to death, those who are sleep deprived, mourning, or depressed all share similar stories of life-altering experiences that they strongly believe to be real. I hope that my personal experiences, along with the medical advances in sleep research and neurology, help bind the gap between your dreams, reality, and acceptance of your spiritual nature. Allow your dreams to occur and be careful not to take control of the content or you may find that you miss important messages you need to receive and emotions you need to feel. Pay attention to details and enjoy the extraordinary encounters you find along the way.

The research in near-death experiences (NDEs) and after-death communications (ADCs) along with the teachings from world famous medium James Van Praagh provided me with the courage and inspiration to share the beliefs and theories I have developed through my lifetime as a person with narcolepsy and an education in the field of sleep. Telling my story and sharing my dreams mean baring my sole to the world. I may not be able to help others understand their dreams and push through their times of crisis, but I can offer assurance that they are not alone.

The spiritual world surrounds us in our daily lives and in our sleep. Be conscious of the signs they provide for guidance and teaching. I demonstrate how accepting the unique characteristics of narcolepsy has helped me explore what Dr. Nelson describes as the "borderlands of consciousness." I encourage you to blend our medical realities with a bit of faith and consider the possibilities. By sharing my personal experiences, I hope to bring affirmation to those who may be questioning their own experiences as coincidence or being "just a dream."

About the Author

BRENDA A. MOORE was diagnosed at the age of twenty with narcolepsy. She received Bachelor of Arts degrees in Psychology and Administration of Justice and a Master of Public Administration degree from the University of Missouri-Kansas City. With a determination to spread awareness and teach others about sleep disorders, she returned to school and received an A.A.S. in Polysomnography and is a registered sleep technologist (RPSGT). Brenda is a mother of two grown children and lives with her husband in Leawood, KS.

www.ingramcontent.com/pod-product-compliance
Lightning Source LLC
Chambersburg PA
CBHW071907290426
44110CB00013B/1309